'I love you sons of bitches. You're the only ones with guts enough to really care about the future, who really notice what machines do to us, what cities do to us, what tremendous misunderstandings, mistakes, accidents, and catastrophes do to us. You're the only ones zany enough to agonise over time and distances without limit, over mysteries that will never die, over the fact that we are right now determining whether the space voyage for the next billion years or so is going to be Heaven or Hell.'

Kurt Vonnegut
God Bless You, Mr Rosewater

WATERSTONE'S GUIDE TO SCIENCE FICTION, FANTASY & HORROR

Edited by Paul Wake, Steve Andrews and Ariel

WATERSTONE'S GUIDES

SERIES EDITOR

Nick Rennison

Contents

Introduction

The *Waterstone's Guide To Science Fiction, Fantasy and Horror* has been compiled as a reader's guide to the very best writing currently available in these genres. On a daily basis the SF booksellers in our shops are asked the following question and variants on it. 'I've read Tolkien. What should I try next?' This guide aims, primarily, to answer those questions. We hope that by using the guide readers will be able to discover new authors, authors who write the kind of SF, fantasy and horror that they enjoy. We have made every effort to ensure that the listings of titles are as comprehensive as possible and to include as many authors as possible. Inevitably our choice has been dictated by what is and is not in print in this country. Some authors we would have liked to include do not have books currently available. Many authors that we have included have written a lot of novels, of which only a handful are available. Where this is the case we have listed only those titles which are in print. We have made a small number of exceptions to these rules. Either these are writers who are central to the history of the genres or they are writers who are particular enthusiasms of the Waterstone's booksellers who have contributed the brief surveys of authors' works which accompany each entry. We are not making any claims to be the most comprehensive guides to the genres. Anyone seeking a more complete understanding of the overall history and development of the genres should look out for John Clute's *Encyclopedia of Science Fiction* and his *Encyclopedia of Fantasy*. These are undoubtedly the foremost reference works for their respective subjects.

The guide has been organised in what we hope will be seen as a logical way. The three broad genre divisions within the guide were chosen because we quickly realised how difficult it would be to place authors accurately within a particular sub-genre. The few sub-genres we have treated separately are intended to provide a pointer towards some different styles of writing in SF and fantasy. We also realised that the labelling of individual authors as 'SF', 'Fantasy' or 'Horror' is a notoriously subjective process and that definitions and choices would vary from reader to reader. In cases where the labelling of writers is debatable, we have placed the writers in question in the section that we believe the general reader would expect to find them. Thus Anne McCaffrey, whose work some would describe as fantasy, has been classified as SF, because that is where we feel most of her public, and Anne McCaffrey herself, would expect to find her. The latest series by Dan Simmons is a powerful futuristic epic but he is a noted horror writer and it is in the Horror section that he is to be found. Other authors, like Fritz Leiber, who are so hugely prolific as to defy categorisation, we have included in the section that best represents the work that is in print.

Science Fiction, Fantasy and Horror are such dynamic and swiftly changing genres that it is just possible we may have omitted one or two authors who will be big names when the guide appears. This is a result of the timing of the selection process rather than a reflection on the writers. We have, however, included a section at the beginning of the guide which represents our Editors' Choice. Not all of these writers are brand new. They range from people like Neal Stephenson, who published his first novel in 1984, to Mary Doria Russell who has published only one book so far. All of them are writers that we are predicting will be among the best known and biggest names in the genres in the future. And if there are writers that we have omitted - don't worry, we'll get you next time.

OPENING THE GATES
by John Clute

The genre's finest historian and critic looks at the writers who lead us through the three gates of Science Fiction, Fantasy and Horror.

Writers in bold in John Clute's text have separate entries in the body of the Guide.

There is no smoke without fire. There is no story without a world to change. There is no science fiction without a march of Time. There is no fantasy without a Dream that says, You must change your life. There is no horror without a panic fear that it all stops here: that Nightmare is all she wrote. This book is about some of the fine people who have been bringing us the smoke.

But three genres, even three closely related genres with their arms around each other for support, do not encompass the entire world. All of science fiction (hence SF) and fantasy and horror together – intertwined, incestuous, jostling and fratricidal – do not even encompass the whole of the world of the fantastic.

This book, *The Waterstone's Guide to SF, Fantasy and Horror* touches only slantingly on the whole of the world of the fantastic, which also includes Myth, Legend, Romance, Allegory, Dream, Surrealism, Magic Realism, and much much more; it has been enough of a task here to glance swiftly over the three genres of the fantastic which dominate the marketplace at the end of the 20th century.

Two of these genres – SF and fantasy – occupy fairly specific domains and do definable things with those domains; the third, horror, is a genre without a home, a genre which, like the cuckoo, takes over the home of others, and colours it black.

Any large bookshop of quality will have selling space devoted to all three genres; and *really* large bookshops may well offer further subdivisions, so that space opera is housed in one rack, women's SF in another, dynastic fantasy on a third, supernatural horror on a fourth, Stephen King all by himself on a fifth, classic SF on a sixth, elf stuff on a seventh, and so on.

The Waterstone's Guide to SF, Fantasy and Horror reflects some of these pragmatic exercises – but be warned. Very few books, except the very worst, fit neatly into any one category. And a whole pre-Copernican maze of genres and subgenres, cooky-cut out of the original three, can be created, for marketing purposes, out of whole cloth; or very nearly.

Procrustean exercises in squeezing round books into square genres are not primarily the fault of bookshop managers, however. They tend to put books where they have been told to put them. What tells them where to put them?

The package.

If the cover of a new, previously unknown, completely unreviewed title comes to the attention of a bookstore manager, and if the cover of that book features a young *deshabillé* woman alone, stumbling aghast and gaping out of a gothic mansion, with one light shining in an upper window, then the bookshop manager will not put that new title in the space opera section. He or she will put it in the Romantic Gothic Horror (Female Author) section.

Even if the Gothic Mansion is in fact a spaceship.

Even if the book was written by a man.

Even if it is *Wuthering Heights: the Sequel.*

It may not be the case that marketing people always know for certain which genre a particular text might occupy, or which of the thousand subgenres within the three main genres that text might be deemed to be an example of; but once they have decided where a book fits 'so it can be sold', the people do know exactly what to do. The cover and blurb codes which tell us that a book is 'being marketed' as SF, or fantasy, or horror, are extremely clear. We know what they mean – they mean that we can find a book whose text *may* fit the cover and the blurb. They mean that we can start our search *here.*

The Waterstone's Guide to SF, Fantasy and Horror starts *here,* too. Most of the writers featured, in the various sections the guide has been divided into, are currently in print. SF publishers, in particular, have managed to keep an unusually high proportion of the masters of the field in print; and it's not an impossible task, therefore, to select a range of in-print writers who reflect both current taste and the history of the SF genre. It is very much harder to do the same with fantasy, a genre whose folk history has in any case (until recently) not been described in an orderly fashion. And horror, which abides darkly in a thousand nests, has as many histories: though it may be possible to discern a spinal column of stories somewhere in the Necroscope.

So. The Guide starts *here,* but it comes from *there.* And it might be an idea to attach the wave of the present, which we might also call the *fin* of time and which marks these pages, to the benthos that made us.

SCIENCE FICTION began, as everyone knows, with Gilgamesh. Or Homer. Or Daedalus. Or Plato. Or Beowulf. Or *The Golden Ass, The Tempest, Gulliver's Travels, Frankenstein, The Time Machine,* or *Ralph 124C 41+*. In the world of SF, in other words, there is a great deal of argument over origins. Significantly, though, whoever happens to win this argument in whatever year it happens to be formulated, the overall shape of SF does not change greatly in the mind's eye as a consequence. We can seek (and find) hints of ur-SF in works that date from the beginning of the written word on Earth, and these hints all tend to foreshadow the same mature literature. (This is not, by the way, an argument about Progress: by 'mature' I mean fully-formed, not higher.) SF, which did not gain its present name and full nature till well into the 20th century, always seems to have been a gleam in the speculative eye of *homo sapiens.*

There has always been a thrust to the edge of things.There have always been wonders beyond the known.

But we call texts written before (roughly) 1800 ur-SF for one very good reason: they lack the dimension of Time. Not until men and women conceived of the wheels of history grinding in one direction, forwards and upwards, through historical Time, could SF stories really be written. Not until the future was invented as a goal we had to change ourselves in order to reach could SF really exist. For SF to inhabit our nights, we had to be able to dream of the transfigured, next thing. The sleep of Reason begets SF.

So Brian **Aldiss** suggests that the first SF novel must be *Frankenstein: Or, the Modern Prometheus* (1818) by Mary **Shelley**. (There are grounds for thinking that it is more important in the history of Gothic Horror; but any good novel, as opposed to any sharecrop, can almost indefinitely be mined for meaning.) *Frankenstein* is a novel from the beginning of Time. We peer back at his face and we see ourselves, and in his rusty amateurish scars we can see the speedlines on our own retro faces, as we slide inexorably into the jaws of our own neighbourhood whore of Time: the Millennium.

However, to think about the future was not yet quite to inhabit the future, even in the sense SF writers and readers might claim to accomplish that feat: that is, in their imaginations. For most of a century after *Frankenstein,* only rarely did an SF text carry its protagonists into the future, and even more rarely (my own memory says: never) before World War One was an SF novel actually set more than a few years into the future. A novel like H G **Wells**'s *The Time Machine* (1895), though its eventual gaze encompasses millions of years, sets off from 1895; and *The War of the Worlds* (1898) may be told some time after the fact by a man who has lived through the eponymous catastrophe, but the Martians' invasion takes place no more than a year or so into the 20th century.

Then came American pulp SF (its texture thickened for a few years by Hugo Gernsback's attempts to use what he called 'scientifiction' as a tool to teach technophilia to young boys); and the future became a platform, an escape clause, a release, an adventure, a coign of vantage, a premise, a landscape in the hands of writers like Edmund Hamilton or Murray Leinster or E E **Smith** or Stanley Weinberg within the pulp empire, Aldous **Huxley** or Olaf **Stapledon** without the walls. But it was only after writers like Isaac **Asimov** and Robert A **Heinlein** began to domesticate it in 1939 that the future became a homestead.

From this point American SF dominated the genre world, and told the Big Story of the American Century, of the forcible taming of the new wilderness of space – though with many a recessional note, like *The Space Merchants* (1953) by Frederik **Pohl** and C M Kornbluth, or *The Stars My Destination* (1956) by Alfred **Bester**, or *Solar Lottery* (1955) by Philip K **Dick**, or *A Canticle for Leibowitz* (1960) by Walter M **Miller** Jr. It was not until Sputnik went into orbit in 1957 and took away our toys – took space and made it part of grimy old human history – that American SF began to lose its creative momentum *as a movement*. From about 1957 until now, the best American SF has been able to do has been to flood the world with retro icons, sci-fi comfort blankets for addicts of 1950.

Individual American SF writers, on the other hand, have continued to flourish and there was more good SF published in the 1990s than perhaps ever before. An author like Gene **Wolfe** – who is discussed here as a fantasy writer, in order perhaps to catch the eyes of readers not yet familiar with his dark daedal universe – could not have existed had there not been an institutional SF to provide him with fuel, grist for his mill; and could not have published had that old SF, which I've taken to calling First SF for a number of arguable reasons, still controlled the markets.

At the end of the century, we have the best of both SF worlds. Many of the classic writers are still in print – Heinlein and A E **Van Vogt**, **Asimov** and Arthur C **Clarke**, George **Orwell**, Theodore **Sturgeon**, John **Wyndham**, and so on. Writers who began to work in the old world, and have flourished in the new, like J G **Ballard** (who rang the death knell of the old order from the day he began publishing), Thomas M **Disch** or Ursula K **Le Guin**, remain available. And the jittery, live-wire SF authors who are young at the end of the century, they continue to bring us face to face with the eye-watering niagaras of the coming worlds, as those worlds intersect our dreams, our VCRs, our Nets. It would be invidious to list just a few of them. The *Waterstone's Guide* is full of them. They are easy to find. They glow in the dark.

FANTASY – SF has a line of descent or two. Fantasy has thousands, or so it seems. It is remarkably difficult to distinguish fantasy (as a term descriptive of a particular genre) from the fantastic in general. As an editor of encyclopedias, I was myself recently embroiled (with John Grant) in an attempt to make sorting sense out of the genre for a first-ever encyclopedia of fantasy. We ended up with several ring-fence criteria which seemed to work.

To begin with, Fantasy (we thought) was unlike SF in its origins. Ur-SF texts might show a 'primitive' precursor relationship to the mature SF of the 20th century; but how could we in all seriousness claim that (say) William Shakespeare's *The Tempest* (performed c.1611; published 1623) was a 'primitive' precursor of (say) Tad **Williams**'s *Caliban's Hour* (1994). We couldn't, and didn't try. Instead of treating the Ocean of Story of World Literature as a set of attempts at writing Fantasy, we trawled that Ocean for what we called Taproot Texts, a category which came to include various Shakespeare plays, and works by Ovid, Geoffrey Chaucer, Sir Thomas Malory, Dante Alighieri, Edmund Spenser, Miguel de Cervantes, and so on: until around the beginning of the 19th century.

At that point, fantasy begins. That is, stories begin to be written by authors who know that they are writing in a genre which is subversive of realistic literature, and which appeal to readers who know what they are reading. Those readers would understand that when (say) E T A Hoffmann wrote a dark fantasy like "*The Sandman*", he was undercutting the daylight world, subverting and mocking it, making a statement that the daylight world – the world of his contemporary Jane Austen – did not exhaust the realms of the imagination.

From this point it is a short step to George MacDonald and Lewis Carroll and William Morris and Lord Dunsany and Kenneth Morris and A. Merritt: it is a short step to the autonomous secondary world. For our encyclopedia, John Grant and I came to the pragmatic conclusion that – although they did not constitute a centre from which all other fantasy stories stemmed – the secondary world tale, like those told by J R R **Tolkien**, was indeed central to our understanding of how fantasy worked at full flood. 'A fantasy text,' we said, 'is a self-coherent narrative. When set in this world, it tells a story which is impossible in the world as we perceive it; when set in an otherworld, that otherworld will be impossible, though stories set there may be possible in its terms.'

Some modern fantasy stories play *trompe l'oeil* games with the 'real' and the Other; some treat the 'real' as an appendage of the Other (and vice versa); and some thin out the magic so fearsomely that they end – and their readers end – adrift in aftermath. Where we live. Modern fantasy, some of it written for children or adolescents doing sensitivity training, is an escape from the real world of the 20th century. Modern fantasy written for adults not only escapes the world: it says the world is 'wrong'. The great modern writers of fantasy include Peter S Beagle, John Crowley,

Stephen R **Donaldson**, E R Eddison, Paul Hazel, Robert **Holdstock**, Fritz **Leiber**, C S **Lewis**, Michael Swanwick, Charles Williams. There are others. Many of them are only intermittently in print.

HORROR is all of these things, but stalled. Horror is an affect. It is, perhaps first and foremost, a way of feeling SF, or Fantasy, or Family Romance, or the Western, or Gothic, or Urban Legend, or Hospital Drama, or Bodice Ripper, or Child Mabuse. But it is more than that.

Over and above the usual themes most typically coloured by Horror novelists – these themes usually have something to do with the violation of the body, the desecration of the land – what most deeply characterizes Horror is stoppage. In a full-fledged Horror novel, a story is told for a while, and then it is stalled – held immobile like the gaze of Saturn eating his son in Goya's terrible vision of appetite stalled in unending appetite – trapped waterless in the midst of the waste land. It is, perhaps, the most modern of all genres. And it is perhaps the most honest – even though much of it consists of unendurably boring doses of splatterpunk interspersed with iterations of Nada nada: nothing nothing.

Its history is a history of the same take on different materials. Edgar Allan **Poe**, Bram **Stoker**, H P **Lovecraft**: the killing grounds may vary, but the gestures are the same. Modern writers of supernatural Horror – like Ramsey **Campbell** or Stephen **King** or Thomas **Ligotti** or Peter **Straub** – incorporate those gestures, that eye of the devouring Saturn, into complex artifacts of enduring merit. But the same acid eats our dreams. Horror devours the stories which tell us we can get out of here.

SF, Fantasy, Horror: Three gates. The rest of *The Waterstone Guide to SF, Fantasy & Horror* is devoted some of those who open the gates. Here's a chance to share some of the thunder they make.

Editors Choice

KICKING THE S*** OUT OF MAINSTREAM FICTION

Ariel, bookseller at Waterstone's in Manchester and one of the editors of this guide, asked Michael Marshall Smith, author of Spares and One of Us, for his thoughts on the future of genre fiction. Here are the outspoken results.

Ariel: SF, Fantasy and Horror are all constantly evolving and rapidly changing genres. Are there any major themes or tropes that you feel will come to dominate (albeit temporarily) any of the genres in the future?

Michael Marshall Smith: One of the interesting things about the sf, fantasy and horror genres is that there always tend to be two strands co-existing within them. At any given time there is more 'classic' material being generated – by which I mean short stories and novels which, while not necessarily mere reworkings of what has gone before, tend to bear a strong resemblance to them: 'classic' space opera, sword-and-sorcery trilogies or blood-drenched horror! novels. Simultaneously there is other material being generated which represents a more 'cutting edge' approach, toying with the possibilities, introducing new ideas and often dragging a genre in entirely new directions. The genres are more prone to these exciting shifts in emphasis than more mainstream literature, because they tend to reflect far more clearly changes in culture and general zeitgeist. What then tends to happen is that a few of the new ideas will earn themselves a role in the overall pantheon of relevant ideas, and things settle down a little – often with a resurgence in interest in the above-mentioned more 'classic' formats – before something new comes along again.

In terms of the new tropes which are coming to dominate, I feel they congregate around the the notion of 'reality'. For a long time all three genres could almost be considered sub-divions of 'fantasy' – in that they generally concerned themselves with distant, rather dream-like meditations on possible futures and worlds. Since the cyberpunk revolution in sf, however, there's been a much grittier, more realistic strand of concern. It may be that when the mainstream finally realises that the genres are no longer always about distant galaxies, unicorns or werewolves, but often very cunning analyses of our own worlds simply mediated through genre tropes, then there might be a blurring of the traditional boundary between us and them.

I'm also pleased to see more and more writers taking a cross-genre approach; people like Kim Newman, Paul McAuley, Jay Russell – bringing different strands, merging them together, mixing it up and coming out with new approaches, ideas and atmospheres . . .

Ariel: To what extent do you think the development and growth of the internet in the future will help or hinder sf, fantasy and horror writing? Will it prove to be the death of the printed word? Will we all end up with electronic books and no paper editions at all?

Michael Marshall Smith: Look at the fate of the so-called 'paperless office' – all that happens is that people print out copies of all of their e-mails and files. We don't trust computer storage of materials yet – and with good reason. They don't have the immediacy of a printed edition, of the 'object' that is a book. We value objects, and not just for the things we store inside them: which is why we love books, and go into shops to buy them, and look after them at home. We don't just regard books as a manifestation of the story within, but also as things in their own right. I don't think computer files have – or ever will have – this degree of emotional trust given to them. They're too easy to delete or corrupt. Books persist. Plus you can use them to prop up tables, which is useful.

And, obviously, a book doesn't require a computer, screen, internet connection and electricity supply. The only real disadvantage that the paper edition has over electronic editions is that you can't search the paper edition as easily – which is a problem for reference books, but not fiction. People have been doomsaying the end of the printed world through film, video, computer games yet it carries on. A printed novel seems to me the perfect vector for a particular type of experience – and evolution tends to favour very well-adapted species.

What we almost certainly will see, however, is the internet as a *medium* having some influence on the progression not just of genre fiction, but of fiction in general. Geoff Ryman's *253* for example – an 'interactive' web-based novel, which was accessible in random and unusual ways. I'm sure that we'll see a growth in this kind of thing: though having just read 253, and as a fan of Geoff's writing, I have to say that I read it in the old-fashioned way, from front to back, and that anyone who doesn't will miss at least some of what the author intended to communicate. It's not just a great idea: it's also a superb story and stories require a degree of linearity. The idea of breaking up the conventional, sequential nature of story-telling has been around for ages – *Slaughterhouse-Five*'s aliens and their arts are just one example – but it remains to be seen whether it actually gives us anything new other than curiosity value. That, and the possibility for true interactivity between a variety of people are the two great possibilities given us by the net – and it'll be interesting to see where it goes. I personally think that our minds work – or like to work – in fairly linear ways, with space for occasional sideways and backwards leaps of association.

My gut feeling is that while the internet will provide another strand to what we consider to be literature or art, it will in no way supersede the more traditional approaches. Part of my reason for believing this is a practical one: most works of art or literature are, initially at least, the work of one person. They are the result of one person seeking to communicate something. They are inherently selfish and personal. Interactivity will never do more than stir the surface of that initial need to communicate.

Games are games, and stories are stories. There may be some cross-fertilisation, but I don't think they'll ever merge. Remember how, in the 1970s, Brian de Palma and those guys experimented with split-screens in the cinema? Didn't last long, did it?

We don't want to be messed about. We don't want to interact. We WANT TO BE TOLD A STORY.

Ariel: I know you are a great champion of the short fiction form as the purest expression of the genre, but do you foresee a growth or decline in popularity for short fiction in the future? Are we likely to see a wider or narrower range of material published?

Michael Marshall Smith: I think it will remain pretty much as it is – for reasons to do with the purest and best form of communicating particular types of idea. In horror, for example, with a very few exceptions, I think the very best work has been done in the short story form – or in shortish novels. And I think this is because of the nature of the experience being communicated. Fear is a quick, vital emotion. Once it stretches past a certain point, it either snaps or becomes something else. It's like if you're being chased by a huge monster or something – it can only go on so long before you either get caught (in which case, end of story) or you have to go to sleep – in which case, you'll either get whacked in your sleep, or wake up refreshed in sunlight and probably not so scared. Obviously that's a ridiculous over-simplification, but you get my point. A horror story taken past a certain length becomes dark fantasy: which may be just as exciting and worthwhile, but it's just . . . different. Less of an immediate 'experience' and more of a 'tale'. Few people – Stephen King is the obvious example – are masters of both horror and dark fantasy. People tend to be good at one or the other.

Similarly, a lot of short sf and fantasy fiction doesn't work for me because you don't get enough of an idea of the world the story is set in – and the world is very often the real star of sf or fantasy fiction. Unless it's set in a previously existing and established world, in which case it becomes like a self-contained chapter of something else.

So, I think the existence of great horror short story writers like Ramsey Campbell, Dennis Etchison, Lovecraft, M. R. James, Kim Newman, Poe and innumerable others is due to the fact that the ideas are perfectly suited to that form. That's not going to change, and therefore the short story is not going to go away, particularly when anthologists like Stephen Jones are doing so much both to revisit the traditional corners of the genre and also to establish and breach new boundaries.

Ariel: Are there any of the current generation of genre writers who you think will go on to become as influential and important as some of the classic authors of the 50s, 60s and 70s?

Michael Marshall Smith: Difficult to predict – because it depends, to a degree, on whether the world happens to lumber along the path they're exploring: whether their take on the fluid reinvention of culture is sufficiently congruent to be dragged along with it. Concentrating on English writers – because somebody ought to . . .

In sf, I think Stephen Baxter, Paul J. McAuley and probably Jeff Noon stand a very good chance of getting up there. In horror Ramsey Campbell must surely already *be* there – and I suspect Kim Newman will soon be joining him. Fantasy I don't know about, to be honest . . .

Oh, and me, obviously: as in 'What was the name of that guy, oh you know . . . Christ, what *was* his name . . . jeez, nevermind.'

Ariel: If there was to be one major change to the way that genre fiction was to be published, marketed, sold and indeed written in the future, what would you like it to be?

Michael Marshall Smith: Personally I would like the genres to gang up on the mainstream, take it outside and kick the shit out of it.

I'm sick of being regarded as a 'mere' genre writer, and of having my books hidden away in the 'genre' sections. It's like many of the booksellers, and even the publishers, are saying 'This is weird stuff, probably got ghosts or robots or something in it. Don't really understand it. And it's all nonsense, obviously. But some of the customers like it, so I guess we have to stock it. But we'll put it on this little table here, near the back of the store, so it's obvious we don't really approve.' There are obvious exceptions, Waterstone's in Manchester, for example: but the general rule unquestionably applies.

Why are my books any less NEW than the books put on the New Releases table? Why do my books and countless others get sidelined straight into 'genre shit'? Is *1984* sf? Is *The Bell Jar* horror? Who cares? In my writing I try to introduce elements from all three genres. My next book, *One of Us*, for example, has a strong dose of crime – because I like reading all types of books, and don't see why I should be constrained by the traditional marketing boundaries. We have access to a range of metaphor and symbolism which more mainstream fiction simply cannot access, and this gives us a magical advantage in telling stories which speak directly to more elemental and vital parts of our imagination.

Literary fiction? Here's one for you: A middle-aged woman goes to Italy on holiday and has a short and doomed affair which leads her to re-evaluate her stalled career in Personnel, whilst favouring us with screeds of mannered descriptions of little back streets and street urchins. Who gives a shit? I'd much rather read something a little scary, something fantastic, something with a sense of wonder – especially if it has been rooted in apparent reality. Such stories can cut to the quick of what our world is about, what it means to be human – while providing just as many insights into the human condition, observations on society or jokes as any other type of writing.

It's time for the genres to strike back and demonstrate that if any strand of writing has a tendency to be limited in the scope of its ideas, environments and use of language . . . it's mainstream literary fiction. Of *course* there's a great deal of excellent literary fiction out there but there's a lot of superb 'genre' fiction too. Stretch yourself, guys:use a little imagination. You want to read a competent description of something you already know about – okay, read a literary novel. I often do. But if you want something new, something exciting, something you may not have experienced or thought about before . . . well, follow me, let us show you some interesting books tucked away on tables at the back of the store . . .

TOM ARDEN

Tom Arden's first novel grabs the reader's attention and refuses to let go. It's a literary fantasy with an intriguingly original setting, a quasi-eighteenth century milieu, but one into which a whole gamut of traditional fantasy tropes has been thrown for good measure, and it is very well written indeed. Arden is reminiscent of Gene Wolfe in the way that he uses non-standard formats to convey a story of great depth and power. This author has a lot of potential and readers of his first book will be looking forward with great anticipation to his next work.

Harlequin's Dance
Gollancz hbk £16.99
0575065176

PAUL DI FILIPPO

Di Filippo is a writer of great ambition and weirdly visionary scope whose elaborately crafted fiction is laced with a healthy dose of humour. *The Steampunk Trilogy* is a gathering of three novellas set in a *very* alternative nineteenth century. Di Filippo's mastery of language shines in his collection *Ribofunk,* a wildly inventive fusion of cutting-edge biology, hence 'ribo', and a deeply funny rock-and-roll ethic, his own brand of 'funk'.

Fractal Paisleys
Four Walls Eight Windows hbk £13.99 1568580320

Ribofunk
Four Walls Eight Windows hbk £13.99 1568580622

The Steampunk Trilogy
Four Walls Eight Windows pbk £7.99 1568581025

KEN MACLEOD

Ken Mcleod, although not derivative, draws some of his inspiration from the same sources as his close friend Iain M Banks. Like Banks, he takes cutting-edge ideas in politics, science and technology and pushes them into the future, mutating them along the way into his own distinct forms. His debut novel, *The Star Fraction,* was set in 21st century Britain, in a world full of struggling anarcho-socialist political groups. In this society the controlling US/UN group has spy satellites equipped with deadly lasers ready to destroy anyone threatening their version of peace. The book was darkly humorous and full of clever and inventive ideas and Macleod built on this impressive debut with *The Stone Canal,* a novel set on a Martian colony in which the action moves through time from the recent past to the distant future. His most recent novel, *The Cassini Division,* confirms categorically his talent. Set even further into the future than his previous books, it asks far-reaching questions about the nature of intelligence in a world where certain members of the human race have decided to move on from the boundaries of flesh and blood, downloading their intelligence and personalities into silicon, simultaneously expanding and mutating their sentience. Once again Macleod shows himself to be a fine proponent of the cool, modern science fiction style used by the best writers in the genre.

The Cassini Division
Legend hbk £15.99 009924022x

The Star Fraction
Legend pbk £ 5.99 0099558815

The Stone Canal
Legend pbk £5.99 0099559013

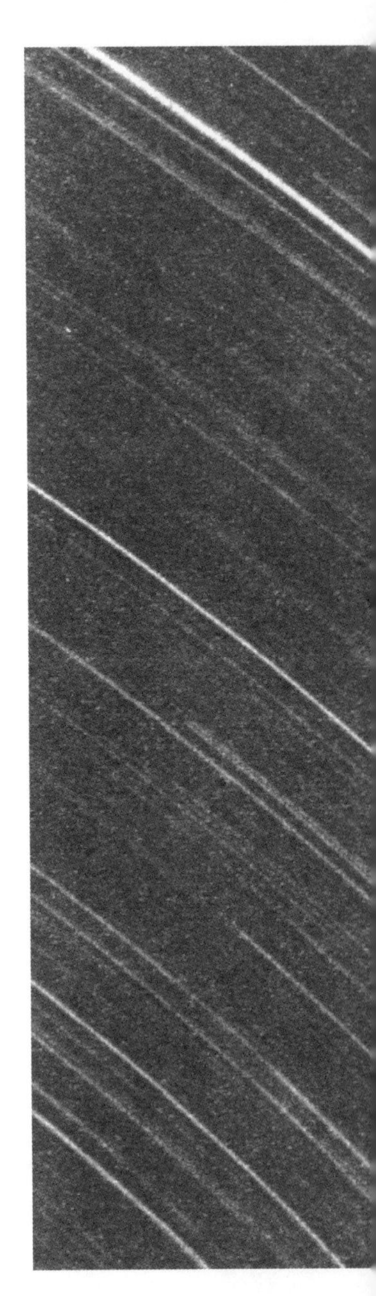

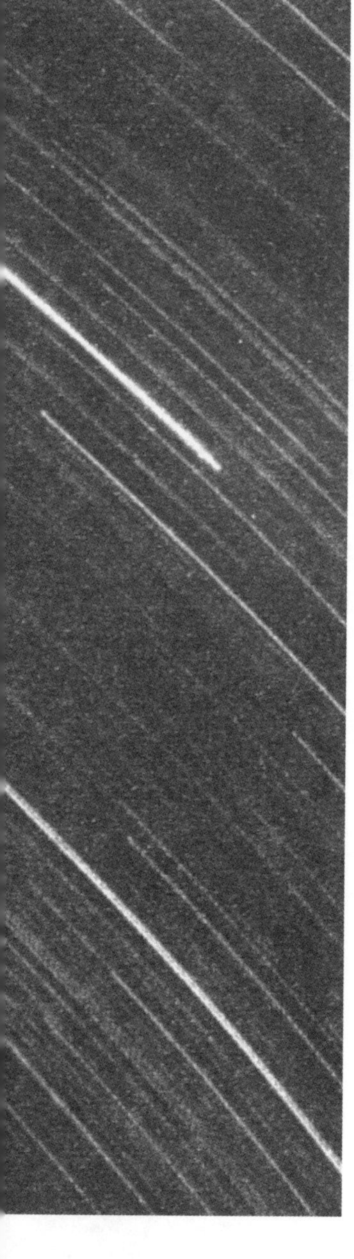

JEFF NOON

Jeff Noon exploded onto the SF scene in 1994 with the publication of his first novel, a surreal coming-of-age odyssey, set in a hip, trippy, Daliesque future Manchester. *Vurt* won him the Arthur C. Clarke award. The sequel, *Pollen,* continued to explore some of the same themes as the first novel - fractal information, the wavering barrier between reality and imagination and the burden of growing up in a world you don't really understand and don't really belong to. In *Automated Alice,* as a tribute to one of his strongest literary influences, Noon subjected Lewis Carroll's pinafore-clad heroine to a Manchester not so far adrift in time from the one we know but infinitely stranger. His most recent book, *Nymphomation,* returns to the same territory as *Vurt.* Manchester's SF maestro probes the concept of sexy information - words and numbers, belief and hallucination, probability and improbability, all of which breed and intermingle to reproduce strange versions of seemingly familiar themes. Jeff Noon is an author who breaks all the rules, an author in love with language who invites the reader to share his addiction. We can expect more surreal and seductive fiction from Noon in the years and realities to come.

Automated Alice
Corgi pbk £6.99 0552144789

Nymphomation
Doubleday hbk £15.99 0385408129

Pollen
Pan pbk £5.99 033033882X

Random Factor
Pulp Books pbk £7.50 1899571043

Vurt
Pan pbk £5.99 0330338811

MARY DORIA RUSSELL

It may be too early to predict with certainty but it seems likely that Mary Doria Russell's first novel *The Sparrow* marks the start of a brilliant career. In this intelligent and beautifully written book Russell tackles two of the most demanding and difficult themes in SF - 'first contact' and 'the future of religion' - and uses them to create a multi-layered narrative that engages both heart and intellect. The book's main character, the Jesuit missionary Emilio Sandoz, willing to bet his life and his faith on first contact with the alien peoples of Rakhat, is a memorable creation. In Sandoz's understanding and misunderstanding of God's other children lies the drama and tragedy of this remarkable book. *The Children of God*, a sequel soon to be published in the US, in which Sandoz returns to Rakhat, looks set to be one of the most sought-after SF books of the year.

The Sparrow
Black Swan pbk £6.99
0552997773

MICHAEL MARSHALL SMITH

Michael Marshall Smith is a writer of great depth and imagination, a wordsmith of the highest order and one of the most entertaining science fiction writers at work today. He is a man of many talents. As a writer of superb short stories he is one of the champions of the very lifeblood of the genre. As the author of three novels to date, he has shown us that science fiction can still be sharp, sexy, dangerous and almost insanely funny all at once. Steven Spielberg certainly seems to think so; he's paid a lot of U.S. Dollars for the film rights to *Spares*. Smith's newest book, *One of Us,* isn't even on the bookshelves yet and already we can expect a movie.

Michael Marshall Smith has a habit of apparently defying the normal sub-genres whilst secretly embracing them all; from high-action adventure to secret-agent intrigue, from psychological horror to bone-dry black humour. His way with words and concepts is pure pleasure to experience and, stylistically, his books are reminiscent of the best Tarantino movies - cool, slick, and exciting. His works to date have everything the reader could possibly want; love, hate, passion, terror, life, death, sadness, joy, blood, sweat, tears, sentient washing machines and colour co-ordinated trousers. Entertaining, thought-provoking, intellectually stimulating and cathartically satisfying, the novels and short stories of Michael Marshall Smith come with the highest of recommendations.

One of Us
Voyager hbk £12.99 0002256002

Only Forward
Voyager pbk £5.99 0586217746

Spares
Voyager pbk £5.99 0586217754

NEAL STEPHENSON (b.1959)

Neal Stephenson sprang into the spotlight and gained both critical acclaim and a cultish following with the 1992 novel *Snow Crash,* in which, in the near future, a strange computer virus strikes down hackers. He seemed to sweep straight into his stride as a mature writer and the early book *Zodiac* is notable for its assured plotting and its direct language. His inventiveness is clear and his speculations have the sound basis in present fact that is the mark of the best SF writers. This was most amply demonstrated by *The Diamond Age,* in which he re-imagines the forms society might take in response to developments in nanotechnology which are equally well-realised. Yet Stephenson is not a solemn writer. The hectic and blackly comic opening scene to *Snow Crash* verges on the slapstick and his storytelling gifts are amongst the brightest in operation in the genre. All Stephenson's novels so far have been very different and it seems safe to assume that he will continue to demonstrate his startling originality in novels to come.

Snow Crash
RoC pbk £5.99 0140232923

The Diamond Age
RoC pbk £5.99 0451454812

Zodiac
Penguin pbk £5.99 0140270388

TRICIA SULLIVAN

Tricia Sullivan's first two novels are amongst the very best to appear in the last few years. Her spectacular first novel, *Lethe*, a far future story about genetic engineering, met with instant critical acclaim and she followed this auspicious debut with *Someone to Watch Over Me*, a wonderfully engrossing near-future novel about technological voyeurism. In both novels Sullivan displays a rare talent for characterisation and explores psychologically complex interpersonal relationships and questions of identity. Not often does a writer show such immediate and diverse talent with just two books and it is safe to assume that Tricia Sullivan will continue to develop and gain recognition as one of the potentially great SF writers of the future.

Lethe
Bantam pbk £5.99 0553568582

Someone to Watch Over Me
Millennium pbk £9.99
1857985249

JACK WOMACK (b.1956)

Jack Womack is five books into a projected six book series of novels set in a near future New York. These first five novels form a loose sequence with overlapping characters and the common setting of a 21st century metropolis which is little short of a warzone. Each book can be read individually or in the following, chronological order: *Heathern, Random Acts of Senseless Violence, Ambient, Terraplane,* and *Elvissey*. Womack's novels are stylish and witty excursions into our very near future, firmly grounded in some of today's harsher realities. Writing in the fading light of cyberpunk Womack considers familiar themes: the fragmented city, the rise of the megacorporation, appalling violence and the loss of belief. His all too human characters play out their lives against a dark urban landscape. Stylistically he demonstrates great flair. His books are sensuous and dense. There is a certain foregrounding of linguistic style and an emphasis on language that provides the greatest challenge in his work and also the greatest reward. In his most recent novel Womack has moved away from SF. *Let's Put the Future Behind Us* is a satire on the state of modern Russia, where Womack seems to have found a contemporary setting suited to many of the issues he explores in his science fiction.

Let's Put the Future Behind Us
Flamingo pbk £6.99 000655007X

Random Acts of Senseless Violence
Flamingo pbk £4.99 0586213201

HARD
SCIENCE FICTION

JEWELS IN THE CROWN: SCIENCE FICTION SHORT STORIES *by* Stephen Baxter

The author of the Xeelee stories runs through a list of his favourite examples of the SF short story.

Science fiction is one of the few literary fields in which the short story form continues to flourish. In fact, some aficionados contend that it is in the short form that SF is at its best, with the startling ideas that characterise the field polished to an economical and jewel-like brilliance.

Most of SF's best-known authors have published short fiction as well as novels. The stories of HG Wells are still well worth reading; seek out *The Crystal Egg*, in which the object of the title offers glimpses of another world. It is well known that Arthur C. Clarke's classic 2001 series developed from ideas he first presented in a simple early story called *The Sentinel*; Clarke's great and poignant short pieces also include *The Star*, in which a Jesuit confronts the reality of the Star of Bethlehem, and *The Nine Billion Names of God*, in which a modern computer helps a group of monks in their task of compiling all the possible names of God. Isaac Asimov's short fiction includes perhaps the most famous SF short story of all, *Nightfall*, about a world without darkness – until a multiple eclipse hides the suns. Asimov's robot stories, collected in *I, Robot* and elsewhere are justly famous for their logic and intricacy. *The Last Question* is a famous piece about a super-computer which, struggling to answer a question about the inevitability of the universe's end, transcends time and space. My favourite of Asimov's is the poignant *Eyes Do More than See* about powerful post-humans mourning the loss of their corporeality. Robert Heinlein, famous for long, discursive novels, gave us such intricate pieces as the astounding time-travel classics *By His Bootstraps* and *All You Zombies*, the latter about a time traveller who becomes his own father and mother. Bob Shaw's moving *Light of Other Days* (incorporated in *Other Days, Other Eyes*) – about 'slow glass', a material which passes light extremely slowly – is one of the finest developments of a new idea in modern SF. James Blish's *Surface Tension*, a tale of microscopic humans struggling to escape from a shallow pond, is a great evocation of wonder and the human spirit. Philip K Dick wrote many fine and intelligent stories, often playing on a sense of the fragility of reality – such as *War Veteran*, whose protagonist mumbles of a war that has yet to be fought.

Many of SF's best authors have reached their artistic peak in short stories. Ray Bradbury's Martian stories, collected in *The Silver Locusts*, are justly prized; other favourites include the time paradox classic *A Sound of Thunder*, in which a clumsy dinosaur hunter steps on a single butterfly and changes the world, *The Veldt*, a sinister story in which the images on the walls of a virtual-reality nursery prove rather more 'real' than expected, *Frost and Fire*, in which humans are stranded on a planet where their lives last just eight days, and *The Pedestrian*, about the last pedestrian in an urban future. Harlan Ellison's stories, including the post-apocalyptic *A Boy and His Dog*, have startled readers for three decades. Robert Sheckley wrote dozens of hilarious and poignant pieces, including *Ticket to Tranai* and *Ask a Foolish Question*. J. G. Ballard's 'space stories' – such as *Cage of Sand*, about the drowning of Cape Kennedy by Martian sand – were ironic responses to the gung-ho American SF of the 1950s.

Classic stories of the past, some by otherwise largely forgotten authors, have helped to shape the field today, and can still be found in the anthologies. *The Cold Equations* by Tom Godwin is a chilling depiction of the remorseless hostility of space. Philip Latham's *The Xi Effect* is an unforgettable depiction of the consequences of the startling discovery that the entire universe is shrinking.

Some authors have developed series of stories against a common background, often called a 'future history', which may also be elaborated in linked novels. The first future history of all was developed by Robert Heinlein; in stories like *The Man Who Sold The Moon* Heinlein set out his vision of an American future in space – a vision now tinged with nostalgia for its lost possibilities. Asimov's Foundation series has its roots in a series of linked stories. My own stories, collected in *Vacuum Diagrams*, form an exploration of a devastating cosmic conflict. Larry Niven's *Known Space* stories set out details of the imaginary universe which includes his famous *Ringworld* novels - though my personal favourite of Niven's is the stand-alone story *Inconstant Moon*, about a man who understands that the reason the Moon is shining so brightly in the California night sky is that the sun has exploded.

Modern short story specialists include the Americans Terry Bisson – who gave us *Bears Discover Fire* (about precisely that) and *The Hole In The Hole*, about a Brooklyn junk yard where tyres from a Lunar Rover turn up – and Howard Waldrop, whose dense, complex and hilarious stories include *The Ugly Chickens*, detailing the fate of the last dodos. The British writer Ian Macleod is comparatively unknown in this country, but he has built a high reputation in the US with a string of intelligent and beautiful stories. A personal favourite is Macleod's *Snodgrass*, about the fate of the Beatles in a reality where John Lennon lived on. Eric Brown, another British writer, has delivered a string of fine short stories including *The Time-Lapsed Man*, about an astronaut whose senses suffer an accumulating – and devastating – time delay.

The Best of Interzone, edited by David Pringle, is a recent compilation from the pages of Britain's top SF short story magazine. *Interzone* and the leading American magazines – *Asimov's Science Fiction, Fantasy and Science Fiction, Analog* and *Science Fiction Age* – can often be found in British stores, or are available on subscription. Gardner Dozois's *Best New SF* series is a reliable annual compilation of the best short SF from both sides of the Atlantic. Tom Shippey's *The Oxford Book of Science Fiction Stories* is a good introduction to the genre, and there are in-print collections by many classic authors such as Clarke, Asimov, Bradbury and Dick, as well as modern authors like myself, Paul McAuley, Eric Brown and Gregory Benford.

BRIAN ALDISS (b.1925)

Once established, many writers are content to dig themselves into comfortable niches and spend the rest of their careers endlessly re-exploring familiar themes. From the outset Brian Aldiss indicated that this was not the route he intended to take. Rarely repeating himself he has shown a need to reinvent himself as a writer with each succeeding work. Unlike most jacks-of-all-trades, he is also master of many and he has written such sub-genre quintessentials as *Hothouse* (dying earth), *Non Stop* (generation starship) and, arguably his finest novel, *The Malacia Tapestry* (alternative universe). However Aldiss's work is very fluid and difficult to categorise, embracing mainstream fiction, genre and literary SF, and pastiche. If influences have to be identified, then he owes as much to Joyce and the *nouveau roman* as to Golden Age SF. This versatility is best reflected in his impressive output of shorter stories, some of which are amongst the few works of experimental SF which genuinely challenge literary conventions and boundaries. His novels and stories reflect the unpredictability of human life. Few reach absolute conclusions and his beleaguered characters often face uncertain prospects. They do, however, undergo fantastic adventures and Aldiss's fecund imagination creates a whole pantheon of bizarre lifeforms, weird ecologies and timeless cities. In his most successful sequence - *The Helliconia Trilogy* - all these factors combine to prove that Aldiss is amongst the finest living writers of SF.

The Detached Retina : Aspects of Science Fiction (essays)
Liverpool UP pbk £11.75 0853232997

The Helliconia Trilogy
Voyager pbk £9.95 0006482236

The Secret of This Book
Voyager pbk £5.95 0006497934

POUL ANDERSON

(b.1926)

Since publishing his first short story as a student in the 40s, Anderson has been a prolific writer of science fiction and fantasy, demonstrating an attention to scientific fact which is a reflection of his own training as a physicist. He is also, however, adept at the creation of exciting and compelling narratives and new worlds which are believable and detailed. His interest in Scandinavian myth is reflected in many of his fantasy novels and his future history of what he calls the Technic Civilization is cleverly informed by his knowledge of political and economic trends in recorded history.

The Boat of a Million Years
Orbit pbk £4.99 074740609X

The Stars Are Also Fire
Tor Books pbk £4.99
0330347071

ISAAC ASIMOV (1920–1992)

Asimov fitted the dictionary definition of a polymath. Over a professional writing career of fifty three years he produced a flood of scientific articles, whodunnits, jokes, limericks, even biblical and Shakespearean commentaries. But it is for his monumental contribution to SF and its development that he will be remembered. His vast array of short stories frequently shows signs of having been written at speed. Indeed he reportedly wrote one of them live on a television chat show in response to a challenge. However the best of them are amongst the best in the genre. *Nightfall,* for example, is an extraordinary tale of a planet which follows a complicated orbit around multiple suns in such a way that night falls every two millennia, bringing the fall of civilization in its wake. At the close of the story it is not the coming of the dark that causes society to collapse but the sudden revelation of millions of stars sparkling in the sky.

Undoubtedly Asimov's two major achievements were the Foundation series and the Robot stories. *Foundation, Foundation and Empire* and *Second Foundation* were written between 1942 and 1950 and originally appeared in instalments in

FOUNDATION SERIES

Prelude to Foundation
Voyager pbk £5.99 0586071113

Foundation
Voyager pbk £5.99 0586010807

Foundation and Empire
Voyager pbk £5.99 0586013555

Second Foundation
Voyager 0586017135 pbk £5.99

Foundation's Edge
Voyager 0586058397 pbk £5.99

Foundation and Earth
Voyager pbk £5.99 0586071105

Forward the Foundation
Bantam pbk £5.99 0553404881

ROBOT SERIES

The Complete Robot
Voyager pbk £9.99 0586057242

I, Robot
Grafton pbk £5.99 0586025324

The Rest of the Robots
Grafton pbk £4.990586025944

Robot Dreams
Vista pbk £5.99 0575601809

Robots and Empire
Grafton pbk £5.99 0586062009

The Robots of Dawn
Grafton pbk £5.99 0586061991

Robot Visions
Vista 0575601523 pbk £5.99

The Caves of Steel
Grafton pbk £4.99 0586008357
A Child of Time
(w.Robert Silverberg)
Pan pbk £5.99 0330325795
The Complete Stories Volume 1
Voyager pbk £5.99 0006476473
The Complete Stories Volume 2
Voyager pbk £5.99 0006476473
Gold
Voyager pbk £5.99 0006482023
Magic
Voyager pbk £5.99 0006482031
Naked Sun
Bantam pbk £4.99 0553293397
Nemesis
Bantam pbk £5.99 055340069X
Nightfall (w.Robert Silverberg)
Pan pbk £6.99 0330320963
The Positronic Man (w. Robert Silverberg)
Pan pbk £6.99 0330330586

John Campbell's *Astounding* magazine. Together they told the huge story of the decay of a galactic civilization in an unapologetically popular and entertaining manner. In the eighties, towards the end of Asimov's career, disappointing sequels followed in the shape of *Foundation's Edge* (1982), *Foundation and Earth* (1986), *Prelude to Foundation* (1988) and *Forward the Foundation* (1992), the latter completed only a few weeks before his death.

The robot series is built around the famous Three Laws of Robotics, a set of guidelines built into his fictional creations. The laws themselves are beguilingly simple but nonetheless leave loopholes and contradictions which supplied Asimov with the raw material for a multitude of stories. The two collections, *I, Robot* and *The Rest of the Robots*, are seminal works of SF. Unfortunately the later sequels *The Robots of Dawn* and *Robots and Empire*, which attempt to blend the Robot series and the Foundation series into one seamless continuum, are less than perfectly judged and often seem slightly frantic in plot and narrative. Of his other works, two novels which combine the SF and crime genres, *The Caves of Steel* and *The Naked Sun*, are highly commended.

The Three Laws of Robotics:
1) A robot may not injure a human being or, through inaction, allow a human being to come to harm.
2) A robot must obey the orders given it by human beings except where such orders would conflict with the First Law.
3) A robot must protect its own existence as long as such protection does not conflict with the First or Second Law.

STEPHEN BAXTER (b.1957)

This British author began writing his Xeelee short stories for *Interzone* before expanding this fascinating and highly detailed 'future history' into a sequence of novels, beginning with *Raft* and continuing with *Timelike Infinity*, *Flux* and *Ring*. Although these tales are set in the far future they contain a wealth of fantastic but plausible devices, which, although the product of Baxter's fertile imagination, are based very much on an extrapolation of today's science. Indeed Baxter has also written more contemporary hard SF, taking an alternative view of real-life events, such as his version of the space programme in *Voyage*, in which America not only lands on the moon but goes on to visit Mars. In all his books, whether he is exploring the solar system in *Titan* or alternative worlds in *The Time Ships*, his sequel to H.G. Wells's *The Time Machine*, Baxter always explains his future society or technology in believable terms. Those who enjoy pure SF in the tradition of Arthur C. Clarke will find much to enjoy in Stephen Baxter.

XEELEE

Timelike Infinity
Voyager pbk £17.95 00647618X

Flux
Voyager pbk £5.99 0006476201

Ring
Voyager pbk £5.99 000648221X

The Time Ships
Voyagerpbk £5.99 0006480128

Voyage
Voyager pbk £6.99 0006480373

Titan
Voyager pbk £6.99 0006498116

Vacuum Diagrams
Voyager pbk £5.99 0006498124

Traces
Voyager hbk £16.99 0002254271

GREG BEAR (b.1951)

After a number of relatively pedestrian works, Greg Bear came into his own in the mid-eighties when he began to produce a seemingly limitless succession of excellent hard SF novels. Often of huge cosmological sweep, his chunky epics are typified by *Eon* and its sequels, which feature an infinite corridor of doorways to alternate realities. Mind-boggling in scope, the worlds visited are lovingly described, replete with exotic inhabitants. Reworking familiar Hollywood stereotypes - ET-like aliens - and classics of children's literature - the Dawn Treader as spaceship - Bear creates a very accessible universe bursting with adventure. However there is a darker side to his work. Bear is also something of a world destroyer as well as world creator, enthusiastically deploying intelligent cells in *Blood Music* to render humanity into something wholly incomprehensible. In *The Forge of God* it is extraterrestrial viral machines that do the job of consuming the earth. Inevitably, Bear allows something to arise from the ashes of destruction, whether it be a new lifeform or refugees eager for revenge, although this never appears cynically manufactured to soften the apocalyptic blow but to emerge from the necessities of the story. Surprisingly his characters are seldom swamped by the spectacle of creation and destruction and his work continues to grow in complexity and sophistication in novels like *Queen of Angels* and *Moving Mars.*

Anvil of Stars
Legend pbk £5.99 0099780402

Blood Music
Legend pbk £4.99 009952340X

Country of the Mind
Legend pbk £9.99 0099350912

Eon
Legend pbk £5.99 0099547104

Eternity
Legend pbk £5.99 009970630X

The Forge of God
Legend pbk £5.99 099618702

Legacy
Legend pbk £5.99 0099350718

Moving Mars
Legend pbk £5.99 009978050X

Queen of Angels
Legend pbk £5.99 0099847701

Songs of Earth and Power
Legend pbk £6.99

Strength of Stones
Gollancz 0575057017 pbk
£3.99

Tangents
Gollancz pbk £5.99
0575047755

The Venging
Legend pbk £4.99 0099964503

GREGORY BENFORD (b.1941)

A Californian physicist, Benford is an author who has shown the influence of both the literary New Wave and traditional SF. Certainly one of the main contenders for Arthur C. Clarke's crown, Benford is adept at the kind of speculation that shows due respect for current scientific knowledge while remaining open-minded about the possibilities of our future as space travellers. He is particularly skilful at conveying the vastness of the universe and the comparative tininess of human lives and human concerns. His depictions of enigmatic aliens will be relished by all fans of *2001: A Space Odyssey*, excellently evoking mysteries which the books only partially resolve. For hard SF readers, however, Benford's greatest virtue must be his ability to describe the lives and work of scientists with a realism unsurpassed by his peers. Drawing on his own experience he conveys a genuine sense of what it is like to be on the cutting edge of scientific research. Together with a willingness to explore issues of gender and race, this quality is one that makes Benford's fiction appeal to a wider audience than that usually available to the writer of traditional SF.

Across the Sea of Suns
Vista pbk £5.99 0575600551

Foundation's Fear
Orbit hbk £16.99 1857234634

Heart of the Comet
Orbit pbk £6.99 1857234367

In the Ocean of Night
Gollancz pbk £5.99 0575600357

Matter's End
Gollancz pbk £5.99 0575600721

Timescape
Gollancz pbk £5.99 0575600500

GALACTIC CENTRE

Sailing Bright Eternity
Gollancz pbk £5.99 0575600470

Tides of Light
Gollancz pbk £5.99 0575058293

Furious Gulf
Gollancz pbk £5.99 0575061006

'Night and day fled across the desert's face, but in the streets of Diaspar it was always afternoon.'

Arthur C. Clarke,
The City and the Stars

ARTHUR C. CLARKE (b.1917)

One of the most influential and prolific SF writers since the war, Arthur C. Clarke established himself in the genre during the fifties, at much the same time as other giants in the field such as Asimov and Heinlein were publishing their best work. Not only has Clarke been a great teller of tales, a master at conveying the wonders and vastness of the universe, he has also been enormously successful in using his scientific background (he studied physics and mathematics at King's College, London) to predict technological advancement. He was describing the possibilities of communications satellites and mobile phones as early as 1945.

Clarke began as a writer of short stories and he has published hundreds of quirky and readable tales, most famously *The Sentinel* in 1951, which was the basis for his turbulent collaboration with Stanley Kubrick in the making of the innovative film *2001 : A Space Odyssey* in 1968 and for the subsequent novel. He has also produced other full-length novels, many of which explore ideas originally raised in the short stories. Among the best of these novels are *Childhood's End, Earthlight, A Fall of Moondust* and *Rendezvous with Rama.* At the age of eighty Clarke continues to write, although in recent years, due to his health, much of his work has been in collaboration with others, particularly the NASA scientist Gentry Lee who has worked with him on sequels to *Rendezvous with Rama.*

As a writer, Clarke lacks the satirical venom and sheer originality of contemporaries like Philip K. Dick or Heinlein, but his sound background in science has made him the arch-exponent of Hard SF, and his imagination and humanity are clear throughout his work. He has helped lay the foundations for many of the SF writers of the last forty years and has provided the ordinary reader with fiction which stimulates a sense of the grandeur and the dangers of the universe.

A Fall of Moondust
Gollancz pbk £4.99
0575060034

Childhood's End
Pan pbk £4.99 0330316613

Cradle
Orbit pbk £5.99 1857230728

Ghost from Grand Banks
Warner pbk £5.99 0751500534

Hammer of God
Orbit pbk £4.99 1857231945

Imperial Earth
Vista pbk £4.99 0575601582

Reach for Tomorrow
Vista pbk £4.99 0575600462

Richter 10
Vista pbk £5.99 0575601108

Songs of Distant Earth
Voyager pbk £4.99 0586066233

Tales of Ten Worlds
Gollancz pbk £4.99
0575061243

The City and the Stars
Gollancz pbk £4.99
0575056754

The Deep Range
Gollancz pbk £4.99
0575057920

The Fountains of Paradise
Vista pbk £4.99 0575601531

The Other Side of the Sky
Gollancz pbk £4.99
0575039884

SPACE ODYSSEY

2001: a Space Odyssey
Legend pbk £5.99 009979800X

2010: Odyssey Two
Voyager pbk £5.99 0586056998

2061: Odyssey Three: Odyssey Three
Voyager pbk £5.99 0586203192

3001: the Final Odyssey
Voyager pbk £5.99 0586066241

RAMA SERIES

Rendezvous with Rama
Orbit pbk £4.99 0708849458

Rama II
Orbit pbk£5.99 0708848265

Garden of Rama
Orbit pbk £6.99 1857230213

Rama Revealed
Orbit pbk £6.99 1857232526

GREG EGAN (b.1961)

In a relatively small number of novels and stories Australian Greg Egan has shown that he is one of the most interesting and demanding of contemporary practitioners of hard SF and fully deserving of the accolade bestowed by one critic – 'one of the genre's great ideas men.' His short stories, collected in *Axiomatic*, explored possible consequences of technologies of the not too distant future. Lovers exchange bodies and minds but sexual experimentation goes too far. Artificial minds replace human brains but the questions of identity and self-awareness persist. The novel *Permutation City* was an engrossing and imaginative reconstruction of virtual realities to which humanity had travelled in search of immortality. What Egan himself calls his 'subjective cosmology' trilogy was begun by *Quarantine* in 1992 and completed by *Distress* in 1996. Readers will anticipate more mind-expanding fiction from Egan in the future.

Axiomatic
Millennium pbk £4.99 1857983092

Diaspora
Millennium pbk £9.99 1857984390

Distress
Phoenix pbk £5.99 1857994841

Permutation City
Millennium pbk £4.99 1857982185

Quarantine
Legend pbk £4.99 0099153815

An Unusual Angle
Norstrilia P pbk £9.50 0909106126

LARRY NIVEN (b.1938)

Larry Niven emerged in the sixties as a new voice in SF and is now recognised as the undisputed king of the blockbusting Hard SF epic. He has the kind of large scale audacity displayed by old masters of the genre like Robert Heinlein and, in an age of pessimism and dystopian visions, is mostly optimistic, an enthusiastic proponent of the power of engineering, maths and space travel to transform the human race. His early future history sequence, *Tales of Known Space*, is an example of the scope of Niven's vision. Humans are placed in a universe populated by various alien races that have influenced the Earth's past and continue to affect humanity far into the future. Spanning millennia, these exciting tales of alien interaction and human conquest are complex and inventive, if sometimes overly militaristic. Niven is, primarily, a hard SF writer who incorporates speculations based on the concepts of modern physics into his work. *Ringworld*, for example, a book about an engineered 'planet' which completely circles a sun, is rigorously defined and skilfully conceived. Niven's most popular works are his collaborations with other authors, particularly Jerry Pournelle. These are massive, compulsive page-turners about alien invasion and planetary colonisation. Although Niven tends towards the right and political correctness is not his forte - he makes environmentalists, for example, the villains in several books - his ability to combine storytelling with world-building and speculative science in one gripping narrative is not in doubt.

Achilles' Choice (with Steven Barnes)
Pan pbk £4.99 0330331043

Dream Park: the Voodoo Game (with Steven Barnes))
Pan pbk £4.99 0330326473

Fallen Angels (with Jerry Pournelle)
Pan pbk £5.99 0330335995

Footfall (with Jerry Pournelle)
Orbit pbk £6.99 1857230973

Guide to Larry Niven's Ringworld
S&S pbk £9.99 0671722050

Limits
Orbit pbk £4.50 0708882013

N-space
Orbit pbk £6.99 1857230035

Oath of Fealty (with Jerry Pournelle)
Orbit pbk £4.99 0708880894

The Barsoom Project (with Steven Barnes)
Pan pbk £4.99 0330316702

The Dragons of Heorot (with J. Pournelle)
Orbit pbk £6.99 1857233735

The Legacy of Heorot (with J. Pournelle)
Orbit1 pbk £6.99 185723134

The Mote in God's Eye (with J. Pournelle)
HarperCollins pbk £5.99 0586217460

The Moat Around Murcheson's Eye (with J. Pournelle)
HarperCollins pbk £5.99 0006476457

World Out of Time
pbk £5.99 0345336968

TALES OF KNOWN SPACE

Smoke Ring
Orbit pbk £5.99 1857233115

Ringworld
Orbit pbk £5.99 1857231694

Ringworld Throne
Orbit pbk £5.99 1857234707

The Ringworld Engineers
Orbit pbk £5.99 1857231112

KIM STANLEY ROBINSON (b.1952)

Everything about Kim Stanley Robinson is big. His name is big, all those syllables. His books are big – veritable breezeblocks, all of them - and his stories contain huge, timeless landscapes from Antarctica to Mars. When things go boom in a Kim Stanley Robinson book, whole universes shake. Robinson is best known for his Mars trilogy which chronicles the colonisation of Mars, the first arrival of one hundred colonists and the progress from outpost to empire.

Although he writes authoritatively about both technology and war, it's clear that, unlike many other SF writers, Robinson is less interested in blowing empires to shreds than in building them back together again. The process of civilization takes precedence over quick and easy displays of violence and one of the joys of reading his books is watching the ways his characters develop against often inimical backgrounds. Yet his worlds are more than backdrops. There are few writers who can conjure up such a sense of place and leave readers with a feeling that they've roamed the craters of Mars, that they've stood on the peaks of the Himalayas, that they too have followed Amundsen and Scott through the vast cold of the Antarctic. *Antarctica,* his latest, sees him at his best. The narrative flows imperceptibly like the silent movement of a glacier. Nothing happens and then everything happens. The book confirms that Robinson is one of the most intelligent and absorbing SF writers around.

Antarctica
Voyager hbk £16.99
0002253593

Down and Out in the Year 2000
Voyager pbk £5.99 0586214976

Icehenge
Voyager pbk £5.99 0006482554

Pacific Edge
Voyager pbk £4.99 0586214577

The Gold Coast
Voyager pbk £6.99 0708882951

The Wild Shore
Voyager pbk £4.99 0006480195

MARS SERIES

Red Mars
Voyager pbk £6.99 0586213899

Green Mars
Voyager pbk £6.99 0586213902

Blue Mars
Voyager hbk £15.99
0246138831

MAIN STREAM

SCIENCE FICTION

A. A. ATTANASIO (b.1951)

Described by one critic as 'one of the most magnificently baroque SF stylists of his generation' and by another as 'one of our most imaginative and visionary writers', Attanasio is best known for his Radix sequence in which he traces a future history of mankind, beyond its extinction, to a time, millennia hence, when aliens resurrect it for their own purposes. He is also the author of gentler, mystical fantasies such as *The Moon's Wife* and, in 1997, *Millennium*, a depiction of the wonders and terrors of the Third Millennium in which scientific and technological advance are seen to transform life both on and off the earth.

Centuries
NEL pbk £6.99 0340666005

Dark Shore
NEL pbk £5.99 034064947X

The Dragon and the Unicorn
NEL £5.99 0340617721

Last Legends of Earth
NEL £5.99 0340674636

The Moon's Wife
NEL £5.99 0450606406

Radix
NEL £5.99 034061840X

Shadow Easter
Hodder hbk £16.99
0340696257

Solis
NEL pbk £4.99 0450606414

JOHN BARNES (b.1957)

One of the best American SF writers of his generation, John Barnes has combined storytelling power and a gift for scientific extrapolation and speculation to great effect in his short stories and novels. *Mother of Storms* looked forward to the 21st century and the potentially disastrous consequences of global warming. *Kaleidoscope Century* was an odyssey through a century of war and plague as experienced by the carrier of a mysterious, rejuvenating virus. Perhaps his most original and enjoyable book is *A Million Open Doors*, which shows the reader a universe of thousands of Earth colonies, each holding a civilization modelled on one from Earth's past history. In all his books Barnes shows generosity of imagination and zestful narrative skills.

Earth Made of Glass
Millennium hbk £15.99 185798465X

Kaleidoscope Century
Millennium pbk £5.99 1857996496

A Million Open Doors
Millennium pbk £4.99 1857981499

Mother of Storms
Millennium pbk £5.99
0752808869

BEN BOVA (b.1932)

On the death of John W. Campbell in 1971, Ben Bova was appointed editor of *Analog* magazine (formerly *Astounding*), an honour which points to the latter's standing in the field of hard SF. However Bova had been producing science fiction for more than a decade before this appointment and his skills in the traditional area of space opera and related fields had been well developed. Since the time of his appointment to *Analog*'s editorial chair, his workmanlike and plausible novels of first alien contact, terraforming, clones and generation starships have appealed to readers devoted to the cardinal virtues of hard SF. Bova is an optimistic visionary whose belief in our need to conquer space is tempered by his knowledge of real science. With his refreshing taste for adventure, his natural ability to convey his awe at the cosmos and his skill at extrapolation of fiction from fact, he is one of the best technical-minded SF authors currently writing.

Brothers
NEL pbk £5.99 0450613356
Death Dream
NEL pbk £6.99 0450588815
Mars
NEL pbk £6.99 0450577171
Moonrise
NEL pbk £6.99 0340682493
Moonwar
NEL pbk £5.99 0340682515
The Trikon Deception
NEL pbk £5.99 0450588823
The Craft of Writing SF That Sells
Writers' Digest hbk £12.95 0898796008

PAT CADIGAN (b.1953)

SF movements have always struggled to accomodate female authors but there is no doubt that Pat Cadigan is the reigning empress of cyberpunk. Like Gibson and Sterling she was first published in the seventies and her excellent short stories (collected in *Patterns*) show her to be an admirable early practitioner of the movement that made genre SF so exciting in the eighties and edged it into the post-modern world. Her writings on the interface between human minds and VR and AI technologies are as striking as the reality will be in the decades to come.

The novels of Pat Cadigan are out of print in the UK. Imports of American editions of her books may be available in some larger branches of Waterstone's.

ORSON SCOTT CARD (b.1951)

American SF writer and devout Mormon burst onto the scene during the eighties and has since been a prolific and energetic producer of highly acclaimed fiction. He began his career with the *Worthing* series, a collection of novellas that reflected many aspects of his Mormon faith. Although sometimes confusing, in their use of ideas and beliefs, to the non-Mormon reader, these all showed a characteristic readability and narrative drive. Card's best and best known work is the *Ender* series, the first two books of which achieved the extraordinary feat of winning the Hugo and Nebula awards two years in succession. The series focuses on a boy called Ender who, in the first book, is indirectly responsible for the virtual elimination of an alien race. In the remaining books what began as tragedy turns into a tale of redemption as Ender aids the recovery of the aliens and comes to be regarded by them as their messiah-like saviour. In the nineties Card has been diversely productive and he has four different series currently underway. He has also turned to the writing of fantasy, although not with the success, either commercial or critical, of his SF. He remains one of the best American SF writers of his generation.

Ender's Game
Legend pbk £5.99 0099496100

Speaker for the Dead
Legend pbk £5.99 0099503204

Xenocide
Legend pbk £5.99 0099525003

SAMUEL R. DELANY (b.1942)

Delany emerged in the sixties as one of the leading lights in the American New Wave. He works in the tradition of the space opera - his epic *Neveryon* series depicts a fantastic empire beyond the borders of history - but has revitalised it with a linguistic sophistication and a willingness to treat complicated themes of gender and sexuality. No less a figure than Umberto Eco has written of Delany that he is 'not only one of the most important SF writers . . . but a fascinating writer in general who has invented a new style.'

They Fly at Ciron
Voyager pbk £5.99 0006499392

Tales of Neveryon
Harper Collins pbk £5.99 0586202706

Neveryone
Harper Collins pbk £5.99 0586202714

CHRISTOPHER EVANS (b.1951)

Since the publication of his first novel in 1980, Evans has been a prolific writer of SF although much of what he has produced has been minor fiction published under pseudonyms. Much his most successful book has been *Aztec Century*, an intricately imagined and cleverly sustained alternative history based on the premise that Cortes gave his support to the Aztecs, who were thus saved from conquest and propelled towards a world-wide empire. More recently *Mortal Remains*, a novel in which the humans of the future are translated after death into a strange, psychic afterlife known as the Noosphere, has also been well received.

Aztec Century
Gollancz pbk £4.99
0575057122

Mortal Remains
Gollancz pbk £5.99
0575600438

PHILIP JOSÉ FARMER (b.1918)

One of the great iconoclasts of SF, Farmer emerged in the fifties as one of the more original writers of that decade. Along with Bester and Dick, Farmer was an important precursor of the New Wave, eager to bring a new psychological and sexual maturity to SF. He is famous for his *Riverworld* novels, in which the entire human race is resurrected on the banks of a seemingly endless river and historic personalities from Jesus to Herman Goering explore this unexpected afterlife, but his work is very diverse. It falls, broadly, into three categories. His adventure novels are often intelligent and interesting and even routine works are marked out by Farmer's original approach to the genre. (One of these, *Flesh*, is about as raunchy as SF of the period gets.) His experimental writing is usually in shorter forms and can be engagingly quirky and verbally gymnastic. However Farmer's best works are his superb parodies and pastiches of other writers' characters and mythologies. In several of these he examines the psyches of Tarzan and Doc Savage and reveals a subconscious fascism in the characters together with a polymorphously perverse sexuality that is unexpected. Funny, scatological and incisive, the finest of these latter works is probably the obscene and brilliant *A Feast Unknown* in which Farmer satirises the Freudian undertones of much fantastic fiction and the adolescent mentality of many of its writers and readers. Much of Farmer's work is out of print in the UK but this imaginative and versatile writer is unlikely to be forgotten.

A Feast Unknown
Rhinoceros pbk £5.99 1563332760
Flesh
Rhinoceros pbk £5.99 1563333031
Image of the Beast
Rhinoceros pbk £5.99 1563331667

JACK FINNEY (1911–1995)

Also a writer of crime and mainstream fiction, Finney is chiefly renowned as one of the authors (Richard Matheson, author of *I Am Legend* and *The Shrinking Man*, is another) who helped to define US paranoid SF movies of the fifties. His classic *The Body Snatchers*, filmed three times (*Invasion of the Body Snatchers*, Don Siegel's 1956 version is perhaps the finest speculative film of its era) takes the concept of Heinlein's *Puppet Masters* to extremes that are as chilling and intense today as they were in the days of cold war fever. Possibly a key influence on the brilliant Nigel 'Quatermass' Kneale, *The Body Snatchers* remains a landmark work of alien possession and human persecution.

The novels of Jack Finney are out of print in the UK. Imports of American editions of his books may be available in some larger branches of Waterstone's.

WILLIAM GIBSON (b.1948)

Hailed by many as the father of cyberpunk, William Gibson can be more accurately described as a major moving force in the popularisation of postmodern SF. Born in the US, Gibson moved to Canada in the sixties and began publishing short fiction in 1977 with *Fragments of a Hologram Rose.* He produced a number of well-received short stories but it wasn't until 1984 that he achieved worldwide recognition for his first novel *Neuromancer*, which won all three major SF awards of the year - the Nebula, the Hugo and the Philip K. Dick award.

Set in a period about seventy years in the future, Gibson's predictions for technology and society combined to create a shockingly real, dystopian vision in which cybernetics and the growth of muti-national computers have meant the death of the nation-state and the birth of vast, commercial sprawls, governed by the law of the survival of the fittest. As Gibson himself describes it in the book, 'Night City was like a deranged experiment in social Darwinism, designed by a bored researcher who kept one thumb permanently on the fast forward button.'

Following the huge success of this first novel, Gibson went on to write two sequels, *Count Zero* and *Mona Lisa Overdrive*, and the three books became known as the 'Sprawl' or 'Cyberspace' trilogy. Although the quality of writing varies in the trilogy, it is at all times amongst the most interesting and rewarding of recent SF. Still best known for his creation, in these books, of the 'consensual hallucination' of cyberspace, Gibson has lately moved away from the study of internal space and virtual realities. With his two most recent books, *Virtual Light* and *Idoru*, he has shown a concern with more immediate questions of personal space and media influence and his writing has exhibited both rich, stylistic development and a new maturity of content.

Burning Chrome
Voyager pbk £5.99 0006480438
Count Zero
Voyager pbk £6.99 000648042X
The Difference Engine
Vista pbk £5.99 0575600292
Idoru
Penguin pbk £6.99 0140241078
Mona Lisa Overdrive
Voyager pbk £5.99 0006480446
Neuromancer
Voyager pbk £5.99 0006480411
Virtual Light
Penguin pbk £6.99 0140157727

'If they think you're crude, go technical: if they think you're technical, go crude. I'm a very technical boy. So I decided to get as crude as possible.'
William Gibson - Johnny Mnemonic

JOE HALDEMAN

(b.1943)

A master of the short story and novella, Haldeman remains best known for his seminal work, drawing on his own experiences in Vietnam, *The Forever War*, a tale of protracted conflict in space. *The Forever War* uses some of the themes and conventions of the genre of military SF but his own knowledge of the realities of war inform what is an almost polemical work, frighteningly convincing in its descriptions of future military technology. The novel is both a product of a particular historical moment and a work of contemporary relevance. The collection *None So Blind* demonstrates Haldeman's brilliance as a short story writer and includes such engaging and unmissable gems as the Hugo and Nebula award-winning *The Hemingway Hoax.*

Worlds Enough and Time
H&S pbk £4.99 0450574040

Joe Haldeman has also written Star Trek stories, some of which are in print published by Titan Books.

HARRY HARRISON (b.1925)

Harry Harrison has been a prolific and professional writer over five decades. Born Henry M. Dempsey, he started out as a commercial artist in New York, working on magazines and comics, before moving into SF as an author and editor. Robert Silverberg is one of the writers who owes his start in the genre to Harrison. Since this time, Harrison has lived in a number of countries. He moved from America to Mexico and then on to Europe, where he has spent time in Italy and Denmark, England and, for a long while, Ireland. This has fostered an international outlook and he was a leading light in the creation of World SF, an organisation for SF professionals from all countries. He is also a proponent of the international language, Esperanto. Indeed the characters in what is, probably, his best known series, the *Stainless Steel Rat* books, are speakers of Esperanto in the far future. The series, built around the exploits of reformed master criminal James Bolivar DiGriz, has a light, humorous tone although serious concerns are sometimes raised. These caper stories have a companion series in the *Bill the Galactic Hero* books which make fun of the space opera genre and its cliches in a more knockabout style. Harrison has also written a number of one-off, more serious novels of which the best known is probably *Make Room!Make Room!*, a dystopian tale of an overpopulated New York which was made into the film *Soylent Green* in 1973.

Bill the Galactic Hero

Bill, the Galactic Hero
Gollancz pbk £3.99 0575047011

Bill, the Galactic Hero on the Planet of Bottled Brains
Gollancz pbk £4.99 0575050047

Bill, the Galactic Hero on the Planet of Robot Slaves
Gollancz pbk £4.99 0575050039

Bill, the Galactic Hero on the Planet of Tasteless Pleasures
Gollancz1 pbk £4.99 057505248

Bill, the Galactic Hero on the Planet of the Hippies from Hell
Gollancz pbk £4.99 057505526X

Bill, the Galactic Hero on the Planet of Zombie Vampires
Gollancz pbk £4.99 0575053208

Bill, the Galactic Hero and the Final Incoherent Adventure
Gollancz pbk £4.99 0575057173

Stainless Steel Rat

The Stainless Steel Rat
Orbit pbk £4.99 1857984986

The Stainless Steel Rat for President
Orbit pbk £4.99 1857232798

The Stainless Steel Rat Is Born
Orbit pbk £4.99 1857232771

The Stainless Steel Rat Wants You
Orbit pbk £4.50 185723278X

The Stainless Steel Rat's Revenge
Orbit pbk £4.99 1857984994

The Hammer and the Cross
Legend pbk £5.99 0099868202

One King's Way
Legend pbk £5.99 0099303086

Stars and Stripes
Hodder pbk £6.99 0340689188

The Turing Option
RoC pbk £5.99 0140129502

ROBERT A. HEINLEIN (1907–1988)

It is almost impossible to overestimate Heinlein's contribution to SF. He started writing in the late thirties and became a mainstay of John Campbell's *Astounding* magazine. He produced a huge series of mutually consistent short stories, sound in their ideas and told in a refreshingly popular idiom, that represented the genre's first serious attempt at a future history.

In the fifties Heinlein turned away from his future history and embarked on a series of impressive juvenile novels. The best of these, *Starman Jones, The Star Beast* and *Have Spacesuit - Will Travel,* still read well today. The rest of his immense body of work is diverse and of varying quality. *Starship Troopers* is a gung-ho, Hugo award-winning story of future war, recently subverted as a satirical film. In *Stranger in a Strange Land,* which became something of a cult novel in the sixties, a human brought up by Martians returns to Earth and becomes a messiah figure. Another Hugo-winner, *The Moon Is a Harsh Mistress,* tells of a revolution on the moon and remains one of the most purely enjoyable SF novels ever written.

Heinlein's later work tended towards an odd form of solipsism. He mixed characters that were clearly his alter-egos with characters from his earlier work in books that were bloated and very nearly unreadable. It was an ignominious literary end for a giant in the field. It is better to remember him for the novels of his prime and for such wonderful short stories as *By His Bootstraps* and *All You Zombies,* the two best time paradox short stories ever written.

Between Planets
pbk £5.99 0345320999

Beyond This Horizon
pbk £5.99 0451166760

The Cat Who Walks Through Walls
pbk £6.99 0441094996

Expanded Universe
pbk £6.99 0441218911

Friday
Orbit pbk £5.99 0450055493

Glory Road
S&S pbk £4.50 0671877046

I Will Fear No Evil
pbk £6.990441359175

Job: A Comedy of Justice
Hodder pbk £5.99 0450058409

The Moon Is a Harsh Mistress
Orbit pbk £5.99 0450002314

The Notebooks of Lazarus Long
pbk £10.95 0876544731

Space Cadet
Hodder pbk £4.50 0450007375

Starship Troopers
Orbit pbk £5.99 0450005739

Stranger in a Strange Land
Orbit pbk £5.99 0450547426

Time Enough for Love
pbk £6.99 0441810764

To Sail Beyond the Sunset
Orbit pbk £6.99 1857231988

K. W. JETER (b.1950)

Jeter's early fiction was strange, disturbing and inventive. The thematic trilogy consisting of *Dr Adder, The Glass Hammer* and *Death Arms,* weirdly imaginative and often violent, was unflinching in its questioning of sexual mores and unsparing in its examination of the potential brutality of technology. More recently Jeter has turned to media tie-in books and has written, amongst other works, sequels to *Bladerunner.*

Blade Runner II: the Edge of Human
Orion pbk £5.99 0752803603

Blade Runner III: Replicant Night
Orion pbk £5.99 0752808621

NANCY KRESS (b.1948)

In the decade since the publication of her first novel *An Alien Light,* a story of a degenerate, warring group of humans coming under the baffled scrutiny of aliens, Nancy Kress has gained a high reputation as a stimulating writer of first-class SF. As Gene Wolfe has said, 'Nancy Kress has idea after idea but she knows that ideas are nothing without people.' Her work in that decade has included some admirable shorter fiction and the novel *Beggars in Spain,* together with its sequel *Beggars and Choosers,* which look at a society in which some individuals require no sleep.

Beggars and Choosers
RoC pbk £5.99 0451454847

Beggars in Spain
RoC pbk £5.99 0451185544

Oaths and Miracles
RoC pbk £5.99 0451455770

JULIAN MAY (b.1931)

Julian May's work, essential reading in fantasy fiction, consists of the quartet, *The Saga of the Exiles,* and a trilogy, *The Galactic Milieu* trilogy, linked together by a single novel, *Intervention.* The basic premises of the series can be easily described. In the twenty second century, humanity has, with the help of alien species, escaped Earth and been given *lebensraum* in the stars. Those few disaffected with the new system can take advantage of a unique, one-way time trip back to Earth's Pliocene period, in the hope of finding a simpler, less demanding and less structured society. Instead they find Pliocene Earth under the benign despotism of another, totally alien race. *The Saga of the Exiles* looks at one group of the disaffected and the very different fates which await its members in the Pliocene. *The Galactic Milieu* Trilogy looks at the society the disaffected have left behind and a rebellion by one enormously powerful family in the new alien/human politics. Most fantasy series have a simplicity of structure but Julian May's work overwhelms the reader with its sheer scope and complexity. All the different threads of the tales - space-age societies, alien interactions, strange technologies, echoes of European myths and legends - are woven together with consummate skill and intelligence. Her novels - hugely creative and deeply involving - demand to be read with some of the same intelligence with which they are written.

Saga of the Exiles

The Many-Coloured Land
Pan pbk £5.99 033026656

The Golden Tore
Pan pbk £5.99 0330267191

The Nonborn King
Pan pbk £5.99 033026902X

The Adversary
Pan pbk £5.99 0330280317

Galactic Milieu

Jack the Bodiless
Pan pbk £5.99 033028553X

Diamond Mask
Pan pbk £5.99 0330322990

Intervention
Pan pbk £5.99 0330303090

PAUL J. MCAULEY (b.1955)

Paul McAuley is a biological scientist who has worked in research and his solid grounding in real-life science has been clear from his first novel, lending an authenticity to his speculations which allows the reader to suspend disbelief with confidence. His novel *Four Hundred Billion Stars* was the first British novel to win the Philip K. Dick Award and he extended this book to a trilogy with two sequels, *Of the Fall* and *Eternal Light.* In his original take on humanity's expansion to the stars, Mcauley used his scientific training to good effect in his ingenious creation of alien life forms and his understanding of human character to people the books with believable and evolving individuals. Further novels such as *Red Dust,* set on a Mars colonised by Chinese communists, seemed but preparation for the spectacular imaginings of *Fairyland.* In this biotechnological pilgrimage to the farther reaches of speculative fiction, McAuley posited a new, genetically altered life form. The fairies of McAuley's new fairyland develop their own societies, some with sinister aims, and social meltdown or apotheosis beckons. Further insights into exotically imagined biologies of the future are eagerly awaited.

Child of the River
Gollancz hbk £16.99 0575065277

Four Hundred Billion Stars
Gollancz pbk £5.99

Eternal Light
Orbit pbk £5.99 1857230159

Fairyland
Gollancz pbk £5.99

The Invisible Country
Vista pbk £5.99 0575601892

Pasquale's Angel
Gollancz pbk £5.99 0575059176

Red Dust
Gollancz pbk £4.99 0575055955

Secret Harmonies
Orbit pbk £4.99 0747405441

JACK MCDEVITT

American writer Jack McDevitt began his career with an episode for *The Twilight Zone,* moved on to short stories and finally published a novel, *The Hercules Text,* a tale of human-alien first contact which won him a prestigious Philip K. Dick Award. The five novels he has written since are notable for the religious, spiritual and mythical motifs which McDevitt works into them. Often his characters grow spiritually as the novel progresses and they discover more about other cultures, the universe and their own place in it. McDevitt has taken standard SF mechanisms, such as the mysterious alien artefact, and breathed new life into an old format. In his last three novels – *The Engine of God, Ancient Shores* and *Eternity Road* – he has used a future archaeology of ancient and alien civilizations to impart that sheer sense of wonder which SF, at its best, is so well able to arouse.

Ancient Shores
Voyager pbk £5.99 0006482287

The Engines of God
Voyager pbk £5.99 0006482279

Eternity Road
Voyager pbk £5.99 0006483089

ANNE MCCAFFREY (b.1926)

McCaffrey struck a blow for female SF and fantasy writers when she published the first of her series of novels about the Dragonriders of Pern, *Dragonflight*, in the late sixties. Winner of all the major SF awards, this first chronicle of the planet Pern began a sequence of many books, as yet unconcluded, which has won a devoted fanbase and countless imitators. The Dragon books follow Pern's uneasy relationship with the elite corps of Dragonriders, men and women chosen at birth by their hatchling dragons with whom they share a strong telepathic bond. They are sworn to protect Pern from the menace of Thread, an invasive organism that rains down every century, killing anything in its path. Also heavily involved in the plots are the planet's various guilds, most notably the Harper Hall, whose charismatic members often act as mediators in the drama.

McCaffrey's personal passion for music and its power is a strong motif in all her work. This is particularly so in *The Crystal Singer* series, a series which also exemplifies another characteristic of many of McCaffrey's books. Most of the central figures in her novels are young women who are disaffected or, in some way, displaced in society. As the plots unfold, the revelation of hidden depths and talents provides them with a way to overcome loneliness, prejudice and social exclusion. This theme is further explored in a book such as *The Rowan*, which starts with a child abandoned in a strange place, unable to communicate.

McCaffrey is, perhaps, not best described as a wholly feminist writer. Her novels have, for example, their fair share of old-fashioned dashing heroes who claim the girl at the end. However it is true that her talent is best seen in the detailed depiction of character and that the emphasis in her work is firmly on empathy and experience rather than epic quest.

The Dragon Books

Dragonflight
Corgi pbk £4.99 0552084530

Dragonquest
Corgi pbk £5.99 0552116351

Dragonsong
Corgi pbk £4.99 0552106615

Dragonsinger: Harper of Pern
Corgi pbk £4.99 0552108812

The White Dragon
Corgi pbk £4.99 0552113131

Dragondrums
Corgi pbk £4.99 0552118044

Moreta: Dragonlady of Pern
Corgi pbk £5.99 0552124990

Nerilka's Story / The Coelura
Corgi pbk £4.99 0552128171

Dragonsdawn
Corgi pbk £5.99 0552130982

The Renegades of Pern
Corgi pbk £5.99 0552130990

All the Weyrs of Pern
Corgi pbk £5.99 0552137294

The Chronicles of Pern
Corgi pbk £4.99 0552139130

Red Star Rising
Corgi pbk £5.99 0552142727

The Dolphins of Pern
Corgi pbk £4.99 0552142700

The Girl Who Heard Dragons
Corgi pbk £5.99 0552144363

The Master Harper of Pern
Bantam Press hbk £15.99
0593037766

The Crystal Singer Series

The Crystal Singer
Corgi pbk £5.99 0552120979

Killashandra
Corgi pbk £5.99 0552125563

Crystal Line
Corgi pbk £4.99 0552139114

The Talent Series

To Ride Pegasus
Corgi pbk £4.99 0552141801

Pegasus in Flight
Corgi pbk £4.99 0552137286

The Tower and Hive Sequence

The Rowan
Corgi pbk £5.99 0552137634

Damia
Corgi pbk £5.99 0552137642

Damia's Children
Corgi pbk £4.99 0552139122

Lyon's Pride
Corgi pbk £4.99
0552139149

The Catteni Sequence

Freedom's Choice
Corgi pbk £5.99 0552142735

Freedom's Landings
Corgi pbk £5.99 0552142719

The Planet Pirates Sassinak
Orbit pbk £5.99 1857230922

The Death of Sleep
Orbit pbk £5.99 1857230051

Generation Warriors
Orbit pbk £5.99 1857230337

The Ship Who Series

The Ship Who Sang
Corgipbk £4.99 0552091154

The Ship Who Searched
Orbit pbk £5.99 1857232054

The Ship Who Won
Orbit pbk £5.99 1857233603

The City Who Fought
Orbit pbk £5.99 1857232607

Crisis on Doona
Orbit pbk £4.99 1857231295

Decision at Doona
Corgi pbk £4.99 0552086614

Dinosaur Planet I
Orbit pbk £4.99 1857230906

Dinosaur Planet II: Survivors
Orbit pbk £4.99 1857230892

Get Off the Unicorn
Corgi pbk £4.99 0552109657

Partnership
Orbit pbk £5.99 1857232046

Restoree
Corgi pbk £4.99 0552083445

Treaty Planet
Orbit pbk £5.99 1857231848

with Elizabeth Scarborough

Powers That Be
Corgi pbk £5.99 0552140988

Power Lines
Corgi pbk £4.99 0552140996

Power Play
Corgi pbk £4.99 0552141003

ANDRE NORTON (b.1912)

One of the *grandes dames* of the genre, Andre Norton has been an astonishingly prolific author over many decades and her oeuvre effortlessly spans both SF and fantasy. Born Alice Mary Norton, she took her pseudonym in the forties because she thought male writers more likely to be published than female. Since then she has published dozens of deeply imagined, pacily narrated novels, often packing more into a couple of hundred pages than some can do in a thousand. She is perhaps best known for her Ross Murdock tales, for the *Witchworld* novels and for books featuring the mysterious Forerunners but she has also written many one-off stories that are just as good. Recurring themes exist in her work - time travel, for instance or the collaborative endeavour of man and animal or man and alien - but she has rarely seemed to repeat herself. Perhaps the fact that many of her books feature self-reliant protagonists who go through a rite of passage which reveals them to have more resources than they believed, or who finally find a place they belong after a lifetime of isolation, explains her lasting appeal for a teenage readership. However there is much in Andre Norton's work to continue to appeal to readers of all ages.

See entry on Mercedes Lackey (p.131)

The novels of Andre Norton are otherwise out of print in the UK. Imports of American editions of her books may be available in some larger branches of Waterstone's.

FREDERIK POHL

(b.1919)

Pohl is one of the great figures in the history of SF who, over a period of more than fift years has produced a massive body of work, as novelist, short-story writer and influential editor of magazines like *Galaxy*. He combines wit and inventiveness with an interest in using the genre as a means of exploring contemporary social issues and examining the role of technology within American society. His most famous work, published in the fifties, was *The Space Merchants,* a collaboration with C.M. Kornbluth, whose own career was cut short by a tragically early death. This tale of an attempt to claim Venus for consumerism is a good example of Pohl's style but he has continued to pour forth novels and short stories in the decades since.

Annals of the Heechee
Orbit pbk £5.99 0708883176

Black Star Rising
Orbit pbk £3.99 0708882188

Heechee Rendezvous
Orbit pbk £3.99 0708881572

RUDY RUCKER (b.1946)

Well-known for his popular science and mathematics books, Rucker was the first winner of the Philip K. Dick Award. He shows the influence of the late master in his quirky humour and approach to character but differs from Dick in his scientific rigour. His melding of hard SF rationalism and scientific extrapolation that is as wacky as it is plausible makes him an important associate of the cyberpunks. As an expert at making physics fun and a skilful creator of fictions, Rucker is an original presence on the contemporary SF scene.

White Light
Hardwired pbk £8.99 1888869178

CARL SAGAN

Sagan was professor of astronomy at Cornell University and a noted writer of popular science books. *Cosmos*, which he presented, was an acclaimed TV series and bestselling book. *The Demon-Haunted World* was a spirited defence of scientific rationalism against the attacks of pseudo-sciences and pseudo-religions. In many ways he was the ideal person to write a novel about the first meeting between man and an alien life-form and *Contact*, first published in the eighties and recently made into a film, was a successful tale of the most awesome encounter in human history.

Contact
Legend pbk £5.99 0099469502

LEWIS SHINER

American writer Lewis Shiner has written numerous short stories across a wide range of genres - crime, horror and fantasy as well as SF. The publication of *Frontera* made him an important figure in contemporary SF and its gritty realism and challenging use of SF icons drew much comment. Shiner has been linked to the 'cyberpunk' movement; his vigorous prose and hard-edged, relentless style betray the influence of the hard-boiled detective fiction which Gibson used as his model. In his third novel, *Slam*, Shiner has moved away from SF but it is to be hoped that this talented and exciting writer will soon return to the genre.

The novels of Lewis Shiner are unavailable in the UK. American editions of his books may be available in larger branches of Waterstone's.

JOHN SHIRLEY

(b.1953)

Bruce Sterling described John Shirley as 'the first and only punk science fiction writer in the world.' Shirley is the only genuine punk among the cyberpunks, heavily involved in the first outbreak of punk on the West Coast, lead singer in numerous punk bands and general hell-raiser. His personal experience of extreme people and extreme states feeds into his fiction which is characterised by its fierce intensity and surreal vision. A strong sense of anger can be felt at the heart of Shirley's most powerful writing, a feeling which is often at its strongest in his shorter fiction. *City Come A-Walkin'* is a vivid precursor to the later cyberpunk novels. However it is in the trilogy, *A Song Called Youth*, that Shirley's most significant work in SF to date can be found.

The novels of John Shirley are unavailable in the UK. American editions of his books may be available in larger branches of Waterstone's.

ROBERT SILVERBERG (b.1935)

Isaac Asimov once said, 'Where Robert Silverberg leads, others follow.' High praise indeed and, in the course of his long career, Silverberg has also won every major award for science fiction several times over. He began young, publishing a fanzine when he was fourteen and a first novel in 1955. In the late fifties, living in the same New York apartment block as Randall Garrett and Harlan Ellison, Silverberg collaborated with them on a number of projects. Garrett and Silverberg used the pseudonym Robert Randall for several collaborations, including the novel, *The Shrouded Planet.* During this same period the often prolific Silverberg was producing so much work (more than two hundred short works and eleven novels between 1957 and 1959) that he was obliged to use several pseudonyms to avoid saturating the market.

In the course of his career Silverberg has, on more than one occasion, announced his retirement from SF but he seems always to return to the genre. Frederik Pohl, when editor of *Galaxy,* is credited with persuading Silverberg, after one furlough, that a different style of story would still sell. Works like *Nightwings, Tower of Glass* and *Downward to Earth* are darker in tone, with ambiguous or downbeat endings. The eighties saw the publication of the Majipoor series, set on the eponymous planet and marked by yet further depth of development in characters and plot. In the nineties he has continued to pour forth fiction of a high quality and a fifth volume of his collected short stories, *Ringing the Changes,* is due shortly. Versatile and, at times, mind-bogglingly productive, Silverberg is a major figure in American SF.

Majipoor Series

Lord Valentine's Castle
Pan pbk £5.99 0330264621

Majipoor Chronicles
Pan pbk £4.99 0330281178

Valentine Pontifex
Pan pbk £4.99 0330287079

Mountains of Majipoor
Pan pbk £4.99 0330335197

The Sorcerers of Majipoor
Pan pbk £6.99 033034269X

Collected Short Stories

Pluto in the Morning Light
HarperCollins pbk £6.99
0586213694

The Secret Sharer
HarperCollins pbk £5.99
0586213708

Beyond the Safe Zone
HarperCollins pbk £6.99
0586213716

The Road to Nightfall
HarperCollins pbk £6.99
0586213724

Ringing the Changes
Voyager pbk £6.99 0586213732

Starborne
Voyager pbk £5.99 0586211098

The Face of the Waters
HarperCollins pbk £4.99
0586211063

CLIFFORD D. SIMAK (1904–1988)

Like Bradbury, Simak was shaped by his midwest roots and upbringing. In his work it can seem as if, instead of leaving Wisconsin for the stars, he brought the stars down to earth. His best works, some of his novelettes, say, or the full-length novels *Ring Around the Sun* and *Time Is the Simplest Thing* have a charm and concern with old-fashioned virtues like forbearance and tolerance which can slip into outright sentimentality in some of his less successful fictions. However Simak is a significant figure in SF history and a reminder that the genre has reflected older and less complex visions of America, human nature and potential futures in its past.

All Flesh Is Grass
Carroll & Graf pbk £4.99
0786700459

Cemetery World
Carroll & Graf pbk £3.99
0881849855

The Goblin Reservation
Carroll & Graf pbk £3.99
0881848972

Ring Around the Sun
Carroll & Graf pbk £3.99
0881848522

The Werewolf Principle
Carroll & Graf pbk £3.99
0786701005

BRUCE STERLING (b.1954)

Although still most widely known for his noisy championing of cyberpunk in that sub-genre's definitive anthology, *Mirrorshades*, and for his collaboration with William Gibson on the alternative history novel, *The Difference Engine*, Sterling is a versatile and incresingly important creative figure in his own right. After two lively but relatively conventional early novels, his first fully achieved fictions were the novel *Schismatrix* and its associated book of short stories *Crystal Express*, telling of a post-human future in which bio-engineered 'Shapers' compete with cyborg 'Mechanists'. The books stood at a distance from cyberpunk writing in their interest in a far rather than near future. More characteristic of the movement was *Islands in the Net*, whose heroine uncovers a vast computer-encoded conspiracy. Sterling's distinctive anarchic vision is probably best expressed in the novel *Heavy Weather*, whose central characters pursue storms in a world where climate has grown violently unstable, and in *The Hacker Conspiracy*, a contentious non-fiction examination of legal issues involved in electronic policing. *Globalhead* is an unevenly brilliant collection of diverse short fiction, whilst the recent novel *Holy Fire* gives further indication of the author's stature and of his growing ambition to let SF reach out to a mainstream audience.

The Artifical Kid
Hardwired pbk £8.99
188886916X

Globalhead
Phoenix pbk £5.99 1857994442

Heavy Weather
Phoenix pbk £5.99 1857992997

Holy Fire
Phoenix pbk £5.99 1857998847

NORMAN SPINRAD

(b.1940)

A bold representative of American New Wave SF, Spinrad caused a sensation with his 1969 novel *Bug Jack Barron* whose language and, for the time, sexual explicitness provoked considerable comment on its first publication. Even more outrageous was *The Iron Dream,* a satire purporting to be an SF novel by Adolf Hitler, which was banned in Germany. Notable later books combining black humour and radical politics within a slangy, vigorous style include *The Void Captain's Tale*, a bizarre sex fantasy, *Little Heroes,* about near future rock music, and *Russian Spring,* set in a collapsing Soviet Union.

The novels of Norman Spinrad are out of print in the UK. Imports of American editions of his books may be available in some larger branches of Waterstone's.

JOHN VARLEY

(b.1947)

Ever since the first appearance of his stories in the early seventies, Varley has shown himself adept at juggling and combining SF themes old and new to produce enjoyable and exuberant fiction. His best known works are a series set in a future in which mankind has been expelled from earth and forced to adapt to life in the solar system in a variety of wondrous ways, and the trilogy (*Titan, Wizard* and *Demon*) set on Titan, the living moon of Saturn. Strong characters, such as the female astronaut Cirocco Jones, and a healthy dose of humour are evident in the sequence and, indeed, in all of Varley's work.

Steel Beach
HarperCollins pbk £4.99

ƆR VINGE

.nor Vinge's approach to SF is that of the classic authors. No idea is too big. *A Fire Upon the Deep*, which shared the 1993 Hugo award, depicts a vast and diversely populated galactic space bound together by communications networks vaguely reminiscent of the Internet. Into this universe is unleashed an unimaginably dangerous and destructive threat left behind by races that have long since transcended physical space. The result is an exuberant and mind-expanding novel. Arguably even more interesting is *Across Realtime*, an omnibus edition of two earlier novels *The Peace War* and *Marooned in Realtime.* Bobbles - spheres in which time stands still - are deployed around weaponry to prevent a war. Years later, in a peaceful society, the bobbles start to burst. The central idea is ingenious and Vinge explores the consequences with energy and imagination.

A Fire Upon the Deep
Orion pbk £5.99 1857981278

Across Realtime
Orion pbk £5.99 1857981472

A.E. VAN VOGT
(b.1912)

From the publication of his first story in 1939, Van Vogt was one of the leading writers for John Campbell's *Astounding* magazine and his work shows both the strengths and the weaknesses of that hothouse for SF talent. His narratives can be confusing and his characters slightly wooden but short stories and novels alike are rich in ideas and his imagination vivid and unique. His earliest, and most successful novels such as *Slan* and *The Weapon Makers,* were published in the forties. In the fifties Van Vogt published little new and became involved in the Dianetics / Scientology movement of fellow *Astounding* contributor L.Ron Hubbard. Further books followed in the sixties and seventies but his most influential and individual fiction remains that which he produced for Campbell.

The Beast
Carroll & Graf pbk £3.99
0881848832

The Book of Ptath
Carroll & Graf pbk £3.99
0881847887

Cosmic Encounter
Carroll & Graf pbk £3.99
0881846775

The House That Stood Still
Carroll & Graf pbk £3.99
0881848840

The Mind Cage
Carroll & Graf pbk £3.99
0881849804

Universe Maker
Carroll & Graf pbk £3.99
0881848417

IAN WATSON (b.1943)

One of the great ideas men to emerge from British SF during the seventies, Watson has always appeared comfortable with the melding of hard and soft SF concepts in his work. Weaving the human sciences of archaeology and linguistics into stories of time travel and extraterrestrials, he has been an important guiding light to the more traditionally-minded young writers on the current UK SF scene. Covering a vast range of topics from the Tunguska event to vegetarianism, from UFO abductions to chessgame planets, Watson's versatile mind encourages his reader's curiosity before confounding expectations with skill and energy. He is a thoughtful writer whose seriousness appears refreshing rather than self-absorbed. By taking nothing for granted and inviting his readers to join him in bold speculation, he has succeeded in producing fiction which is intelligent and intensely readable.

The Coming of Vertumnus
Gollancz pbk £5.99 0575059214

The Fallen Moon
Gollancz pbk £5.99 0575060980

Hard Questions
Gollancz pbk £5.99 0575600675

Lucky's Harvest
Gollancz pbk £5.99 0575057793

The Martian Inca
Gollancz pbk £3.99 0575055588

Oracle
Gollancz hbk £16.99 0575064870

Stalin's Teardrops
Gollancz pbk £3.99 0575052813

DAVID WINGROVE
(b.1954)

Co-author, with Brian Aldiss, of *Trillion Year Spree*, one of the best histories of SF, now sadly out of print, David Wingrove is also the creator of a vast saga of future history, *Chung Kuo*. This is set in a 23rd century ruled by the Chinese in which society has been strictly stratified and formalized into different levels along neo-Confucian lines. The massive sequence is strong on epic setpieces of battle and conflict between rulers and ruled but Wingrove is adept at ensuring that individual and believable characters are not lost amidst the large-scale dramas.

Chung Kuo Series

The Middle Kingdom
H&S pbk £6.99 0450516105

The Broken Wheel
H&S pbk £8.95 0450528634

The White Mountain
H&S pbk £5.99 0450568474

The Stone Within
H&S pbk £6.99 0450579638

White Moon, Red Dragon
H&S pbk £5.99 0340639717

Beneath the Tree of Heaven
H&S pbk £6.99 0450602990

Days of Bitter Strength
H&S pbk £6.99 0340672536

Marriage of the Living Dark
H&S pbk £5.99 0340688858

Myst Series

Myst: The Book of Atrus
Corgi pbk £4.99 0552143863

Myst II: the Book of Ti'Ana
Corgi pbk £5.99 0552143871

Myst III: the Book of D'Ni
Bantam hbk £17.99
0593040260

JOHN WYNDHAM (1903–1969)

In the thirties John Wyndham had some success with short stories aimed at the American pulp magazine market but it wasn't until after the Second World War that, appalled by the time of mass destruction he had lived through, he wrote the full-length novels for which he is remembered. Clearly influenced by the war and by the new nuclear threat, these often follow man's struggle to survive and adapt to a sudden, catastrophic breakdown of society. Usually the books are written in the first person and Wyndham's narrators are usually very similar - educated, thirty something, middle class men with the knowledge and determination to survive. Bill Mason, in *The Day of the Triffids,* retains his sight and can use his expert knowledge when most of the population has been suddenly blinded and the world has been overrun by the triffids, sentient and carnivorous plants. Mason faces a moral dilemma. Should he attempt to help the 99% of the population who are blind and helpless or should he concentrate on his own survival? It is the kind of dilemma which echoes throughout Wyndham's novels. In *The Midwich Cuckoos* the authorities wrestle with the problem of dealing with a group of alien children whose intelligence and ruthlessness make them a danger to mankind. To kill them ensures the survival of the human race and yet they shrink from killing children. Immensely readable, many of Wyndham's novels were bestsellers when first published. Since then his work has been regularly filmed for cinema and TV and has transcended its genre definition, even becoming required reading on many GCSE syllabuses.

Chocky
Penguin pbk £4.99 0140031219
The Chrysalids
Penguin pbk £4.99 0140013083
The Day of the Triffids
Penguin pbk £5.99 0140009930
The Kraken Wakes
Penguin pbk £5.99 0140010750
The Midwich Cuckoos
Penguin pbk £5.99 0140014403
The Seeds of Time
Penguin pbk £4.99 0140013857
Trouble with Lichen
Penguinpbk £5.99 0140019863
Web
Penguin pbk £4.99 0140053387

ROGER ZELAZNY

(1928–1995)

The death in 1995 of Roger Zelazny means that there will be no more of his mythic narratives to enjoy and that readers will need to look elsewhere for a writer who, in both SF and fantasy, can blend stirring adventure with a twisted use of world mythologies and cosmologies. Well known for early novels such as the Hugo-award winning *The Immortal* and for the brilliant Amber sequence, Zelazny wrote fiction that travels at a breakneck speed, fueled by laconic dialogue and an ability to move swiftly between the vernacular and a highly formal language, between comedy and deep emotion.

Knight of Shadows
Sphere pbk £4.99 0747449570

A Night in the Lonesome October
Orbit pbk £4.99 1857232178

DAVID ZINDELL

(b.1952)

Zindell moved from prizewinning short-story writer to highly acclaimed creator of an epic and panoramic world when he published *Neverness* in the late eighties. This novel demonstrated clearly the broad sweep of Zindell's imagination and the technical skill with which he brought to life his universe and the peoples and entities who populate it. This universe, with its extraordinary beings, is also the setting for the trilogy *The Requiem for Homo Sapiens* of which Zindell has so far published two parts.

The Broken God
HarperCollins pbk £5.99 05865211896

The Wild
Voyager pbk £5.99 0006497128

Neverness
HarperCollins pbk £5.99 0586205365

Space

Opera

FROM SCIENCE FICTION TO SPECULATIVE FICTION *by* Peter F. Hamilton

The author of The Reality Dysfunction and The Neutronium Alchemist describes what SF means to him.

Tough call, trying to define Science Fiction; worse still written SF. Science Fiction is now in vogue in a big way, so everyone has their own idea of what it is. Ask anybody in the street what they know about the genre, and they'll close their eyes, think for a minute and probably say something like; *Men in Black, Red Dwarf, Star Trek* in all its multiple franchise variants, *Starship Troopers* and good old Arnie in the *Terminator* films. (If you're of my generation, you'll add *Thunderbirds* and *Stingray* to the list.) They might even occasionally say *The Lord of the Rings.* Oh, and what about that computer guy, William Gibson.

Science Fiction, as Hollywood and advertising agencies have discovered, is a fabulously visual medium. As far as presenting vistas and imaginative visions to the public is concerned, it's unparalleled. In the search for ever bigger thrills and spectacle to pull in the ticket sales, you have to come up with the new and the fresh. Decades of TV have made us completely familiar with our own world. Drive down any motorway in the country and you can see speeding cars performing the kind of insane manoeuvres that would leave Steve McQueen in his *Bullitt* days a nervous wreck. If directors and producers want that precious novelty value they have to venture outside the world of the present day. What's more, with the near flawless computer-generated imagery we have now, they can realise any vision, however bizarre or colossal. The sky is no longer the limit, we can go much further than that.

This really should be good for me, an author who's writing the stuff everyone flocks to see. Unfortunately all too many of the Science Fiction blockbusters are of the leave-your-brain-behind-in-the-lobby variety. They have spectacle in abundance, but no story whatsoever. Last year's *The Fifth Element* was a superb example of this. Visually, it was stunning. The plot...what plot? Nit-picking is a wonderful post-cinema sport, but this went way beyond having holes in the structure. The structure itself was just empty space, with every act simply another excuse to parade the creator's admittedly sumptuous vision.

And this is one of the main reasons SF still gets tagged as the genre of the perpetual adolescent. Preconception has us as literature's poor relation; as Terry Pratchett once put it rather nicely, the victims of the Hampstead sneer. Now, much as I'd like to, I can't just blame Hollywood and the men in red glasses of the advertising world for this. Although our heritage might be the scientific romances of Jules Verne and H. G. Wells, modern SF's true origins are the pre-war American pulp magazines. Comic books without the pictures. Their stories, by and large, were absolute drivel. Of course, the cover paintings were wonderful - but that's another story. Written by adolescents for adolescents, the pulps featured space rockets roaring off into the void, and men from Venus armed with ray guns, and robots who lusted after girls with an extraordinary dress sense. Well, everyone's got to start somewhere.

The pulps sold in quantity for one reason. They provided escapism, the most precious commodity for people trapped in mundane reality. It was the reason I started reading the genre. In a way, I was lucky growing up when I did, a child of the space age. Apollo had taken us to the moon. Skylab and the early Salyut stations were happening. Who then didn't believe NASA would reach Mars by the end of the eighties. Certainly I signed up to that. To an early-teens kid of that time, Science Fiction was the blueprint of the future. I read it avidly. John Christopher's Tripod books are the first I can remember. After that it all blurs together as I started to discover the Names: Asimov, Heinlein, Clarke, Wyndham, Van Vogt, Aldiss, E. E. Doc Smith (wonderful when you're thirteen). Then, with my teens coming to a swift end in tandem with the Space Age, my tastes started to change. But, there was always a genre book that suited. And that's where Science Fiction, for me, came into its own and finally proved itself. The vast majority of those pulp writers faded away into well-deserved obscurity, but some kept going and developing and writing better stories. Asimov is the classic example, evolving with his readership.

Science Fiction was no longer action adventure novels set in the future. There were also books that made you think, that drew on aspects of modern life and projected them into the future, questioned where they would take us. There were satires, polemics, comedies, hard-science, alien biology puzzles, altenative histories, detectives...Today the range of writing on offer in the SF section of your local bookshop is so broad that it can no longer be defined and bound by a single classification. Science Fiction has become Speculative Fiction. It has grown beyond the kind of trivial future-scenery yarn devoured so desperately by its cousins of the visual media. Today it's a literature that does the job which all great writing is supposed to do, interpreting and rewiring the world in a blaze of imagination. There are no hard and fast predictions. Instead we have a spectrum of possibles and what-ifs that avalanche through a receptive reader and create a sense of wonder. There's still plenty of dross to be found in the genre, lurking among the more garish colours, but what section of a bookshop's shelves doesn't have its share of that? The fun comes in reading through it, and discovering something you never believed existed before.

Good hunting.

IAIN M. BANKS (b.1954)

Iain M. Banks is fast becoming one of the best known of all British SF writers. He has also written mainstream fiction under the name Iain Banks, including his notorious first novel *The Wasp Factory*, but it is science fiction writing that is his first and true literary love. To date his SF novels have been largely space-operatic, although they have expanded beyond the narrow themes of conflict and epic confrontation that characterise that particular sub-genre. The Culture novels (*Consider Phlebas, The Player of Games, The Use of Weapons* and *Excession*) explore an idyllic far-future in which, through advances in technology and medicine, humans have transformed themselves into beings of great longevity, whose main purpose is the pursuit of experience in all its forms. The Culture represents a state of advancement which often comes into conflict with other, less developed societies and it is the interplay between different mind-states and philosophical attitudes that really interests Banks. Machine sentience is another concept that fascinates him, the idea that citizens of the Culture need not be only human. So the reader is introduced to vast space habitats, starships and drones, all of which have unique personas, needs and interests. Banks is also interested in psychology and his narratives (*Feersum Endjinn*, for example, and *Against a Dark Background*) are often a means of examining some of the darker and more complex aspects of the human psyche. Banks's work is entertaining, amusing and challenging and he regularly turns preconceived notions and SF stereotypes on their heads in favour of diversity and eclecticism. He is highly recommended for readers who like high adventure to be mixed with high intelligence.

Against a Dark Background
Orbit pbk £6.99 1857231791

Consider Phlebas
Orbit pbk £6.99 1857231384

Excession
Orbit pbk £6.99 185723457X

Feersum Endjinn
Orbit pbk £5.99 1857232739

The Player of Games
Orbit pbk £6.99 1857231465

The State of the Art
Orbit pbk £5.99 1857230302

Use of Weapons
Orbit pbk £6.99 185723135X

MARION ZIMMER BRADLEY (b.1930)

In this country Marion Zimmer Bradley remains best known for *The Mists of Avalon* (1983), her feminist retelling of Arthurian mythology . This and similar works, however, form only a small part of her output. She is one of the *grandes dames* of SF and fantasy who has been a prolific novelist in both genres for many decades. Undoubtedly her major work, the work to which she returns time and again, is the Darkover sequence. Darkover is a lost Earth colony dominated by a telepathic elite. Technologically backward and chauvinistic in its attitude to women, Darkover culture is nonetheless highly sophisticated in its use of PSI power. The main driving force behind most of the books in the sequence is the clash between *Darkover* and the highly technological, space-faring society of Earth and its empire. One of the fascinations of the Darkover books is to watch Bradley's increasing sophistication as a writer and the increasing exploration of feminist themes in the sequence. She has even returned to the earliest and crudest books, *The Sword of Aldones* and *The Bloody Sun,* to rewrite and reintegrate them into the expanding series. Darkover is now one of the great SF sequences, comparable to Andre Norton's *Witchworld* and Anne McCaffrey's Pern books. Marion Zimmer Bradley has also done fine work as an editor and encourager of new talent and new writers, especially women. She has edited collections of stories about Darkover by new authors, many of whom have gone on to become professional SF and fantasy writers themselves. It is to be hoped that more of Marion Zimmer Bradley's extensive backlist is made available in the UK.

The Firebrand
Penguin pbk £6.99 0140177205

Forest House
Penguin pbk £6.99 0140177213

Lady of Avalon
Michael Joseph pbk £9.99 0718138562

Lady of the Trillium
Voyager pbk £5.99 0006496601

The Mists of Avalon
Penguin pbk £6.99 0140177191

Some larger branches of Waterstone's may stock American editions of the Darkover books.

DAVID BRIN (b.1950)

A US writer and accomplished scientist, David Brin burst dramatically onto the Hard SF scene with the publication of his first novel *Sundiver* in 1980. This highly enjoyable novel of galactic intrigue began his ongoing *Uplift* series in which all sentient beings have been 'uplifted' by older races through the use of advanced genetic engineering. The second in the series, *Startide Rising*, won both the Hugo and Nebula awards for best novel and one of his stand-alone novels, *The Postman*, has been filmed by Kevin Costner. Thoughtful and compulsive reading, David Brin's work is amongst the best in its field.

Brightness Reef
Orbit pbk £6.99

Earth
Orbit pbk £6.99 1857232

Glory Season
Orbit pbk £6.99 185723202X

Heart of the Comet
Orbit pbk £6.99 1857234367

Infinity's Shore
Orbit hbk £17.99 1857234871

Otherness
Orbit pbk £5.99 1857233107

Startide Rising
Orbit pbk £5.99 1857233727

Sundiver
Orbit pbk £5.99 1857233700

The Postman
Orbit pbk £5.99 1857234057

The River of Time
Orbit hbk £5.99 1857234138

The Uplift War
Orbit pbk £6.99 1857233719

JOHN BRUNNER (1934–1995)

Brunner published his first novel when he was still in his teens and went on to produce many literate examples of the space opera. He was a leading campaigner for CND and for human rights and his concern for the present and future state of the world was reflected in many of his works, particularly the acclaimed dystopian novels *Stand on Zanzibar* and *The Sheep Look Up*. Seriousness of subject matter - overpopulation, pollution - was tempered by insight and readability. Ambitious themes were matched, in *Stand on Zanzibar*, by literary techniques more often associated with mainstream, modernist fiction.

Stand on Zanzibar
Legend pbk £4.99 0099191105

LOIS MCMASTER BUJOLD (b.1949)

Bujold's stories of her space-faring hero Miles Vorkosigan could be described as space opera's finest *roman fleuve* and she herself is one of the best writers in that particular sub-genre. A proven adept at using the conventions of classic space opera, Machiavellian intrigue, political shenanigans and skilful world-building, Bujold regularly goes beyond the limits of the genre. Her entertaining and chameleon-like hero, Vorkosigan, is an original creation and her books provide intelligent reading in a sub-genre where intelligence is not always at a premium.

Barrayar
Pan pbk £5.990330317202

Memory
Earthlight pbk £5.99
0671016075`

Mirror Dance
Pan pbk £6.99 0330334220

The Vor Game
Pan pbk £5.99 0330321986
New title forthcoming from Earthlight

JACK CHALKER (b.1944)

A prolific author of undemanding but exciting adventure stories, Jack Chalker began publishing in the seventies and has since produced a large number of single novels and multi-volume series. His *Well World* books are generally considered to be his most enjoyable work and, although his novels are currently unavailable in this country it seems safe to assume that this energetic writer will return to print before long.

The novels of Jack Chalker are out of print in the UK. Imports of American editions of his books may be available in some larger branches of Waterstone's.

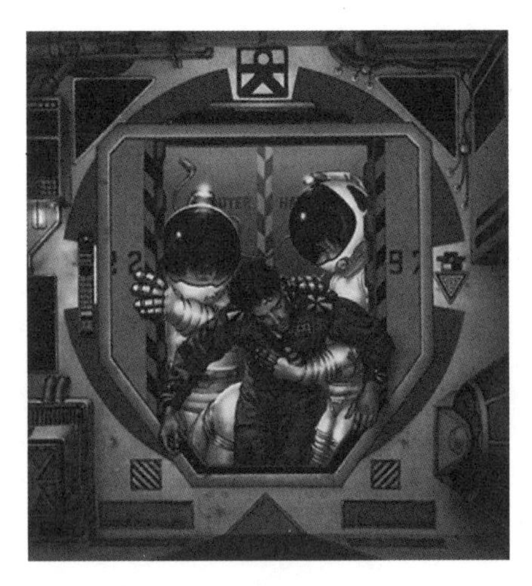

C. J. CHERRYH (b.1942)

A prolific and popular author of both SF and fantasy, Cherryh is most widely known for the mighty *Union/Alliance* series of novels. These trace the ongoing tension between the hardy, spacefaring 'merchanters' and the aggressive capitalist Union that uneasily contains them as they come into contacct with a wide range of highly developed alien civilizations. Key novels in this dense, complex and still unfinished future history include *Downbelow Station, Merchanter's Luck, Forty Thousand in Gehenna* and the huge *Cyteen.* The latter is one of the masterpieces of eighties SF, detailing the impact of advanced genetic technologies on Union politics and culture. Packed with vividly drawn characters and exciting action, Cherryh's fiction can appear old-fashioned but it is always carefully planned and written and considerable moral subtlety and narrative sophistication lie beneath the space opera conventions. Recent books, such as the tense and economical *Tripoint,* show no decline in power, whilst her fantasy series, starting with *Rusalka,* further demonstrates the scope and inventiveness of a seemingly inexhaustible imagination.

Cloud's Rider
Hodder pbk £5.99 0340689129

Cuckoo's Egg
Mandarin pbk £3.50
0749300163

Finity's End
Hodder pbk £5.99 0340695781

Fortress in the Eye of Time
Voyager pbk £5.99 0006482201

Goblin Mirror
Legend pbk £4.99 0099250713

Heavy Time
Hodder pbk £4.99 0450565378

Hellburner
Hodder pbk £4.99 0450572919

Invader
Legend pbk £5.99 0099444216

Rider of the Gate
Orbit pbk £5.99 0340638281

Tripoint
Hodder pbk £5.99 0340638303

GORDON R. DICKSON (b.1923)

Dickson's novels of military enterprise among the stars are old-fashioned, indeed questionable, when they reveal their author's obvious belief in man's manifest destiny to conquer and colonise other worlds. However the loosely connected future history that is depicted in his best work is ambitious and interesting. Dickson is, undeniably, a skilful writer and demonstrates a clear grasp of the unglamorous realities of warfare.

The novels of Gordon R. Dickson are out of print in the UK. Imports of American editions of his books may be available in some larger branches of Waterstone's.

DAVID FEINTUCH

David Feintuch used a lifelong interest in British naval history and the Napoleonic era to great effect in writing his Seafort saga. Starting with *Midshipman's Hope*, the series follows the career of Midshipman Nicholas Seafort, an earnest young man who is thrown into command at an early age, aboard the U.N.S. Starship Hibernia. Feintuch's use of genuine naval terminology and practice and his rip-roaring Hornblower-like style mix perfectly with the military SF genre to create a highly enjoyable series.

Seafort Saga

Midshipman's Hope
Orbit pbk £5.99 1857234340

Challenger's Hope
Orbit pbk £5.99 1857234359

Prisoner's Hope
Orbit pbk £5.99 1857234391

Fisherman's Hope
Orbit pbk £5.99 1857234405

Voices of Hope
Orbit pbk £5.99 1857235169

ALAN DEAN FOSTER
(b.1946)

Foster has been a highly productive author and has written both space opera and humorous fantasy. However he is best known for his movie novelisations, most famously the trilogy which consists of *Alien*, *Aliens* and *Alien 3*. These books, shaped by Foster's professionalism and skill and by his own desire, as he has said, 'to tie all three books together so that they can actually be read as a trilogy' are amongst the most rewarding examples of what can be a bastardised and uninteresting format. His own original novels are sometimes marred by the fact that all his characters, wherever they come from, act and talk as if they were contemporary Americans but they are always well-plotted and competently written.

Alien
Warner pbk £4.99 0751503428

Aliens
Warner pbk £4.99 0751503436

Alien 3
Warner pbk £4.99 0708852408

Alien Omnibus
Warner pbk £9.99 0751506672

A Call to Arms : Book 1 of The Damned
Legend pbk £5.99 00999954400

The False Mirror: Book 2 of The Damned
Legend pbk £5.99 0099164922

The Spoils of War: Book 3 of The Damned
Legend 0099225522 pbk £5.99

Cat-a-Lyst
Orbit pbk £4.99 1857230116

Codgerspace
Orbit pbk £4.99 1857230353

Cyber Way
Orbit pbk £4.99 1857230108

Dinotopia Lost
Bantam pbk £4.99 0553504959

Greenthieves
Orbit pbk £4.99 185723216X

The Howling Stones
Orbit pbk £5.99 1857235320

Life Form
Orbit pbk £5.99 1857233581

Mid-Flinx
Orbit pbk £5.99 1857233980

The Spellsinger Series

Spellsinger
Orbit pbk £5.99 1857231627

Spellsinger 2: The Hour of the Gate
Orbit pbk £5.99 1857231449

Spellsinger 3: The Day of Dissonance
Orbit pbk £5.99 1857231430

Spellsinger 4: Moment of the Magician
Orbit pbk £5.99 1857232313

Spellsinger 5: Paths of the Perambulator
Orbit pbk £5.99 1857230914

Spellsinger 6: The Time of the Transference
Orbit pbk £5.99 1857232496

Son of Spellsinger
Orbit pbk £5.99 1857231805

Chorus Skating: A Spellsinger Adventure
Orbit pbk £4.99 1857233131

SIMON R. GREEN

In the great tradition of epic and uncomplicated space opera, of intergalactic warfare and might fighting against right, Simon R. Green's books make exciting and enjoyable reading. Although he has published other sequences his principal work is the *Nightstalker* series. Its protagonist, Owen Deathstalker, has been wrongfully exiled by the evil Empress Lionstone XIV, an exile which sparks off a rebellion against her tyranny. As the rebellion spreads to worlds throughout the empire, the Empress responds ruthlessly and the stage is set for a life and death struggle.

Deathstalker
Vista pbk £5.99 0575601604

Deathstalker Rebellion
Vista pbk £5.99 057560011X

Deathstalker War
Vista pbk £5.99 0575600616

Down Among the Dead Men
Gollancz pbk £4.99 0575056207

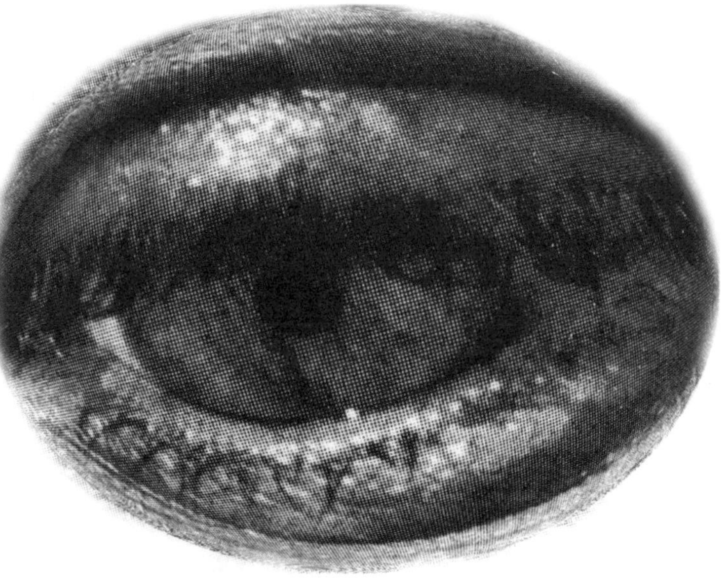

PETER F. HAMILTON (b.1960)

Peter F. Hamilton came to widespread notice in 1993 with the publication of his first novel, *Mindstar Rising*, the first of three books following the adventures of private eye Greg Mandel, ex-Captain of the Mindstar Brigade, a secret army project to implant psi-hormone glands into the heads of soldiers. Set mainly in and around Peterborough and Hamilton's own home near Rutland Water in the Fen Country, the books are an original blend of detective story and psychic cyber-thriller and provide an interesting take on potential socio-political developments from a British perspective. Hamilton's second series, the *Night's Dawn* trilogy, marks a significant break away from his first. Averaging 1000 pages per massive volume, *The Reality Dysfunction* and *The Neutronium Alchemist*, the two so far published, form what many see as the freshest and most compelling space opera of the nineties. Told from several narrative viewpoints, the story develops multiple plotlines and events unfold simultaneously in various far-flung parts of the galaxy. This is dark, epic space opera at its best and most compulsive and Hamilton is surely one of the most important British SF writers of the decade.

Mindstar Rising
Pan pbk £5.99 0330323768

The Nano Flower
Pan pbk £4.99 0330330446

The Neutronium Alchemist
Macmillan pbk £9.99 0333722422

A Quantum Murder
Pan pbk £5.99 0330330454

The Reality Dysfunction
Pan pbk £7.99 0330340328

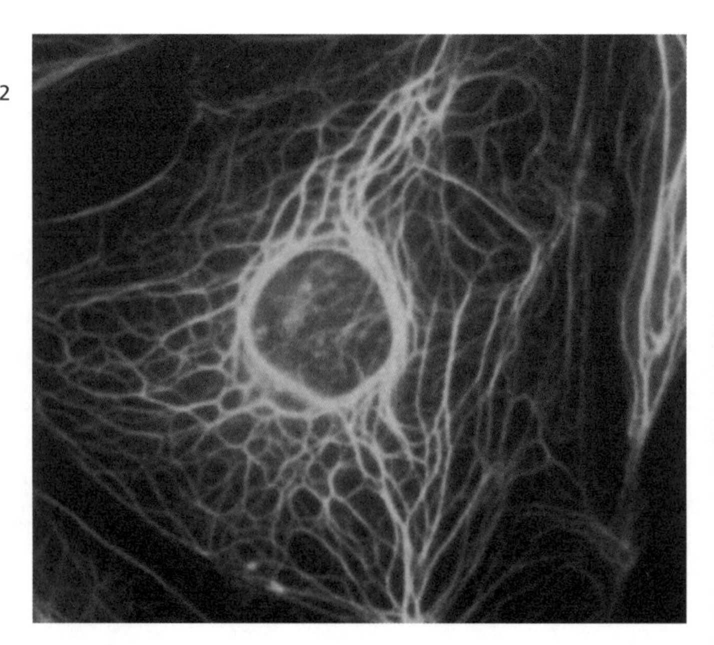

FRANK HERBERT (1920–1986)

In much of his writing Frank Herbert chronicled the future histories of mankind and the societies it created. Several novels considered the interplay of humanity and environment and these narratives were set in harsh landscapes in which humans learn to survive despite the oppressiveness of their surroundings. His famous *Dune* books, set on the desert planet Arrakis, trace the rise of a feudal society to a significant civilization, only to record its return to its original level by the end of the series. Herbert takes the trappings of space opera and uses them, particularly in the original book, to create novels of depth and intensity. Seldom in SF has a planetary environment been so well realised and a galactic history so well documented. *The Jesus Incident* and its sequels deal with humanity's need for a messiah figure to save it from the system it has created. However new-found hope is shown to be illusory and no escape is possible. As a creator of new worlds and a writer of ideas and intelligence, Frank Herbert was one of the major figures in post-war American SF.

Dune Series

Dune
Orbit pbk £6.99 0450011844

Dune Messiah
Hodder pbk £6.99 0450022854

Children of Dune
Orbit pbk £6.99 0450034275

God-Emperor of Dune
Hodder pbk £6.99 0450052621

Heretics of Dune
Orbit pbk £6.99 0450057771

Chapterhouse Dune
Orbit pbk £6.99 0450058867

JERRY POURNELLE (b.1933)

Pournelle has written a number of solo novels which combine hard science with a celebration of the unfashionable virtues of military life. Not likely to appeal to the politically correct or to those out of sympathy with an old-fashioned view of American morality and righteousness, Pournelle's work is nonetheless skilfully crafted. His best work has been done in collaboration, particularly with Larry Niven. *The Legacy of Heorot* treats of a future society, idyllic within its boundaries, but threatened by dark forces without. *The Mote in God's Eye* and its sequel, *The Moat Around Murcheson's Eye*, examine confrontations between men and the alien life forms, the Moties.

Janissaries
Orbit pbk £4.99 0708880843

see also entry for Larry Niven on page 31

E. E. DOC SMITH (1890–1965)

Smith began writing space soap opera for the pulp magazines when he was in his twenties and continued to turn out his particular brand of SF, in books and magazines, for the next fifty years, often using the same characters for long periods of time. By no standards known to man (or, in all likelihood, alien) can Smith's writing be described as demanding or sophisticated but his work can still be read with enjoyment.

The Lensman Series

Triplanetary
Ripping Publishing pbk £5.99 1899884122

First Lensman
Ripping Publishing pbk £5.99 1899884130

Galactic Patrol
Ripping Publishing pbk £5.99 1899884149

Children of the Lens
Ripping Publishing pbk £5.99 1899884211

Grey Lensman
Ripping Publishing pbk £5.99 1899884157

Second Stage Lensman
Ripping Publishing pbk £5.99 1899884165

Master of the Vortex
Ripping Publishing pbk £5.99 1899884173

S. M. STIRLING (b.1954)

Although little of his work is available in this country, Canadian novelist S.M. Stirling has been a prolific contributor to the sub-genre of military SF. He has written novelisations from TV series such as *Babylon 5*, collaborated with Anne McCaffrey and David Drake, among other writers, and produced his own Draka series of alternative world adventures. Like most writers of military SF, Stirling is not notable for his liberal credentials but he is a workmanlike author with a strong sense of narrative pace.

The City Who Fought (with Anne McCaffrey)
Orbit pbk £5.99 1857232607

The Ship Avenged
S&S pbk £5.99 0671878611

PATRICK TILLEY

(b.1928)

Tilley's multi-volume saga of conflict and warfare in a post-holocaust America has been rightly hailed as one of the most compelling adventure series in recent SF. In the 30th century two very different societies are vying for power. The Trackers are descendants of military personnel who have lived underground since the nuclear apocalypse. The Mutes dominate the surface and have developed an immunity to radiation sickness. The Trackers have the Amtrak system which moves men and materials across the devastated land. Some of the Mutes have exceptional psychic powers and await the fulfilment of a prophecy which predicts a new apocalypse and the death of all their enemies. The stage is set for the ultimate struggle to rule the earth.

Amtrak Wars Volume 1
Orbit pbk £6.99 1857235355

Amtrak Wars Volume 2
Orbit pbk £6.99 1857235363

Amtrak Wars Volume 3
Orbit pbk £6.99 1857235371

Amtrak Wars Volume 4
Orbit pbk £6.99 185723538X

Amtrak Wars Volume 5
Orbit pbk £6.99 1857235398

Amtrak Wars Volume 6
Orbit pbk £6.99 1857235401

HARRY TURTLEDOVE (b.1949)

In several sequences of books the American writer Harry Turtledove has shown an enjoyable ability to meld alternative history, informed by a genuinely wide-ranging historical knowledge, with the narrative excitement of the best military SF. An early trilogy was built on the notion that Mohamed did not found Islam but became a Christian saint. Thus Byzantium endures. In the more recent series which began with *Worldwar: In the Balance* he looks at what might have happened had the parochial struggle, in the context of the universe beyond Earth, known as World War II, been interrupted by an invasion of murderously unfriendly, reptilian aliens.

Worldwar Series

Worldwar: In the Balance
Hodder pbk £6.99 0340618396

Worldwar: Tilting the Balance
Orbit pbk £6.99 0340648996

Worldwar: Upsetting the Balance
Orbit pbk £6.99 0340666986

Worldwar: Striking the Balance
Orbit pbk £5.99 0340684917

Fox and Empire
Pocket Books pbk £4.99 0671878581

The Guns of the South
Ballantine pbk £9.99 0345413660

How Few Remain
Orbit hbk £16.99 0340715405

King of the North
Pocket Books pbk £4.99 0671877151

Krispos of Vedessos
Ballantine pbk £3.99 0099954206

Krispos Rising
Ballantine pbk £3.99 0099954109

TIMOTHY ZAHN

(b.1951)

Beginning as a writer of acclaimed and award-winning short stories, Zahn moved on to write a series of books about warrior-machines of the future in *Cobra* and its sequels. More recently he has been making a no doubt comfortable living from *Star Wars* novelisations but he has also written the *Conquerors' Trilogy* in which the space-ships of a future Earth and the alien civilisation of Zhirrzh attack one another with gusto. Zahn neatly undercuts one of the conventions of military space opera (no subtlety allowed) by telling the second of the trilogy from the Zhirrzh perspective.

Conquerors' Trilogy

Conqueror's Pride
Bantam pbk £4.99 0553408534

Conquerors' Heritage
Bantam pbk £4.99 0553408542

Conqueror's Legacy
Bantam pbk £4.99 0553408550

Star Wars Trilogy

Heir to the Empire
Bantam pbk £5.99 0553404717

Dark Force Rising
Bantam pbk £5.99 0553404423

The Last Command
Bantam pbk £4.99 0553404431

Literary
Science Fiction

BALLARD (b.1930)

In 1984, after twenty five years in which his work had been acclaimed within the genre (and by some perceptive mainstream critics), Ballard published *Empire of the Sun*, the novel based on his formative experiences as a child in a Japanese POW camp during World War II. It was shortlisted for that year's Booker prize and was a bestseller. This powerful book provides perhaps the cardinal insight into Ballard's psyche and into the worldview expressed in his SF. The mental landscape of a boy, on the verge of adolescence, trapped in a nightmare environment that is also strangely seductive, may hold the key to his inspiration.

Together with William S. Burroughs, Ballard was the model for many British writers in the sixties and his famous dictum that SF should deal with the 'inner space' of the human mind rather than outer space became a rallying call for the New Wave in the UK. 'Earth,' he wrote, 'is the only alien planet.' His early short stories about spaced-out astronauts predate David Bowie's *Space Oddity* and his tales of overpopulation, media saturation and cold war psychosis can be chillingly entertaining - *The Terminal Beach* is, perhaps, his finest collection.

Character is important to Ballard but it is in the interface between the interior landscapes of his protagonists, the exterior landscapes of the real world and the media landscape created by the fusion of mind and technology that his particular genius lies. In many ways he was a prophetic writer, one ahead of his times and it is only now, in the era of the postmodern, that the world has begun to catch up with him. From his early inversions of the classic British catastrophe novel to the outrages of his mid-seventies trilogy (*Crash, High Rise* and *Concrete Island*) Ballard has expressed his personal vision by exposing fearlessly his own obsessions and fetishes - drained swimming-pools, crashed automobiles and the worship of celebrity.

Although acknowledged as a brilliant stylist and a major, world-class writer, Ballard and his work, *Empire of the Sun* aside, remain largely unexplored by the general reader. The recent furore surrounding David Cronenberg's film of *Crash* and excellent reviews for his latest novel *Cocaine Nights* have ensured that these books have reached a wider audience. Perhaps this will encourage readers to try all Ballard's work, books which no serious lover of SF (or fiction per se) can afford to disregard.

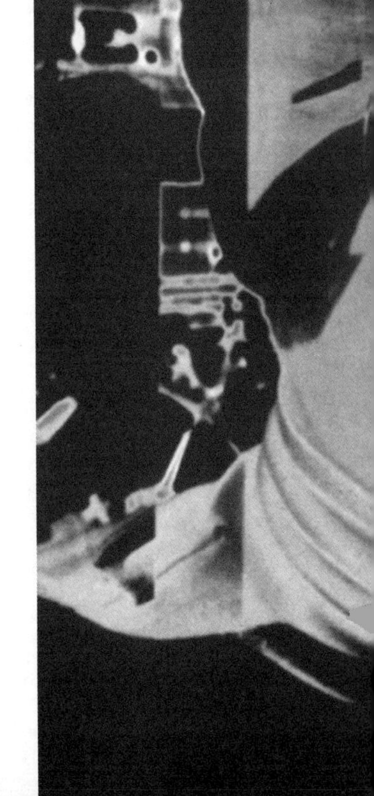

'Everything is becoming science fiction. From the margins of an almost invisible literature has sprung the intact reality of the twentieth century.'

J. G. Ballard

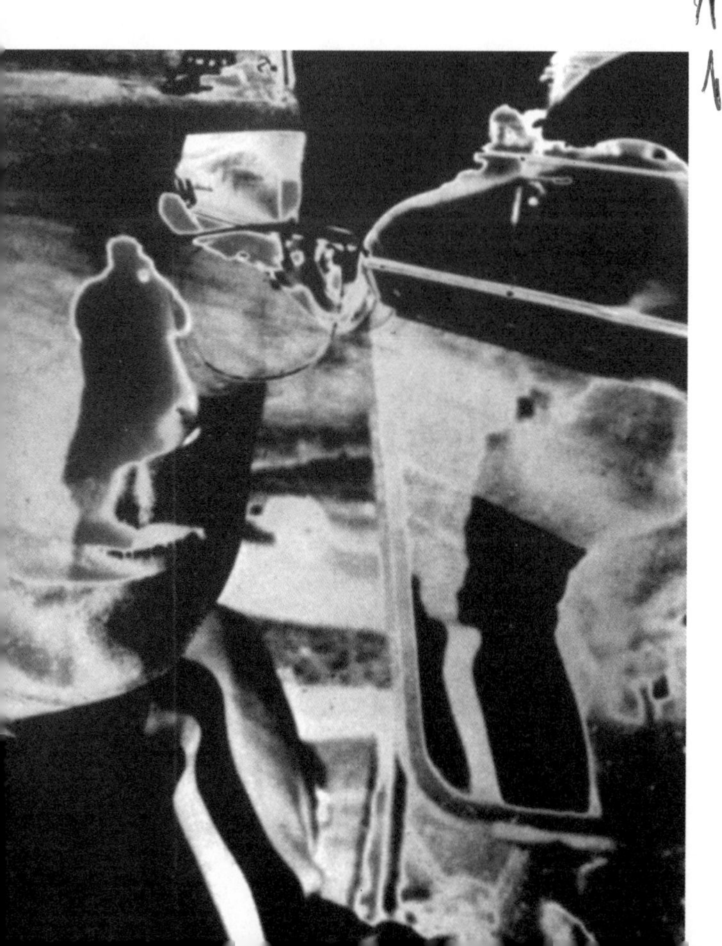

Concrete Island
Vintage pbk £5.99 009933481X

Crash
Vintage pbk £5.99 0099334917

The Drought
Flamingo pbk £5.99
0586089969

The Drowned World
Indigo pbk £5.99 057540129X

Hello America
Vintage pbk £5.99 0099265915

Myths of the Near Future
Vintage pbk £5.99 0099334712

Rushing to Paradise
Flamingo pbk £6.99
0006548148

The Terminal Beach
Indigo pbk £5.99 0575401311

The User's Guide to the Millennium
Flamingo pbk £6.99
0006548210

The Venus Hunters
Grafton pbk £4.99 0586051872

Vermilion Sands
Phoenix pbk £4.99 1857990056

The Voices of Time
Indigo pbk £5.99 0575401303

War Fever
Paladin pbk £4.99 0586090630

EDWARD BELLAMY

(1850–1898)

Bellamy was a nineteenth century American novelist and social theorist who is now remembered solely for his Utopian fantasy *Looking Backward*, first published in 1888. This is the story of a young Bostonian, Julian West, who falls into a hypnotic sleep in the year 1887 and emerges from it in the year 2000 to find a world in which social and scientific developments have produced a society redeemed from the ills of the nineteenth century. It is difficult today to appreciate the impact Bellamy's book had on his contemporaries. Bellamy societies were founded all over the States to promote his ideas. A political party came into being to advocate his principles. Reading the book in the late twentieth century one is haunted by the differences between the actual history of the century and Bellamy's optimistic imaginings.

Looking Backward
Penguin pbk £6.99 0140390189

ALFRED BESTER (1913–1987)

One of the most influential writers in SF since the fifties, Bester was one of the first to bring sophisticated literary techniques to the genre and to traditional motifs of space travel, teleportation and telepathy. Experimenting with typographic layout and employing a baroque prose style that dazzles the imagination, Bester was also possessed of narrative gifts that were charged, frenetic and driven by an energetic sense of drama. Reading Bester's work from the fifties, especially the brilliant short stories, one gets the feeling that at last the genre had a writer who chose every word for deliberate impact and the result is SF of the highest order. His mastery of technique was melded with the traditional craft of tight storytelling and Bester has been a popular writer and an influence on many other writers, from traditionalists to cyberpunks. His early novels, *The Demolished Man* and *Tiger! Tiger!* (also known as *The Stars My Destination*) are essential reads for anyone interested in SF. Although less well known, Bester's latter three SF novels and two thrillers are also well worth reading.

The novels of Alfred Bester are out of print in the UK. Imports of American editions of his books may be available in some larger branches of Waterstone's.

JAMES P. BLAYLOCK (b.1950)

Arguably the most original fantasist of his generation, Blaylock is one of the key 'California Dreamers' who, with Tim Powers and K.W. Jeter, formed a fertile cadre of writers around their mentor Philip K. Dick. A kind of Ray Bradbury on acid, Blaylock has a child-like enthusiasm for the outre and his characteristic oddness, though witty and colourful, is often scary in the manner of Lewis Carroll's Alice stories. Verbally rich and skilled in subgenres as diverse as steampunk SF, Tolkienesque fantasy and parodic scientific romances, Blaylock is the writer Angela Carter would have been had she been a male child of baby-boom America raised on jelly donuts, maple syrup, pancakes and crazed pulp magazines. He was the winner of the World Fantasy Award for *Homunculus.*

Digging Leviathan
Morrigan hbk £11.95 1870338200

Homunculus
Morrigan hbk £11.95 1870338405

Magic Spectacles
Morrigan hbk £13.95 1870338952

JAMES BLISH (1921–1975)

Much of Blish's earli from the fifties and sixties, is erudite, philosophically interesting and scientifically plausible. *Cities in Flight,* his best known work, is an omnibus volume of linked stories in which tramp cities, plucked from their terrestrial settings, wander the universe. In his later career Blish worked largely on novelisations of Star Trek stories although he continued to produce thoughtful and richly imagined science fiction in novels such as *The Day After Judgement* and *Midsummer Century.*

Apart from a small number of Star Trek novelisations, the novels of James Blish are out of print in the UK. Imports of American editions of his books may be available in some larger branches of Waterstone's.

RAY BRADBURY (b.1920)

Bradbury began as a fan of SF in the thirties and was the editor of a fanzine for a short spell before being published for the first time in 1941 in *Super Science Stories.* Leigh Brackett offered to coach his writing skills and, by 1947, he was fully into his stride and had published a first collection, *Dark Carnival.* Perhaps the dominant experience of Bradbury's teenage years had been the uprooting from his beloved mid-west and a move to Los Angeles, and many of his stories contain a sentimental view of small town, mid-West USA, albeit coupled with a weird sting in the tail.

His most famous, and arguably most successful collection is *The Martian Chronicles.* These brilliant interlinked stories catalogue man's colonization of the red planet and show, through brief contact with the vanishing indigenous race, how our prejudices are ageless. Even in these stories Bradbury's nostalgic longings are clear and they have a deep sense of melancholy and loss. In the fifties Bradbury entered a golden period of story-telling, producing some of his best work, including *The Illustrated Man* and *Golden Apples of the Sun. Fahrenheit 451,* famously filmed by Francois Truffaut, is a fiercely dystopian tale contrasting a world of technological censorship with a pastoral society in which books, otherwise banned, represent a glowingly remembered tradition. Meanwhile Bradbury found work as a screenwriter although his best work in this field is not SF but the screenplay for John Huston's *Moby Dick.*

In recent decades Bradbury's themes have appeared repetitive and cosy. As SF concerned itself with grimmer contemporary issues, he seemed more and more like a man out of his time. His work had always contained elements of other genres and he began to turn to horror and to crime fiction - *Death Is a Lonely Business,* for example, and *Graveyard for Lunatics.* These confirmed that he retained his skill as a storyteller. Although he can seem quaint and old-fashioned in comparison with current practitioners of SF, it should be remembered that Ray Bradbury invented a large number of the ideas which are now commonplace in the genre. He remains a giant in the field.

Fahrenheit 451
Flamingo pbk £5.99
0006546064

The Illustrated Man
Flamingo pbk £5.99
0006479227

The Martian Chronicles
Flamingo pbk £5.99
0006479235

Quicker than the Eye
Earthlight pbk £6.99
0671017845

'Do you mind if I ask? How long have you worked at being a fireman?' 'Since I was twenty, ten years ago.' 'Do you ever read any of the books you burn?' He laughed. 'That's against the law.'

Ray Bradbury - Fahrenheit 451

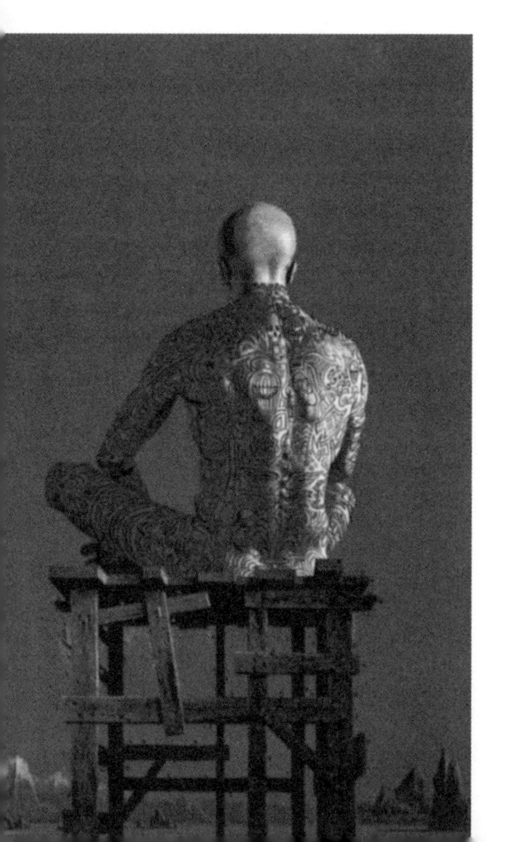

OCTAVIA E. BUTLER
(b.1947)

Male writers outnumber women writers in SF. Black writers are rare. Black women writers of SF are very rare indeed. Octavia Butler draws on Afro-American history in *Kindred,* a tale of time travel to the slaveholding past, and explores a multi-racial, multi-cultural future in her *Xeno-genesis* seies. The sensitively drawn characters in her novels grapple with real issues of power, responsibility and love.

Kindred
Women's Press pbk £6.99
070434162X

Parable of the Sower
Women's Press pbk £6.99
0704344211

ANTHONY BURGESS (1917–1993)

A much admired literary mainstream writer, Anthony Burgess was one of the most versatile writers since the war. However he will probably be best remembered for his dystopian SF novel, *A Clockwork Orange.* It is set in a near future totalitarian welfare state in which teenage gangs run criminally rampant. The gang members have their own argot derived largely from corrupted Russian words and this language and its users are both known as Nadsat, meaning 'teenage'. Amphetamine and psychedelic drugs are legally available to the Nadsats who also place great importance on fashion. However their chief recreations are sex and violence. The novel is told in the first person by nadsat-speaking Alex, a thug who adores Beethoven as much as he does shattered glass and flowing blood. When the state exposes Alex to technology which prevents him doing ill even if he wants to, the book becomes a classic moral fable, a meditation on free will and human choice between good and evil. The novel's cult status has grown since the release of Kubrick's film version, released in the early seventies and since withdrawn from circulation by the enigmatic director. Although Burgess himself viewed the book as a minor work, *A Clockwork Orange,* with its dazzling verbal inventiveness and its crystal-clear plotting, is a major dystopian novel. Other dystopian fictions by Burgess have been collected in a volume called *Future Imperfect.*

A Clockwork Orange
Penguin pbk £5.99 0140188827

Future Imperfect
Vintage pbk £6.99 0099225018

'If I bring back the ashtrays, can I have my pre-frontal?'
Philip K. Dick – VALIS

PHILIP K. DICK (1917–1982)

One of the most complex and prolific SF writers ever, Philip K. Dick was responsible for some of the most interesting novels and short stories in the genre. Dick, who lived most of his life in California, had a troubled personality from childhood onwards and suffered from various emotional problems throughout his life. More than one observer has suggested that he might have been schizophrenic. Certainly Dick's writing displays an ongoing interest in different perceptions of reality and many of his main characters suffer from doubts, addictions and an array of neuroses. The effects of his own paranoia and heavy drug use are clearly evident in much of his work, although they seem to add to, rather than detract from, its arresting originality. *Time Out of Joint*, a good early demonstration of Dick's growing paranoia, in which the main character is kept in a simulated environment as the authorities exploit him to help win a war, is also one of his most striking and successful novels.

Dick's abundant storytelling gifts and the need to express his inner struggles combined to produce some of the most groundbreaking novels and ideas to emerge from SF in the fifties and sixties. Giant multinationals, cybernetic prosthetics, wisecracking household appliances and artificial intelligence machines are just a few of the novelties that appear in novels such as *The Man in the High Castle, Martian Time Slip, Do Androids Dream of Electric Sheep* and *The Three Stigmata of Palmer Eldritch.* As he grew older, Dick became more and more obsessed with theology and philosophy and, during March 1974, he underwent some kind of religious experience, the exploration of which led to his one truly great novel of the seventies, *VALIS* (Vast Active Living Intelligence System), an autobiographical work in which he attempted to come to terms with the experience.

Although the quality of his work is uneven, Philip K. Dick not only produced some stunning short stories and novels, he has also been a major influence on SF in the years since his death and is likely to remain one of the most celebrated and admired writers in the genre.

Collected Stories

Beyond Lies the Wub
HarperCollins pbk £7.99
0586207643

Second Variety
HarperCollins pbk £6.99
0586207651

The Father-Thing
HarperCollins pbk £6.99
0586207678

The Days of Perky Pat
HarperCollins pbk £7.99
0586207686

We Can Remember It for You Wholesale
HarperCollins pbk £7.99
0586207694

Clans of the Alphane Moon
HarperCollins pbk £5.99
0006482481

The Divine Invasion
HarperCollins pbk £5.99
0006482503

Do Androids Dream of Electric Sheep
HarperCollins pbk £5.99
0006482805

Dr Bloodmoney
Carroll & Graf pbk £3.99
088184389X

Flow My Tears, The Policeman Said
HarperCollins pbk £5.99
0006482473

The Game Players of Titan
HarperCollins pbk £5.99
000648249X

The Man in the High Castle
RoC pbk £5.99 014017172X

Now Wait for Last Year
HarperCollins pbk £5.99
0006482449

Our Friends from Frolix 8
HarperCollins pbk £5.99
0006482821

A Scanner Darkly
HarperCollins pbk £5.99
0006482465

Time Out of Joint
RoC pbk £5.99 0140171738

We Can Build You
HarperCollins pbk £5.99
0006482791

The Zap Gun
Carroll & Graf pbk £3.99
0881845531

THOMAS M. DISCH (b.1940)

Alongside Samuel R. Delany, Disch is considered to be the finest literary SF writer to emerge from the American New Wave of the sixties. But unlike Delany and Ellison, Disch committed himself to the pioneers of literary SF in the UK when he, like Norman Spinrad, moved to London for a while to be nearer the hub of New Wave activity, Michael Moorcock's *New Worlds* magazine. Most famous for his work during that turbulent decade, Disch has quietly continued to produce novels and short stories that make him the envy of all kinds of writers. A versatile talent, he has written accomplished poetry, in addition to his fiction. Perhaps the most directly humane of New Wave writers, Disch is seen at his best in such works as the excellent dystopian novel *334*, with its genuine and dignified sympathy for minorities, and in the seventies novel *On Wings of Song*. Earlier key works *Camp Concentration* and *The Genocides* (a groundbreaking book that depicts the total destruction of humanity during an extraterrestrial invasion with a chilling matter-of-factness) are sadly out of print in the UK. In recent years Disch has once again demonstrated the breadth of his talent and has produced superior metaphysical fantasies such as *The Priest*.

Black Alice
Carroll & Graf pbk £3.99 088184506X

On Wings of Song
Carroll & Graf pbk £3.99 0881844438

The Priest
Orion pbk £5.99 0752800094

HARLAN ELLISON (b.1934)

In terms of number of awards received Ellison is the most 'decorated' SF author ever but he remains relatively unknown outside the genre and its readership. His influence on SF in the cinema and on TV has been large but, perhaps because he has concentrated on the short story (although he has also been energetic as editor, anthologiser and encourager of new talent), he has never become a famous name in the same way as, say, Asimov or Heinlein. The key to Ellison is his intensity. He is a polemical writer with strong views to express and razor-sharp prose with which to express them. His best works, the stories of the late fifties and sixties, are those of a man in tune with the zeitgeist. Civil rights, urban blight, drugs and totalitarianism are all covered with pinpoint fineness in a style that owes almost as much to classic, hard-boiled crime as to the SF genre. His combination of directness and gritty romanticism was new to SF and Ellison had great impact, becoming the self-appointed focus of the New Wave in the USA. Some of his very best work is collected in *The Beast That Shouted Love at the Heart of the World* which includes the seminal *A Boy and His Dog*, a post-holocaust tale of telepathy and treachery that has influenced not only later cyberpunk writers but also David Bowie and George Miller, director of the *Mad Max* movies. Ellison, who has also been a highly successful screenwriter for TV, has had further influence on movie stories. *The Terminator*, for example, borrows its time-travelling warrior and machine-dominance motifs from two Ellison short works. His many fine fantasy stories also demonstrate clearly his unique talents. Ellison's work is currently undergoing a reissue programme in the UK and the scope and commitment of his work is once again becoming clear.

The Essential Ellison
Morpheus pbk £14.99
0962344745

The City on the Edge of Forever
White Wolf pbk £9.99 Star Trek Teleplay 1565049640

Edgeworks Series : The Collected Ellison - Volume 1 : Over the Edge (Stories) / An Edge In My Voice (Essays)
White Wolf hbk £14.99
1565049608

Volume 2 : Spiderkiss (Mainstream novel)/Stalking the Nightmare (Stories)
White Wolf hbk £14.99
1565049616

'I would get back to Atlantis, and tell them that time was, indeed, circular. That New York City had risen.'

Harlan Ellison Phoenix

MARY GENTLE (b.1956)

In her work Mary Gentle has shown herself a very capable practitioner of both thought-provoking science fiction and, more recently, of fantasy. She remains best known for her novels of the eighties, *Ancient Light* and *Golden Witchbreed*, in which the tough but sensitive diplomat Christie explores the alien world of Orthe. The Ortheans, their history, religion and culture are well realized but Gentle also succeeds in maintaining the tempo of what are exciting and pacy narratives.

Ancient Light
Vista pbk £6.99 0575601124

Golden Witchbreed
Vista pbk £5.99 0575600330

Left to His Own Devices
Orbit pbk £5.99 1857232755

COLIN GREENLAND (b.1954)

Born out of an acute understanding of genre conventions, Greenland's fiction is suggestive of many eras but remains uniquely and intelligently his own. Cold and dark, his early fantasies retread the alleyways of Gormenghast, populated by antiheroes reminiscent of Michael Moorcock's. His exuberant romp through space opera with Tabitha Jute and her voyaging planetoid, Plenty, is fast-paced and gritty fun. As an aside, almost, he paid homage to the scientific romance in *Harm's Way*, a large novel (sadly out of print) set in an imaginary Victorian age in which the British Empire embraces the stars and grand wooden ships sail between planets. This was accomplished with a Dickensian panache and Greenland's customary skill.

Take Back Plenty
HarperCollins pbk £5.99 0586213392

Seasons of Plenty
HarperCollins pbk £4.99 000647344X

The Plenty Principle
HarperCollins pbk £5.99 0006499066

Mother of Plenty
HarperCollins pbk £5.99 0006499074

URSULA K. LE GUIN (b.1929)

Earthsea

The Earthsea Quartet
Puffin pbk £8.99 0140348034

A Wizard of Earthsea
Puffin pbk £4.99 0140304770

The Tombs of Atuan
Puffin pbk £4.99 0140306323

The Farthest Shore
Puffin pbk £4.99 0140306943

Tehanu
Puffin pbk £4.99 0140348026

A Fisherman of the Inland Sea
Vista pbk £5.99 0575602392

Four Ways to Forgiveness
Vista pbk £5.99 0575601752

The Left Hand of Darkness
Virago pbk £6.99 1860491898

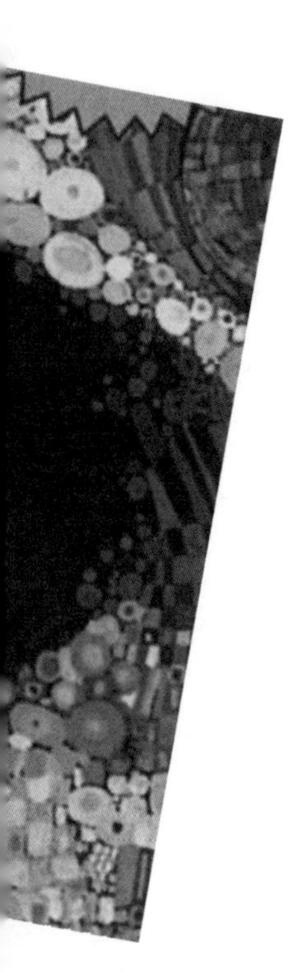

Ursula K. Le Guin is less concerned with the mechanics of space travel than with the experiences of the people travelling. In her novels both characters and readers embark on a voyage of discovery which is as much about inner as outer space. Le Guin's views of her fictional worlds are appropriate for the daughter of an anthropologist. She is widely regarded as a feminist writer, which may be as much a description of her writing style, stressing character, community and society rather than flashy space-opera special effects, as a comment on the novels themselves.

Her major novels, *The Left Hand of Darkness* and *The Dispossessed*, both of which won the Hugo and Nebula awards, follow the anthropological pattern, examining culture clashes and their effects on ordinary people. The anarchist society of *The Dispossessed* comes into conflict with a nearby planet run on capitalist principles; the hermaphrodite culture of *The Left Hand of Darkness* is observed by a traveller from Earth. The latter is also, at one level, a straightforward adventure story, as the characters battle the arctic conditions of a planet called Winter. In a more recent book, *Always Coming Home*, Le Guin leaves the storytelling to the inhabitants of a future society living somewhere in California, and their songs, legends and paintings tell us about their culture in what the author has called an 'Anthropology of the Future'.

In her award-winning *Earthsea Quartet*, written for children but possessing universal appeal, LeGuin turns to myth and Jungian archetypes in her tales of the wizards of The Archipelago. The books tell the story of Ged, a young wizard from the island of Gont, who must set out on a quest to overcome the Shadow he has conjured up in a fit of pride. LeGuin's prose is spare, almost stark, as if telling an old Icelandic saga, and she cleverly employs images of the sea and the natural world appropriate to the portrayal of an island society. She also creates magical reworkings of standard trappings of fantasy fiction such as castles, dragons and labyrinths. Compelling and mystical, the Earthsea novels, like all Le Guin's best work, leave an indelible impression on the reader.

M. JOHN HARRISON (b.1945)

Harrison started his career as a short story writer and critic for Michael Moorcock's *New Worlds* magazine and his work reflected new wave preoccupations with decay and post-industrial alienation. Many of his short stories reveal a loner's sensibility and a love both of rock-climbing and philosophical musings on entropy and the interplay of chance and necessity. Harrison's work has always existed on the periphery of SF. *The Machine in Shaft Ten* betrays the influence of Ballard whilst subsequent works, *The Committed Men* and *Centauri Device*, contain views of a world in decline or rushing headlong into destruction. By the early seventies Harrison had invented a template on which to test his ideas - the city of Viriconium. Peopled by baroque sword and sorcery stereotypes (*The Pastel City*) or Kafkaesque artisans (*In Viriconium*), these novels indicated that Harrison was moving even further away from straight SF into his own realm of existential reverie, climbing and ambivalent reality. The novel *Climbers* took this process a stage further and by the time of the 1992 novel, *The Course of the Heart,* all SF elements had been subsumed into Harrison's own particular, harsh vision.

Signs of Life
Flamingo pbk £6.99 0006546048

Viriconium Nights
Indigo pbk £5.99 0575401206

ALDOUS HUXLEY

(1894–1963)

The grandson of Darwin's colleague T.H. Huxley, Aldous Huxley was a writer of great versatility who produced such diverse works as *Antic Hay* and *Eyeless in Gaza,* satirical novels of the twenties and thirties, *The Devils of Loudon,* a study in sexual hysteria, and *The Doors of Perception,* which describes his experiments with hallucinogenic drugs. His most popular work has been the famous dystopia, *Brave New World* (1932) in which, convincingly anticipating the dangerous potential of genetic engineering, he depicted a society in which babies are chemically adjusted to grow into the body type required and the drug Soma is used for social control. He explored other utopias / dystopias in *Island* and *Ape and Essence.*

Ape and Essence
Flamingo pbk £6.99
0006547400

Brave New World
Flamingo pbk £5.99
0006545793

Island
Flamingo pbk £6.99
0006547346

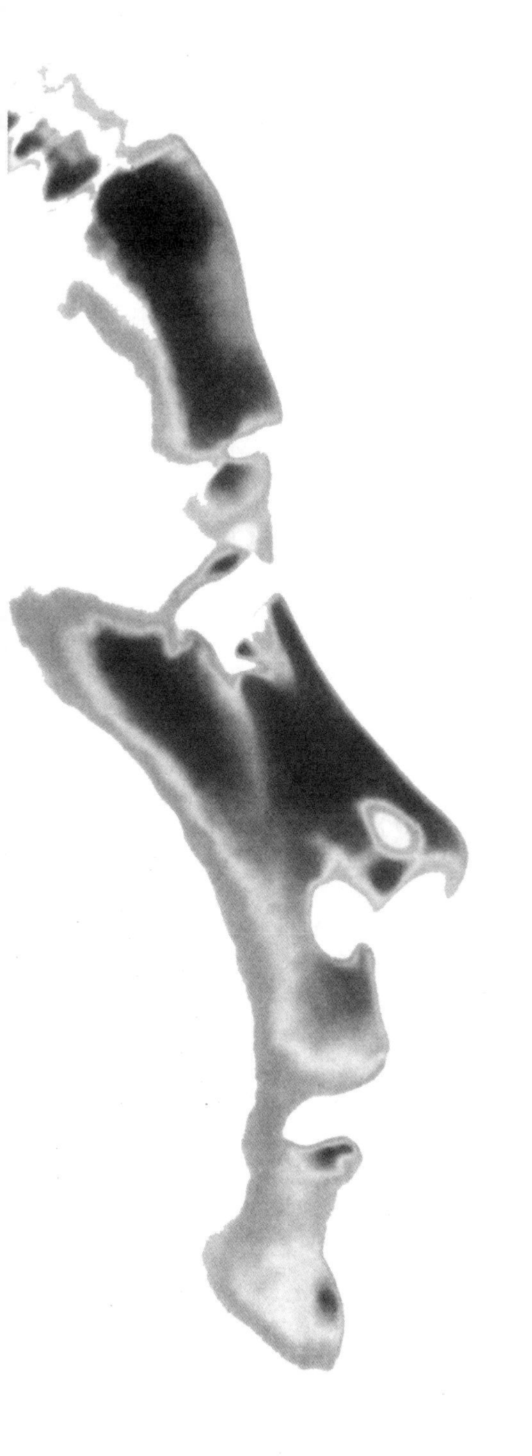

GWYNETH JONES

(b.1952)

Under the nom de plume of Ann Halam, Gwyneth Jones is the author of some of the finest of contemporary SF novels for children. Under her own name she is one of the keynote thinkers and writers in the renaissance of British SF over the last fifteen years, both as critic and award-winning novelist. Her best work has been the moving narratives in her series of novels which look at a collective of sensual alien traders stranded on Earth. In a triumph of imagination, she brings to life creatures who are at once real characters yet truly and convincingly alien. Jones is a demanding and sometimes difficult writer but she is producing exciting and moving work, science fiction which is satisfying, moving and fully engaged. She's the genuine stuff.

Kairos
Gollancz pbk £5.99
0575060670

North Wind
Gollancz pbk £5.99
0575602481

Phoenix Cafe
Vista pbk £5.99 0575600756

White Queen
Vista pbk £5.99 057560378X

DANIEL KEYES
(b.1927)

Brought to a wider audience by the academy award-winning film *Charly*, Daniel Keyes's sixties book *Flowers for Algernon* is one of the most accomplished SF novels ever written. His poignant fable about an experiment to enhance the intelligence of a retarded man and its tragic, all too human consequences is a fine example of just how beautifully written some of the best SF can be. Never shy of difficult themes, Keyes went on to explore the mind in a number of other works, none of which gained the attention given to *Flowers for Algernon*.The great respect in which Keyes is held by so many SF readers and writers is justified, despite being out of all proportion to the small body of work he has produced.

Flowers for Algernon
Indigo pbk £5.99 057540020X

STANISLAW LEM (b.1921)

A former medical student and mechanic, Lem came to SF with a perspective formed under the years of Nazi occupation of his native Poland and the subsequent Soviet domination. As a scientist in Cracow he ran foul of Stalinism and turned to writing as both philosophical exercise and subtle satire. From 1956 onwards Lem wrote prolifically. His works ranged from Swiftian comedy (*The Star Diaries, Memoirs of a Space Traveller*) in which the hapless Ijon Tichy encounters all kinds of political, social and cosmic absurdity, to satirical contemplation of man's arrogance (*Cyberiad*), reflected in a fairy-tale world where robots are the highest form of intelligence. In Lem's more serious works man is forced to face up to his limitations by confronting the unknowable nature of alien intelligence (*The Invincible, Eden, Fizsco*). His best known novel *Solaris* was filmed by Tarkovsky and shows a world which communicates by bringing men's obsessions to life with horrific results. Lem is now resident in Italy. His most recent book, *Peace on Earth*, published in 1989, pokes fun at man's foibles and at the foolishness of the wars he fights, once again showing Lem's brilliant ability to use SF as a tool to reflect our own paradoxical nature.

Eden
A. Deutsch Hbk £11.95 0233985174

Hospital of the Transfiguration
A. Deutsch Hbk £11.95 0233983856

The Investigation
A. Deutsch Hbk £12.99 023398772X

Memoirs Found in a Bathtub
A. Deutsch Hbk £12.99 0233987894

Mortal Engines
A. Deutsch Hbk £12.99 023398819X

One Human Minute
A. Deutsch Hbk £9.95 0233979808

Peace on Earth
A. Deutsch Hbk £14.95 0233989358

Solaris
Penguin Pbk £5.99 0140112731

C. S. LEWIS (1898–1963)

An Oxford academic and literary critic, Lewis wrote on a wide range of subjects from medieval and renaissance literature to popular theology. His Narnia books, published in the fifties, rapidly became children's classics and the magical land reached through the old wardrobe is familiar to many. Although considered children's books, the Narnia sequence has had a major influence on fantasy writing. For many people, the Narnia books are amongst the few works of fantasy they have read ; for others they become stepping stones to a wide variety of imaginative fiction. Lewis's adult science fiction, published earlier in his career, consists of *Out of the Silent Planet* and its two sequels. These tell of the linguist Ransom and his travels to other planets. Like the Narnia books, the trilogy was intended as religious allegory but Lewis's ability to conjure up vivid imagery of alien landscapes is considerable and the books work very well as straight SF.

The Dark Tower and Other Stories
Fount 0006266363 Pbk £4.99

The Ransom trilogy by C.S. Lewis is out of print in the UK.

DORIS LESSING

(b.1919)

Lessing, brought up in southern Africa, came to Britain in the forties and is best known for her quintet of novels tracing the life story of Martha Quest and for *The Golden Notebook*, a landmark feminist novel. Her sequence of SF novels, published in the seventies and eighties, mark her out as a fine example of a 'literary' novelist who has recognised the freedoms provided by the forms of Science Fiction.

Canopus in Argos Series

Shikasta
Flamingo pbk £7.99
0006547192

The Marriages Between Zones 3,4 & 5
Flamingo pbk £7.99
0006547206

The Sirian Experiments
Flamingo pbk £7.99
0006547214

The Making of the Representative for Planet 8
Flamingo pbk £7.99
0006547184

The Sentimental Agents in the Volyen Empire
Flamingo pbk £7.99
0006547222

RRY MALTZBERG (b.1939)

ce the death of Philip K. Dick, Maltzberg has some claim to ing the finest and most serious literary writer in American SF. The author of over seventy novels Malzberg has, like Dick, suffered from neglect and been unjustly ignored. A master of the grimmest kind of existentialism, Malzberg rivals even J.G. Ballard in his harrowing first-person narratives of cosmic angst and joyless lust set in the traditional SF surroundings of space exploration and dystopian futures. Sadly only two novels by this intense and uncompromising writer are currently available in the UK.

Beyond Apollo
Carroll & Graf pbk £3.99 0881845515

Galaxies
Carroll & Graf pbk £3.99 0881844918

'The speed of light is one hundred and eighty six thousand miles a second, which would seem to be fast enough, and yet in astronomical terms, in terms of space exploration, it would be the Seventh Avenue local with brake trouble.'

Barry Maltzberg – Galaxies

MAUREEN F. MCHUGH (b.1959)

SF often mishandles the future; it can come across as unbelievable, ersatz or just plain dumb. Not so in the fiction of Maureen McHugh who manages to create credible futures that are imbued with a sense of inevitability. Current global trends - overpopulation, the growth of far eastern economies - are carefully extrapolated in her work which introduces a future in which underwater cities are constructed in the Caribbean and China, the ultimate tiger, takes on the mantle of world economic domination. Society and technology may advance but people don't, retaining their characteristic racism and sexism. Victimised for being gay, of mixed race, or merely for being poor, McHugh's protagonists inhabit deceptively simple plots that nonetheless allow for rich character development and serious cultural analysis. Whether writing of political intrigues in a dark aquatic metropolis or the anguish of a Chinese-American engineering student striving to find his niche in an intolerant world, McHugh is always intelligent and engaging.

Half the Day Is Night
Orbit pbk £6.99 185723362X

h

WALTER M. MILLER JR. (1922–1996)

Walter M. Miller Jr. is one of the most interesting US writers of the Cold War period. Although his output was tiny - just two small collections of short stories and one novel during his lifetime - he is responsible for what is, arguably, the best post-holocaust SF novel ever written. *A Canticle for Leibowitz* is an immensely powerful examination of beliefs, religion and humanism, told in three parts and focusing on a Benedictine-style monastery and its struggle to preserve knowledge through a new dark age of several hundred years. A second novel, published shortly after Miller's death, runs parallel to the first and takes an interesting look at similar questions, without the Cold War emphasis of the first.

A Canticle for Leibowitz
Orbit pbk £5.99 1857230140

St. Leibowitz and the Wild Horse Woman
Orbit pbk £6.99 1857235614

MICHAEL MOORCOCK (b.1939)

Amongst the most prolific of all British SF authors, Moorcock began his career in a fifties London in which areas flattened in the Blitz still remained desolate, a London also inundated by pulp fiction from the USA. Both elements - the consequences of random acts of history, and the pleasures of pop culture - were to inform his own work until his move to America in the 80s.

Moorcock began as a precocious editor of the Sexton Blake Library. By the early 1960s, under influences as disparate as Mervyn Peake and Fritz Leiber's *Grey Mouser* series, he began to produce what was to become his bread and butter fiction - sword and sorcery novels. Central to all of these books are the twin concepts of infinite universes and infinite histories and the eternal hero caught up in a struggle between entropy and order. Moorcock's heroes took many forms (Corum, Hawkmoon, Von Bek) but the most enduring was Elric of Melnibone, albino prince with a soul-draining sword and a nice line in existential angst.

Together with the mainstream SF he wrote, these books allowed Moorcock to explore more avant-garde literary forms. As editor of *New Worlds* in the mid-to-late sixties, he nurtured a new wave of SF writing and encouraged writers like Norman Spinrad, J.G. Ballard, Samuel Delany and M. John Harrison to produce genre-stretching work. Moorcock's own contribution to the revolution was to mix pop culture with post-apocalyptic alienation in the brilliant Jerry Cornelius Quartet (*The Final Programme, A Cure for Cancer, The English Assassin* and *The Condition of Muzak*) which gradually dispenses with linear narrative as its amoral anti-hero drifts through numerous alternative 20th centuries.

By the late seventies Moorcock was producing mainstream literary fiction, although littered with characters from his earlier work, and *Byzantium Endures* and *The Laughter of Carthage*, for example, won acclaim from critics not usually enamoured of SF. With *Mother London*, published in 1988, he finally fused all of his themes into a novel of startling originality in a contemporary setting. In his inspiring career Moorcock has moved from his position as sword and sorcery's greatest ally (and its sternest critic), through the dramas of the new wave years, to his present role as genre-hopping maverick.

The Tale of the Eternal Champion Series

Von Bek
Millennium pbk £6.99
1857984366

The Eternal Champion
Millennium pbk £6.99
1857982509

Hawkmoon
Millennium pbk £6.99
1857984374

Corum
Millennium pbk £6.99
1857983149

Sailing to Utopia
Millennium pbk £6.99
1857983068

A Nomad of the Time Streams
Millennium pbk £6.99
185798448X

Dancers at the End of Time
Millennium pbk £6.99
0752806173

Elric of Melnibone
Millennium pbk £6.99
0752806327

The New Nature of the Catastrophe
Millennium pbk £6.99
0752806009

The Prince with the Silver Hand
Millennium pbk £6.99
075280877X

Legends at the End of Time
Millennium pbk £6.99
0752806491

Stormbringer
Millennium pbk £6.99
0752809067

Earl Aubec
Millennium pbk £6.99
0752809121

Blood : A Southern Fantasy
Millennium pbk £4.99
1857982363

A Cornelius Calendar
Millennium pbk £14.99
1897580657

The Cornelius Quartet
Millennium pbk £14.99
1897580509

JAMES MORROW
(b.1947)

James Morrow straddles the boundaries of science fiction and fantasy with the darkly satirical novels for which he is best known. *This is the Way the World Ends* is a grim fable in which the unborn stand judgement over those responsible for nuclear devastation. Other novels, like *Towing Jehovah*, explore the religious themes which preoccupy Morrow, the conflict between faith and reason and the darkness that lurks within us all.

The novels of James Morrow are out of print in the UK. Imports of American editions of his books may be available in some larger branches of Waterstone's.

GEORGE ORWELL (1903–1950)

Eric Blair, who wrote under the name of George Orwell, was a novelist, journalist and pamphleteer and undoubtedly the greatest political writer of the century. He is best remembered, however, for two novels published in the last few years of a life cut short by tuberculosis. *Animal Farm* is an involving small scale study of revolution and the betrayal of revolutionary ideals put into the form of an animal fable. *1984* is Orwell's vision of a totalitarian future and one of the most influential and widely read of SF books. The language of *1984* has entered everyday conversation and 'Big Brother', the 'Thought Police', 'Newspeak' and 'Doublethink' continue to have a chilling resonance. The date for Orwell's future may have passed but his vision of a society in which the individual will is ruthlessly crushed has not lost its relevance. Many people now encounter the book first at school, where it is often a set text, but it is always worth revisiting for the sheer relentless power of Orwell's imagining of the grim world in which his protagonist, Winston Smith, makes his futile bid for freedom.

1984
Penguin pbk £6.99 0140182349

TIM POWERS (b.1952)

Onetime winner of the World Fantasy Award, Powers is one of the key California Dreamers to emerge from the Golden State. His best known work is his skilful amalgam of fantasy and anglophile steampunk SF, *The Anubis Gates.* He is particularly adept at such exercises in cross-fertilising genres and has performed the often difficult task of blending SF and fantasy with an elegance that is cool and impressive. The sheer quality of his writing is matched by his rich imagination. His protagonists, doom-laden losers ready for a saving moment of epiphany, inhabit strange and ornate worlds full of zombie pirates and obscure poets, time travellers and the ravages of atomic destruction.

The Anubis Gates
Legend pbk £6.99 1857236181

Earthquake Weather
Legend pbk £5.99 0099560216

CHRISTOPHER PRIEST (b.1943)

Nearly thirty years after the publication of his first novel, Christopher Priest remains one of British SF's best-kept secrets. He is, undoubtedly, a demanding author but one who deserves to be much better known. His earlier work is often claustrophobically concerned with internal, psychological processes, exceptions being *Fugue for a Darkening Island*, which is a bleak, political vision of a near-future Britain, and *The Space Machine*, an ebullient celebration of the work of H.G. Wells, in which Wells himself appears as a character. His most recent novel, *The Prestige,* uses a more conventional narrative to tell the story of two stage magicians vying with one another at the turn of the century. The SF element of the story is a long time coming, although all the more effective for that, and this exciting book demonstrates once again Priest's skill in creating and interpreting character.

The Affirmation
Pocket Books pbk £6.99
0684816148

The Glamour
Pocket Books pbk £6.99
0684816156

The Prestige
Pocket Books pbk £6.99
0684817551

KEITH ROBERTS (b.1935)

One of Britain's finest yet most neglected literary SF writers, Roberts is best known for his brilliantly realised work of alternative history, *Pavane.* This shares with Philip K. Dick's *The Man in the High Castle* the accolade of greatest novel to emerge from this demanding sub-genre. Where Dick focussed on an America in which occupation followed Axis victory in World War II, Roberts creates a world in which the Protestant Reformation did not take place, the Spanish Armada sailed to victory and Elizabeth I was assassinated. It is the late nineteen sixties in Britain and the Catholic church has suppressed the advance of science for centuries. However the times are changing, the voice of reason will be denied no longer and the Enlightenment revolution is coming at last. Roberts sustains his conceit superbly and his prose works to make believable both his characters and a Britain both similar to and radically different from the one we know. The only other work by Roberts in print is a collection of ghost stories, at least one of which bears comparison with the best of M.R.James.

Pavane
Gollancz pbk £5.99 0575061030

Winterwood & Other Hauntings
Morrigan hbk £13.99 1870338707

'I had reached the age of six hundred and fifty miles.'
Christopher Priest Inverted World

JOANNA RUSS (b.1937)

Critic, novelist and short-story writer, Joanna Russ has written some of the most provocative and thoughtful SF and fantasy of the last thirty years. Her best known work is *The Female Man*, a superbly sustained diatribe against injustice and female stereotyping which appeared in the midst of a new wave of feminist fiction, of all genres, in the mid-seventies. Her clever reworking of fixed notions of gender and her shrewd assessments of the structures of power have been embodied in compelling narratives and characters.

The Female Man
Women's Press pbk £6.99 0704339498

To Write Like a Woman: Essays in Feminism and Science Fiction
Indiana UP pbk £9.99 0253209838

ROBERT SHECKLEY (b.1928)

Sheckley published his first novel in the late fifties and has, for nearly four decades, produced some of the most amusing and satirical of science fictions and fantasies. He has been compared by some to Kurt Vonnegut, in his largely benign examinations of human follies and self-delusions, and he was one of Douglas Adams's inspirations for the Hitchhiker books. Sheckley is a writer of some subtlety and his tales of Candide-like innocents, placed in awkward circumstances by those more devious, are cleverly constructed and written but they are, above all, great fun.

Apart from a number of Star Trek and other film novelisations, the novels of Robert Sheckley are out of print in the UK. Imports of American editions of his books may be available in some larger branches of Waterstone's.

MARY SHELLEY
(1797–1851)

First published in 1818, Mary Shelley's *Frankenstein* was written two years previously as part of a story-telling competition with her husband, the poet Percy Shelley, and Lord Byron. The tale of the idealistic Frankenstein and the monster he inadvertently creates is a clear precursor of many modern novels of science gone awry and of horrors unwittingly unleashed. The story, made familiar from countless film versions and variants played upon its basic theme, has become one of the archetypal myths of the modern age.

Frankenstein
Penguin pbk £2.50 0140433627

Frankenstein
Oxford UP pbk £2.50 0192815326

The Last Man
Oxford UP pbk £6.99 0192831526

LUCIUS SHEPARD (b.1947)

After a nomadic and adventurous early life as rock musician, Shepard emerged during the eighties as an assured writer of generically unclassifiable fiction, often set in exotic locales, with the novels *Green Eyes* and *Life During Wartime* and the short story collection *The Jaguar Hunter*. These all brought great literary finesse to bear on their SF/Horror materials. The romantic and political pessimism of his work arguably owes as much to Conrad and Graham Greene as it does to genre models. In the nineties Shepard has continued to produce original and stimulating work from the brilliant tale of vampires, *The Golden*, to impressively varied and stylish collections of shorter fiction like *To the Ends of the Earth* and *Barnacle Bill the Spacer*.

Barnacle Bill the Spacer
Orion pbk £5.99 0752816098

To Ends of the Earth
Orion pbk £5.99 1857981693

The Golden
Orion pbk £5.99 1857981111

Life During War Time
Orion pbk £5.99 0752816144

ALISON SINCLAIR

Alison Sinclair is one of the most widely praised of recent British SF writers. Lucius Shepard described her first novel as 'the kind of book that first attracted me to Science Fiction, the sort one sees too rarely these days.' Alison Sinclair, a research fellow at Leeds University, is a professional scientist with interests in molecular biology and neuroscience and this is reflected in the scrupulously imagined worlds she conjures up in her two novels, *Legacies* and *Blueheart.*

Blueheart
Millennium pbk £5.99 0752810820
Legacies
Millennium pbk £5.99 1857984013

JOHN SLADEK (b.1937)

Sladek is a significant American New Wave writer, although not a prolific one, and his quirky, offbeat humour is reminiscent of Vonnegut. Sharing Vonnegut's playfulness, if not his bleak view of life and the universe, Sladek is an adept satirist of both men and machines. References to other authors, from Asimov to Smollett, pepper his books but his own, often parodic imagination is wholly original. This witty and incisive writer, who has been an influence on many younger writers, deserves greater acknowledgement as one of the leading US fabulists of his generation.

The Muller-Fokker Effect
Carroll & Graf pbk £3.99 0881845485
Roderick at Random
Carroll & Graf pbk £3.99 0881843415
Black Alice (with Thomas M. Disch)
Carroll & Graf pbk £3.99 088184506X

CORDWAINER SMITH

Cordwainer Smith (real name Paul Linebarger) was a much lauded SF author and expert on pyschological warfare, whose knowledge of brainwashing techniques, possibly the product of his extensive military experience, was used to great effect in his *Instrumentality of Mankind* sequence. A series of short stories, novellas and one novel, the Instrumentality is an eon-spanning montage of terraforming, Huxleyesque eugenics, immortality and, tellingly, given Smith's background in US intelligence, astronauts whose work results in the crippling of their sensoriums. Always more discussed than read, Smith's work nonetheless remains amongst the most fascinating and mysterious in the traditional SF canon.

The novels of Cordwainer Smith are out of print in the UK. Imports of American editions of his books may be available in some larger branches of Waterstone's.

BRIAN STABLEFORD (b.1948)

An historian and critic of SF, Stableford has been a prolific and often uncategorisable writer since the late sixties. He has produced highly regarded work which ranges from space opera to the trilogy beginning with *The Werewolves of London,* an astonishing historical fantasy in which Stableford fashions a world where all distinctions between waking and dreaming have been lost, a world where the angels reveal their true nature and the full consequences of their interference in the affairs of humanity. In his most recent sequence Stableford's knowledge of biology - he has been described as 'the genre's number one expert in designing exotic biosytems' - has been put to good use. *Serpent's Blood, Salamander's Fin* and *Chimera's Cradle,* in which hero Andris Myrasol and heroine Princess Lucretzia journey towards a land of mystery and revelation, form a narrative which combines enjoyable melodrama with serious biological speculation.

Werewolves of London Trilogy

The Werewolves of London
Pan pbk £4.99 0330322672x

The Angel of Pain
Pan pbk £4.99 0330326074

The Carnival of Destruction
Pocket Books pbk £4.99
0671851985

Genesys

Serpent's Blood
Legend pbk £6.99 0099443414

Salamander's Fire
Legend pbk £6.99 0099443619

Chimera's Cradle
Legend pbk £6.99 0099443813

OLAF STAPLEDON (1886–1950)

Stapledon used the developing genre of Science Fiction to embody his own ideas about evolution and ethics he was also a teacher and writer of philosophy. His most famous works are *Last & First Men,* a spectacular future history of man's progress across billions of years from First Men (us) to Eighteenth Men, and *Star Maker,* described by Brian Aldiss as 'a chronicle, hardly a novel, of combined science and poetry, brilliant, durable and irresistibly readable.'

Last & First Men/Starmaker
Dover pbk £9.95 0486219623

Odd John/Sirius
Dover pbk £9.95 0486211339

The Olaf Stapledon Reader
Syracuse UP pbk £14.50
0815604300

THEODORE STURGEON (1918–1985)

Emerging as one of the finest Golden Age writers who helped maintain *Astounding* as the premiere SF magazine of the forties, Sturgeon differed from such stablemates as Asimov and Heinlein in his focus. Always more interested in men than machines, he was a precursor of the more psychologically oriented writers of the fifties and it was during this decade that his work flowered. Primarily a writer of short stories, Sturgeon produced a magnum opus in the novel *More than Human.* Originally a series of short stories published in *Galaxy* magazine, the novel chronicles the isolation, despair and final transcendental melding of those who share the common bond of psionic powers. Widely admired by other writers for tackling themes such as homosexuality when they were still taboo subjects in the genre, Sturgeon is well worth reading alongside other social SF stalwarts as Bester, Dick and (especially) Farmer to give the reader a fuller picture of the genre's growing sophistication in the early fifties. After that decade new work appeared infrequently but it is available in a number of short-story collections still in print.

More Than Human
Vista pbk £5.99

The Dreaming Jewels
Carroll & Graf pbk £3.99 0881843512

Some of Your Blood
Carroll & Graf pbk £3.99 078670103X

The Golden Helix
Carroll & Graf pbk £3.99 0881844500

The Complete Short Stories :

Volume One
North Atlantic hbk £21.00 1556431821

Volume Two
North Atlantic hbk £20.00 1556432135

Volume Three
North Atlantic hbk £20.00 1556432275

Volume Four
North Atlantic hbk £20.00 1556432526

JAMES TIPTREE JR. (1915–1987)

During the sixties and seventies James Tiptree Jr was a well-known, prolific and reclusive short story writer. His writings challenged the assumptions of sixties America, while he himself challenged (and antagonised) female participants at a conference he 'attended' by correspondence. Then, in an astonishing disclosure 'he' was unmasked as a woman, former CIA agent Alice Sheldon, who allegedly took her pseudonym from the name of the jam manufacturer. Although a couple of novels appeared under the *nom de plume*, it is the short stories which represent Tiptree's best work. They tackle big themes with speedy narratives and an ironic use of staple SF motifs. The plots seem routine. A spacecraft is flung three hundred years into Earth's future (*Houston, Houston, Do You Read?*); a disfigured woman agrees to operate a beautiful robot body (*The Girl Who Was Plugged In*). Yet they are tackled with one wry eye on conventional SF, the other on a world filled with more disturbing possibilities. Fast, funny, challenging and smart, Tiptree's short stories are classics of the genre.

The novels of James Tiptree are out of print in the UK. Some large branches of Waterstone's may stock American editions.

JACK VANCE (b.1916)

Renowned for his baroque style and mordant wit, Jack Vance is one of the undoubted greats of post-war American SF. He has been demonstrating his talents as a novelist and his inventiveness in building new worlds since the forties and has been responsible for some of the most popular and critically acclaimed of SF series. The *Planet of Adventure* series was begun in the sixties and so too was the complex and imaginative *Demon Princes* saga which Vance brought to a conclusion in the early eighties. Perhaps his most popular sequence has been the *Lyonesse* fantasy novels but he has continued to produce SF novels of high quality, including the *Cadwal Chronicles* which turned an unillusioned eye on the activities of a bunch of developers keen to exploit a planet's resources.

Ecce & Old Earth
Hodder pbk £5.99 0340577252

Night Lamp
Voyager pbk £5.99 0006482112

JULES VERNE (1828–1905)

After spending some years as a writer of opera libretti, Verne eventually found lasting fame and a more rewarding career in penning novels which exaggerated and often anticipated the possibilities of nineteenth century science. He represents, in many ways, the link between Poe's tales of mystery and imagination and the scientific romances of Wells. Certainly Wells was deeply influenced by Verne's writing. Of the dozens of novels which Verne wrote between the eighteen sixties and his death in 1905 two of the best known, which can be definitely classified as science fiction, and which are still in print, are *Journey to the Centre of the Earth* and *Twenty Thousand Leagues Under the Sea.* The former is a reflection of contemporary speculation that the earth might be hollow, a theory that had not been wholly discredited at the time Verne wrote; the latter is the story of the submarine the Nautilus and its misanthropic captain, the mysterious Nemo.

From Earth to Moon
Sutton pbk £5.99 0750908246

Journey to the Centre of the Earth
Penguin pbk £4.99 0140022651

Journey to the Centre of the Earth
Oxford UP pbk £4.99 0192829009

Twenty Thousand Leagues Under the Sea
Oxford UP pbk £4.99 0192828398

JOAN D. VINGE

(b.1948)

Joan D. Vinge won her first Hugo award for her short story *Eyes of Amber,* an intriguing tale of communication between two people from completely different worlds. *The Snow Queen,* a lyric fantasy novel based on the classic Hans Christian Andersen story, won her a second Hugo. In this book, its sequels and in her Psion cycle Vinge made good use of her training as an anthropologist as she created complex worlds and societies and played skilfully with ideas and theories. She has been sidetracked recently into the production of movie novelisations but she remains a writer who can be trusted to supply intelligent fiction with vivid characterisation, a solid grounding in science and technology and enough mystery and magic to keep the reader hooked.

Catspaw
Pan pbk £4.99 033031551X

KURT VONNEGUT (b.1922)

How should Vonnegut's work be defined? Does he write SF or not? His most famous book, *Slaughterhouse-Five,* blends historical facts about the fire-bombing of Dresden, at which Vonnegut was famously present as a POW, with life on the distant planet of Trafalmadore. Yet the book does not sit comfortably within the genre. It may be that other works are more successful as genre works. His first novel, *Player Piano,* was startlingly predictive of the impact of a completely mechanised and automated society and the triumph of a technologically expanding America over a failing Russian social system. The black humour and pessimism that characterise all Vonnegut's work, both SF and non-SF, was evident in *The Sirens of Titan,* in which human history is seen as of little significance, the chance consequence of an alien search for a spare part for a spaceship. *Cat's Cradle,* which features the illusory religion of Bokoninism and the planet-ending invention of ice-nine, was filled with the same laughter in the dark. Vonnegut has written many novels which have little or no SF element to them and he is one of the most admired American writers of his generation. However his work is defined, his books are to be celebrated for the wit and invention with which he mixes his bleak view of the universe and man's place in it.

Cat's Cradle
Penguin pbk £5.99 0140023089

Hocus Pocus
Vintage pbk £6.99 0099877104

The Sirens of Titan
Indigo pbk £5.99 0575400234

Slapstick
Vintage pbk £5.99 009984270X

Slaughterhouse Five
Vintage pbk £5.99 0099800209

H.G. WELLS (1866–1946)

Born in Bromley, Wells began his working life as an apprentice draper and only escaped from this drudgery by winning a scholarship to the Normal School of Science in South Kensington where he was taught by the great scientist T.H. Huxley. He published articles, short stories and textbooks in the late eighties and nineties and his first novel, *The Time Machine*, the story of a man who travels into a future where man has evolved into two distinct species, the gentle but vacuous Eloi and the troglodytic Morlocks, appeared in 1895. From then on he earned his living as a writer and his literary output was enormous and varied, from comic novels of lower middle-class life to outlines of world history, from political theory to autobiography. His most famous works, however, remain the scientific romances which followed *The Time Machine*. Most notable amongst these are *The War of the Worlds*, in which the inhabitants of Mars invade the Earth, *The Island of Dr Moreau*, in which an arrogant vivisectionist rules his own kingdom of creatures, half-man and half-beast, *The Invisible Man* and *The First Men in the Moon*. In his political and social writing, Wells was an advocate of science, reason and socialism as the only hopes for mankind. In his novels, science plays a far more ambivalent role and nature is always ready to reassert itself. The creatures of Dr. Moreau, turned into 'humans' by his scientific genius, revert to the beasts after his death, as 'the stubborn beast flesh grows day by day back again'. The Martians, with their advanced and seemingly unstoppable technology, are defeated by terrestrial bacteria, 'the humblest things that God, in his wisdom, has put upon the earth.' Wells, the founding father of modern science fiction, had the open-mindedness of the true artist and his ideas and influence have been evident in the last hundred years of the genre.

The Science Fiction Volume 1
Phoenix pbk £9.99 1857993527

The Science Fiction Volume 2
Phoenix pbk £12.99
1857994345

The Invisible Man
Everyman pbk £4.99
0460876287

The Island of Dr Moreau
Everyman pbk £4.99
0460872583

The Shape of Things to Come
Everyman pbk £4.99
0460873512

The Time Machine
Everyman pbk £3.99
0460877356

The War of the Worlds
Everyman pbk £4.99
0460873032

CONNIE WILLIS (b.1945)

An acclaimed American writer of short fiction and novels, Connie Willis is probably best known for her 1992 work *Doomsday Book.* In this massive and densely wrought story of time travel a scholar plans to return to the historical period she is studying but lands instead in the midst of the 1348 Black Death. Past and present become intertwined as the Oxford she has left behind is infected by disease from the era she is visiting. She has also written another novel of time travel, *Lincoln's Dreams,* and a number of highly praised short stories and novellas.

Doomsday Book
Hodder pbk £5.99 0450579875

Uncharted Territory
Hodder pbk £5.99 0450617483

'Yet, across the gulf of space, minds that are to our minds as ours are to those of the beasts that perish, intellects vast and cool and unsympathetic, regarded this earth with envious eyes, and slowly and surely drew their plans against us.'

H. G. Wells – The War of the Worlds

YEVGENY ZAMYATIN (1884–1937)

A Russian novelist and satirist, Zamyatin was a Bolshevik before the October Revolution but, as one of nature's nonconformists, became rapidly disillusioned with the new society being created in the twenties. He asked Stalin for permission to emigrate and left Russia in 1931, settling eventually in Paris. His most famous work was an anti-Utopian fantasy, *We*, in which he imagined a state from which passion and creativity had been banished, one in which workers lived in glass houses, had numbers rather than names and dressed identically. Zamyatin was influenced by H.G. Wells, whose work he had edited in Russian, and influenced in turn Orwell's *1984*. The seemingly obvious influence on *Brave New World* was always denied by Aldous Huxley.

We
Penguin pbk £6.99 0140185852

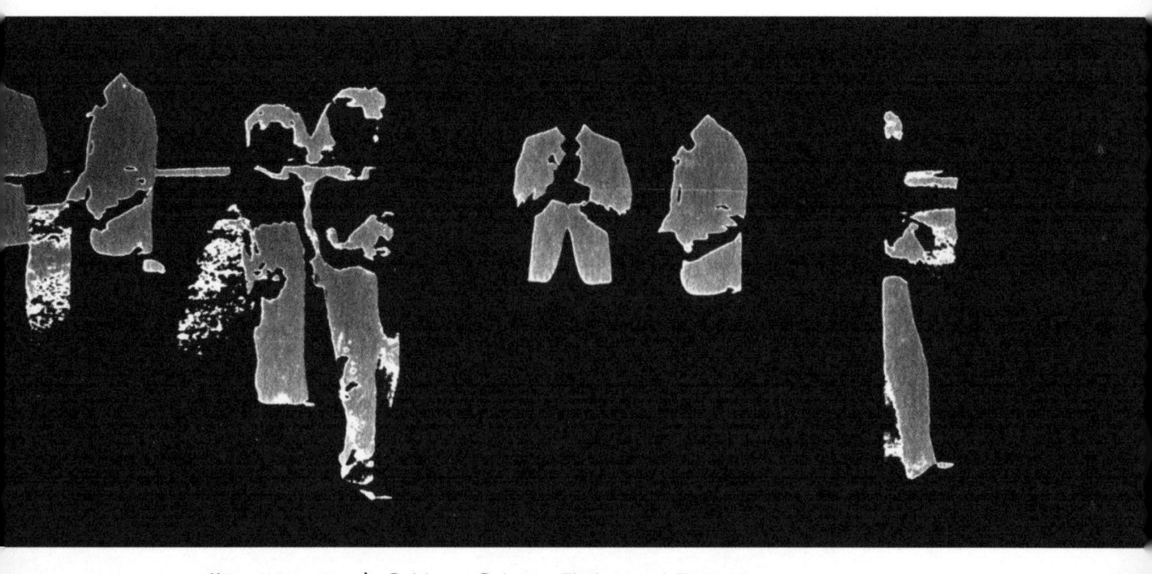

Humourous Science Fiction & Fantasy

WHAT I'M DOING HERE

We asked Robert Rankin, author of The Brentford Trilogy, a trilogy in four books, to explain what led him to the writing of comic science fiction. We expected something a little different. We got it.

Many years ago in a time we now call the nineteen seventies, I began writing. It was my bold intention when I started out to create an entirely new literary genre. I did this for two reasons. Firstly, I had no wish to compete with another living writer. And, secondly, I thought it would get me my own special section in W. H. Smith's. Well, if you don't start out thinking BIG, what's the point in starting out at all?

Things did not go quite the way I'd planned and I began in the general fiction section. Where I vanished without trace. Several publishers later, a very wise man named Patrick Janson-Smith said, 'This man is writing science fiction. Let's put him in the science fiction section.' And that is what I'm doing here.

Now, the thing about being here is this. If you write science fiction as opposed to 'ordinary' fiction, people keep asking you, 'Where do you get your ideas from?' I have no particular problems with this question, because I know exactly where all my ideas come from, or rather from *whom* they come. The man at the back of it all is my late dad. I describe myself as a teller of tall tales and my work as *far-fetched fiction*, the section you don't see in W. H. Smith's. And I inherited the storytelling gene from my dad.

My earliest memory comes from my first term at infants school. The teacher asked us to draw a picture of what our fathers did for a living, and so I drew mine and the teacher was so impressed that she put the picture up in the hall. A great honour. When open evening came around, the teacher hastened over to my dad and asked him whether he would consider coming into school to give the children a talk about what he did for a living. My dad, a carpenter by trade, asked why.

'Well', said the teacher, 'You're the first father we've had who's a whaler.'

You see, my dad had given me a whale's tooth as a present and told me a great tale about how he'd pulled it from the jaw of the whale during one of his many voyages. He had just been entertaining his young son with a tall tale well told, and that's what I'd passed on to the teacher. Any 'normal' father would have owned up and laughed it all off. Not my dad. Without a moment's hesitation he agreed to give the talk, went home and fashioned a harpoon to demonstrate throwing techniques. His talk was a big success and even the headmistress came to listen. I was quite a hero amongst the other kids throughout the second term.

The apotheosis of my father's tall tale telling career came at his funeral and paid a posthumous tribute to his supreme mastery of the craft. No one expects to leave his father's funeral with tears of laughter in his eyes but I did. The vicar was one of those young, eager, fresh-faced bods and he climbed into the pulpit and launched into a discourse on my dad.

'I've only been in the parish for nine months', he began, 'and so I've only known Mr. Rankin through the last stages of his long illness. But it soon became clear to me during our many talks that Mr Rankin was a most extraordinary man, who had lived the kind of life that most of us only read about in books. H had scaled some of the world's highest peaks. Walked alone across the Kalahari desert, where he met the bushmen and became a tribal chief. He had sailed alone around Cape Horn and he was twice decorated during the Second World War for feats of outstanding bravery.'

I nearly fell out of my pew when I heard this lot. My first thought was that this stupid vicar was talking about the wrong old man. My father had never done any of these things. He had lived a very quiet life. I was about to jump up and take issue with the erring clergyman, when I heard the laughter. It came in little muffled bursts from my father's old cronies. The vicar didn't hear it and he continued to eulogise my father and the things he had supposedly done. His world wanderings and his uncanny knack of always being in the right place at the right time when history was being made. The laughter rose and rose but the vicar never heard it. My dad had spent the last nine months of his life winding up the gullible young man. He had the last laugh and he let me share it.

I left the church with tears of laughter in my eyes. But the best bit was still to come and it was almost as if my dad had planned it that way. Thinking back, I am sure that he did.

'Will you come back to the house for some tea and cakes?' I asked the vicar. 'I'd like to have a chat with you.'

The vicar agreed and we went back to dad's place. And we hadn't been there five minutes when it came. The vicar pointed to a sword fish saw that hung above my dad's fireplace. 'That can tell a tale or two, can't it?' he said.

I glanced up at the thing. As far as I knew, it had been utterly mute since the day my father purchased it at a Hastings antique market. But then, it might well have confided something to him.

'Would you care to refresh my memory?' I said.

'Indeed', said the vicar. 'Your father told me about the time he was fishing for sailfish off the Florida keys. He was all alone in a small boat when a storm blew up. It was the infamous Hurricane Flora that swept across America in 1968 and your father was one of the first men to be caught in it. The storm hit his boat and his oars were blown overboard. Being the pious man he was, and fearing that his time had come, he prayed to the Lord. There was a flash of lightning and a swordfish burst its saw, that very one hanging up there, through the bottom of his boat. Using the skills he had acquired whilst working as a circus strongman, your father snapped off the saw, thrust his foot into the hole and, using the saw as a paddle, rowed safely back to land.'

Now, to say that I was speechless, would be to say that I was SPEECHLESS! After the vicar left, my mum took me quietly to one side.

'I think it would be best if none of this was ever spoken of again, don't you, dear?' she said. And I nodded thoughtfully.

And so that's how it works, really. I am merely following in my father's footsteps. The only difference between him and me is that I am lucky enough to be able to do it for a living.

DOUGLAS ADAMS (b.1952)

With the *Hitch-Hiker's Guide to the Galaxy* Douglas Adams single-handedly recreated and reinvigorated humorous SF. Originally it was a radio series broadcast in 1978. Adams reworked the script into the first of a 'trilogy' of five bestselling novels which followed the adventures of Arthur Dent, a perpetually confused earthling cast adrift in a surreal and monstrously unfair universe when the Earth is demolished to make way for a hyperspace bypass. Less well known than the Hitchhiker books, but just as funny, are Adams's other novels - *Dirk Gently's Holistic Detective Agency* and *The Long Dark Tea Time of the Soul*, bizarre collisions between SF and pulp crime genres. These are rooted in the present day but feature such fantastical elements as a sulky God of Thunder, an asylum patient telepathically bonded to Dustin Hoffman and a broken Electric Monk that believes the world is pink. Beneath all the humour Adams's view of the universe is, perhaps, a bleak one. Death is sudden and often highly embarrassing. Even the most enlightened alien races are just as stupidly bureaucratic as humans. At one point he even proves mathematically that there are no people in the entire universe. Yet his books, nonetheless, are wildly funny. Twenty years after the original radio broadcast Douglas Adams is now working on a Hitchhiker screenplay and a new book. No doubt SF's answer to Joseph Heller will give his readers another caustic masterpiece.

Hitchhiker Books

The Hitchhiker Omnibus
Pan pbk £9.99 0330316117

The Hitch Hiker's Guide to the Galaxy
Pan pbk £5.99 0330258648

The Restaurant at the End of the Universe
Pan pbk £4.99 0330262130

Life, the Universe, and Everything
Pan pbk £4.99 0330267388

So Long, and Thanks for All the Fish
Pan pbk £4.99 0330287001

Mostly Harmless
Pan 3 pbk £5.99 033032311

Dirk Gently

Dirk Gently's Holistic Detective Agency
Pan pbk £4.99 0330301624

The Long Dark Tea-time of the Soul
Pan pbk £5.99 0330309552

ROBERT ASPRIN

Although none of his books is currently in print, Robert Asprin has been a prolific author of light, humourous SF fantasy and it is safe to assume that his work will be available again in the UK before too long. He has written several books featuring Willard Phule, the galaxy's youngest trillionaire, and his struggles to turn a bunch of space misfits into a formidable fighting force. However he is best known for the *Myth* series. Mischievously he described this as 'a series to take very, very seriously' but novels which have titles like *Hit or Myth* and... and feature characters like Aahz, the clapped-out demon, and Gleep, a dragon of little brain, are unlikely to be read very solemnly.

The novels of Robert Asprin are out of print in the UK. American editions of his books may be available in larger branches of Waterstone's.

JAMES BIBBY

James Bibby has, in three books so far, had great fun in mocking (amiably enough) the more mockable aspects of old-fashioned sword and sorcery fiction. His hero Ronan the Barbarian (who can that be a reference to?) was required, in the first book, to find the Singing Sword and put to death the evil necromancer Nekros, tasks which he achieved as much through luck as through design. In succeeding volumes the intrepid Ronan has fallen into the clutches of a voluptuous sorceress named Shikara and come up against nefarious members of the Orcbane Sword Corporation. The series promises to be one which can last and the humour, if not in the Pratchett league, is genuine.

Ronan the Barbarian
Millennium pbk £4.99
1857983084

Ronan's Rescue
Millennum pbk £4.99
0752808761

Ronan's Revenge
Millennium hbk £16.99
1857985265

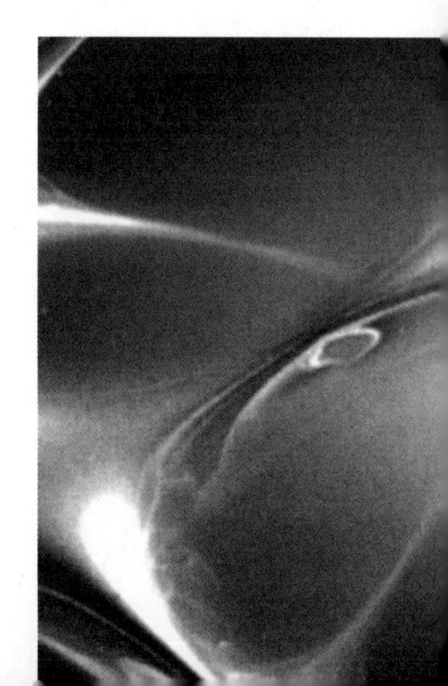

JOHN BROSNAN

A versatile writer, Brosnan has written an excellent history of SF in the movies, *The Primal Screen*, and adventurous space opera in novels like *The Opoponax Invasion*. His most recent work is a trilogy of light-hearted, humorous fantasy novels, beginning with *Damned and Fancy*, in which investigative journalist Travis Thomson wakes up in a leafy glade wearing blue tights and a bright red codpiece. He is paying an unscheduled visit to the land of Samella and, although he makes his escape he finds, in the second novel *Have Demon, Will Travel*, that he has brought with him a fairy-tale princess and that a foul-mouthed demon has taken up residence in his fridge. In the third book, *Lights, Camera, Magic!* he returns to Samella in the hope of filming a fantasy epic there and earning a fortune. These undemanding and funny books are further proof of the range of Brosnan's writing talents.

Damned and Fancy
Legend pbk £4.99 0099512211

Have Demon, Will Travel
Legend pbk £4.99 0099512319

Lights, Camera, Magic
Legend pbk £4.99 0099512416

The Opoponax Invasion
Gollancz pbk £4.99 0575058277

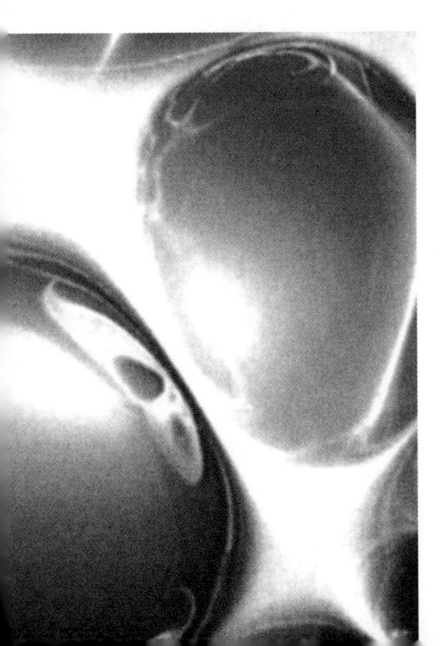

ANDREW HARMAN

In the last few years Andrew Harman has emerged as one of the most ingenious and energetic writers of humorous fantasy. 'the nearest', as one reviewer noted, 'to a genuine rival to Terry Pratchett.' His books, largely set in the twin kingdoms of Rhyngill and Cranachan and the hellish city of Mortropolis, are jam-packed with appalling puns, unashamedly juvenile humour and even a sprinkling of good jokes. Whether revealing the Ultimate Weapon – Rana Militaris, the Frogs of War – or showing how vegetarians and carnivores can be united by implanting chicken genes in corn, Harman gives value for money.

A Midsummer Night's Gene
Legend pbk £4.99 0099788810

Fahrenheit 666
Legend pbk £4.99 009949891X

The Deity Dozen
Legend pbk £4.99 0099681013

The Frogs of War
Legend pbk £4.99 0099284812

The Scrying Game
Legend pbk £4.99 0099499010

The Sorcerer's Appendix
Legend pbk £4.99 0099284715

The Tome Tunnel
Legend pbk £4.99 009928491X

101 Damnations
Legend pbk £4.99 0099498812

TOM HOLT (b.1961)

Over the last few years Tom Holt has developed into one of the best British writers of comic fantasy. Books like *Expecting Someone Taller,* in which the protagonist runs over a badger which turns out to be Ingolf, last of the Giants, *Djinn Rummy,* a work of comic genies, *Who's Afraid of Beowulf,* an engaging mixture of P. G. Wodehouse, Norse mythology and Laurel and Hardy, and *Open Sesame,* set intriguingly in Baghdad and Southampton, have shown the truth of John Clute's assessment of Holt's work. 'This is comedy with a very wide grin.'

Djinn Rummy
Orbit pbk £5.99 1857233638

Expecting Someone Taller
Orbit pbk £4.99 1857231813

Faust Among Equals
Orbit pbk £5.99 1857232658

Flying Dutch
Orbit pbk £4.99 1857230175

Grailblazers
Orbit pbk £4.99 1857231910

Here Comes the Sun
Orbit pbk £5.99 1857231872

My Hero
Orbit pbk £5.99 1857233875

Odds and Gods
Orbit pbk £4.99 1857232992

Open Sesame
Orbit pbk £5.99 1857235568

Overtime
Orbit pbk £5.99 1857231260

Paint Your Dragon
Orbit pbk £5.99 1857234561

Who's Afraid of Beowulf?
Orbit pbk £5.99 1857231961

Wish You Were Here
Orbit hbk £15.99 185723555X

Ye Gods
Orbit pbk £4.99 1857230809

GRANT NAYLOR (ROB GRANT & DOUG NAYLOR)

Grant Naylor is the gestalt entity created by the writing partnership of Rob Grant and Doug Naylor who worked together for a number of years. They were the chief writers on *Spitting Image* for a period in the eighties and produced the acclaimed series *Son of Cliche* for Radio Four. However their great claim to fame is that they were the creators of the Emmy award-winning, comic SF series *Red Dwarf.* The epic adventures of a clapped-out spaceship run by a clapped-out crew consisting of unwilling space traveller (Lister), bad-tempered hologram (Rimmer) and deranged mechanoid (Kryton), the series developed from cult status to international success. Books have spun off from the series, originally written by the two co-creators. More recently Doug Naylor has taken on the task of novelisation himself, producing *The Last Human* as a solo undertaking.

Better Than Life
Penguin pbk £5.99 0140124381

Red Dwarf Omnibus
Penguin pbk £9.99 0140174664

Red Dwarf: Infinity Welcomes Careful Drivers
Penguin pbk £5.99 0140124373

TERRY PRATCHETT

Terry Pratchett is *the* fantasy humourist *par excellence.* The author of twenty one Discworld novels (so far) and several other titles, he is one of the most successful genre writers ever. His books have been published in dozens of languages in countries all around the world. They have been taped, mapped, gazeteered, televised, dramatised and graphic novel-ised. And Pratchett's fans will tell you that, from the start of the first book to the last word of the latest, no novels keep them laughing longer and nobody writes comic fantasy better than their hero.

At the centre of the Pratchett books is the Discworld itself. This is a pancake-flat world supported by four giant elephants, which stand on the shell of a gigantic star-turtle that swims through space. It is a world powered by magic, where the possible is only limited by the scope of Pratchett's imagination and where the impossible is merely a temporary inconvenience. The wonder of Discworld is that there is no concept or idea that can't be explored, exploded, prodded, tweaked and thoroughly expounded within the confines of Ankh-Morpork, Lancre and beyond. So, alongside the lampoons of classic fantasy tropes that are found in earlier books like *The Colour of Magic, The Light Fantastic* and *Equal Rites,* Pratchett also finds room in many of his later books to do a number on other, more serious issues. Philosophy, organised religion, metaphysics, astrophysics, the nature of death, Hollywood, music-with-rocks-in, and the anthropomorphic personification of Jungian mythological-psychological archetypes - all these and more are grist to

Discworld Novels

The Colour of Magic
Corgi pbk £5.99 0552124753

The Light Fantastic
Corgi pbk £5.99 0552128481

Equal Rites
Corgi pbk £5.99 0552131059

Mort
Corgi pbk £4.99 0552131067

Sourcery
Corgi pbk £5.99 0552131075

Wyrd Sisters
Corgi pbk £5.99 0552134600

Pyramids
Corgi pbk £5.99 0552134619

Guards! Guards!
Corgi pbk £5.99 0552134627

Moving Pictures
Corgi pbk £5.990552134635

Reaper Man
Corgi pbk £4.99 0552134643

Witches Abroad
Corgi pbk £4.99 0552134651

Small Gods
Corgi pbk £5.99 0552138908

Lords and Ladies
Corgi pbk £5.99 0552138916

Men at Arms
Corgi pbk £5.99 0552140287

Soul Music
Corgi pbk £5.99 0552140295

Interesting Times
Corgi pbk £5.99 0552142352

Maskerade
Corgi pbk £5.99 0552142360

Feet of Clay
Corgi pbk £5.99 0552142379

Pratchett's mill. Enough to confound any critic who claims that his work is childish or unsophisticated. Above all, perhaps, it is the strength and depth of Pratchett's characterisation that make him such a huge success. His characters are truly memorable, lovable or hate-able on demand, and instantly recognisable. Heroes, villains and supporting cast all come together in a cauldron of anarchic fun.

Fun is the word that explains Pratchett's success, his enormous following and bestseller status, better than any other. Witty and droll, sharp and subtle one moment, indulging in slapstick the next, Terry Pratchett is always enormously entertaining and, quite simply, a lot of fun to read.

Hogfather
Corgi pbk £5.99 0552145424

Jingo
Gollancz hbk £16.99
0575065400

The Discworld Mapp
Corgi 0552143243 £5.99

The Streets of Ankh-Morpork
Corgi £6.99 0552141615

The Discworld Companion
Gollancz pbk £4.99
0575600306

The Carpet People
Corgi pbk £4.99 0552527521

The Dark Side of the Sun
Corgi pbk £4.99 0552133264

Diggers
Corgi pbk £4.99 0552525863

Eric
Gollancz pbk £4.99
0575600012

Good Omens (w.Neil Gaiman)
Corgi pbk £5.99 0552137030

Johnny and the Bomb
Corgi pbk £3.99 0552529680

Johnny and the Dead
Corgi pbk £4.99 0552527408

Only You Can Save Mankind
Corgi pbk £4.99 0552139262

Strata
Corgi pbk £4.99 0552133256

Truckers
Corgi pbk £4.99 0552525952

Wings
Corgi pbk £3.99 0552526495

The Pratchett Portfolio
Gollancz pbk £7.99
0575063483

ROBERT RANKIN

Robert Fleming Rankin is a very funny man. He is also somewhat strange and so are his novels. A typical Rankin plot might involve the Great Pyramid, flying saucers, Adolf Hitler, time-travelling Elvises, a host of dead film stars, a fistful of sprouts and the odd pint of large. Of course there is no such thing as the typical Rankin plot. The publication of the *Brentford Trilogy*, four books written between 1981 and 1984, placed Rankin at the forefront of British humorous fantasy writing. Against the seemingly mundane backdrop of suburban Brentford the Powers of Darkness arise and the fate of the world rests in the none too stable hands of Rankin's greatest double act, dedicated pint-of-large fancier Jim Pooley and professionally unemployed ladies' man John O'Malley. Like all Rankin's work, the Brentford Trilogy subverts the cliches of SF, fantasy and horror and blends them with a healthy measure of genuine weirdness and a warm, if often warped, sense of humour. Rankin has followed these books with the *Armageddon* and *Cornelius Murphy* trilogies and a string of loosely connected novels. He has been called 'a stark raving genius.' This is a fitting description of the man. He is one of the few comic fantasists worthy of adult attention.

The Brentford Trilogy

The Antipope
Corgi pbk £4.99 055213841X

The Brentford Triangle
Corgi pbk £4.99 0552138428

East of Ealing
Corgi pbk £4.99 0552138436

The Sprouts of Wrath
Corgi pbk £4.99 0552138444

The Armageddon Trilogy

Armageddon the Musical
Corgi pbk £5.99 0552136816

Armageddon the B-Movie
Corgi pbk £5.99 0552138320

Armageddon the Remake
Corgi pbk £5.99 0552139238

Cornelius Murphy Trilogy

The Book of Ultimate Truths
Corgi pbk £4.99 055213922X

Raiders of the Lost Car Park
Corgi pbk £4.99 0552138339

The Greatest Show Off Earth
Corgi pbk £4.99 0552139246

The Brentford Chainstore Massacre
Doubleday hbk £16.99
0385407076

The Dance of the Voodoo Handbag
Doubleday hbk £16.99
0385409206

A Dog Called Demolition
Corgi pbk £4.99 0552142131

The Garden of Unearthly Delights
Corgi pbk £4.99 0552142123

The Most Amazing Man Who Ever Lived
Corgi pbk £4.99 0552142115

Nostradamus Ate My Hamster
Corgi pbk £5.99 0552143553

Sprout Mask Replica
Corgi pbk £5.99 0552143561

The Suburban Book of the Dead
Corgi pbk £4.99 0552139238

BOB SHAW (1931–1996)

Bob Shaw once published a book of advice to the would-be writer of SF and fantasy. Few British SF writers could have been better equipped to write such a book. From the first short stories he published in the fifties to the many novels he wrote between 1967 and his death, his work consistently demonstrated his versatility and imagination. His best known work was, probably, the trilogy consisting of *The Ragged Astronauts*, *The Wooden Spaceships* and *The Fugitive Worlds*, but he also wrote humorous SF about galactic troubleshooter, Warren Peace.

Other Days, Other Eyes
Orbit pbk £4.99 1857232216

The Ragged Astronauts
Orbit pbk £3.99 0708882277

The Shadow of Heaven
Gollancz pbk £3.99 0575052945

Warren Peace
Gollancz pbk £4.99 057505719X

How to Write Science Fiction
Allison & B pbk £6.99 0749001356

Fantasy

Anne McCaffrey

The author of *Dragonflight* and *The Crystal Singer* series describes what Science Fiction and Fantasy mean to her and what the difference is between them.

Ever since Uhuru manned the comdesk on the USS Enterprise, women have decided that science fiction is not all that difficult to understand – and enjoy. For which I, as one science fiction writer, am extremely grateful. When *Star Trek* had that long hiatus between Enterprises, women readers turned to women writers of science fiction and fantasy for a hit. The reading base broadened exponentially. And the number of writers increased.

However it is important to point out that there is a distinction between science fiction and fantasy – at least as far as this author is concerned because *her* dragons are science-fictional, not fantasy. The Dragons of Pern® were biogenetically engineered from an indigenous life form on the planet that was being colonised by Terrans. They are certainly not traditional dragons as they do not eat virgins, terrify villagers and only flame what their riders point them at – Thread, the mycorrhizoid organism that falls through Pern's skies and needs to be scorched out of the air before it can fall to the surface and eat anything organic. Since the dragons chew a phosphene-bearing rock, the phosphene gas they burp, as all chemistry students know, ignites on contact with oxygen. Therefore there is a scientific basis for fire-breathing dragons. (Robert Heinlein had his dragon in *Glory Road* use methane gas for the same purpose.) The Pernese dragons are an ecological necessity on a planet that requires a renewable air force. Hence I write science fiction and stick within the generally accepted Newtonian principles of science and logic.

Fantasy, on the other hand, is defined by parameters set by the author and generally includes some element of magic. Horror and the Occult are considered by most members of Science Fiction Writers of America to be sub-genres of Fantasy.

There are two types of science fiction. Hard science fiction is written by scientific minds like Larry Niven, Jerry Pournelle, David Brin, Sir Arthur C. Clarke, Isaac Asimov, Robert Sawyer, Pamela Sargent and others in which a scientific discovery or extrapolation is the dominant topic under discussion. Soft science fiction, which is what I and most of my colleagues write, is scientifically accurate as far as the premises go (although occasionally modern science overruns us with harder facts) but plot, characterization and content are more important than the scientific structure used.

Frankly it doesn't much matter so long as the story is good, the characters stick in the mind when the book is finished and the reader is satisfied with the occupation of reading it.

I was reading science fiction and fantasy long before I put those labels on my choice of reading material. As a child I was introduced to Rudyard Kipling's Mowgli and then *Kim*. I was more fascinated by Edgar Rice Burroughs's John Carter of Mars than Tarzan, and always had my nose in any utopian or dystopian novel I could find. *Islandia* by Austin Tappan Wright, which I read at the age of fourteen, has had a lifelong effect on me. I wrote my senior thesis at Harvard on Evgeni Zamiatin's *We*, comparing it to Huxley's *Brave New World*, that was published six years later. There were parallels between the novels that contributed to to the merit of my honors' thesis. Now those novels are all included in the general science fiction section.

As it happens the first real science fiction and fantasy magazine, *Amazing Stories* published in April 1926, the month and year of my birth, by Hugo Gernsback, now remembered by the SF award bearing his name. So you might say there was a natal connection which would take twenty eight years to fulfil its promise: twenty eight years before I published my first SF story in the late Sam Moskowitz's magazine, *Science Fiction+*.

Why do I write science fiction? Well, for one thing I can sell the stories I write in that genre. Secondly, I happen to have that sort of imagination, so such storytelling comes easily. Most of the time, I enjoy 'what-iffing', extrapolating both traditions and innovations as far as they will logically go. Logically, I said, and that logic is one of my strengths as a writer. It adds to my credibility. It helps me when I truly *believe* that I am where my characters are, doing what my characters need to do or should do, and coping with the sort of lifestyles they must manage. Gordon R. Dickson, one of my long-time SF friends, once said that if you, the writer, knew what was in every drawer in the desk, hanging in the closet, stored under the bed, the reader would too, without your ever having to describe the contents. Cecilia Holland, who wrote the memorable historical novel *The Firedrake*, gave me an invaluable clue to add to Gordie's; she only mentioned those things that would have been unusual to someone living in 1065, the year in which the novel is set. So one does not have to read all about castle barbicans, crenellations, outer and inner keeps . . . because her hero knew all about *them*. But he was surprised to see so many banners from the last big joust in the hall of the keep, and he worried about the amount of fleas bedding in dirty straw on the floor and if he'd irritate his chillblains as he backed up the roaring fire on the hearth. Instantly the reader has a feeling for his problems – not that I suspect many of you of having fleas and fewer of you of having chillblains.

Since, from the thirties to the mid-sixties, science fiction was definitely oriented to a male readership, 'science' dominated and emotion was rarely a facet of the science fiction yarn. I used emotions deliberately, as a facet of storytelling. Some twenty years after I had first written it, I watched BBC cameramen weeping as I stammered through the final paragraphs of *The Ship Who Sang*. The story is *charged* with emotion, mainly grief, and evokes the feeling soldiers get at hearing the Last Post as a requiem or, if you're American, Taps. I did it on purpose. I have made a lot of readers reach for the tissue box. Good therapy. For both reader and writer. And it's an essential part of good storytelling to generate emotions. Even Spock had a few.

Compare the bridge and Enterprise design of the earliest *Star Trek* episodes with those in the *Next Generation* or *Deep Space Nine* and *Babylon Five*. There's been a similar updating and reconstituition of written SF as well. As indeed there should be.

In my days as secretary-treasurer of Science Fiction Writers of America in the late sixties, I was able to read every short story, novella and novel that was printed. Nowadays I'm lucky if I've read one or two of the novels put forward for awards each year. I don't even try to keep up with short fiction. There are such marvellous new writers, too, exploding onto the scene and this improves the field for every one of us. Sometimes our themes might offend the purist or intolerant but if I can make just one of my readers *think* a little more about what I'm saying, I'll have done my job.

Who knows what the future will bring? Let us hope that the worst case scenarios do not erupt over us. Let us pray that the Brave New World of the millennium will be taken from one of the more optimistic futures we science fiction writers have envisioned, with peace (I always put that first), prosperity and promise to all peoples. If enough folks read what could be, maybe they will strive the harder to achieve it. As the poet once said:–

> The problem, yours and mine, is not to wonder
> What were fair in Life.
> But finding what may be,
> Make it fair up to our means.

And a free autographed copy of my latest book to whoever first tells me where that quote comes from because I've forgotten!

PIERS ANTHONY (b.1934)

Piers Anthony began as a new wave writer in the sixties but he soon demonstrated his facility in writing both SF and humourous fantasy. Over the last three decades he has been a highly prolific author and only a proportion of his work, largely consisting of the Xanth series, is in print in this country.

Xanth Series

Heaven Cent
Hodder pbk £4.99 0450537196

Isle of View
Hodder pbk £4.99 0450571130

Man from Mundania
Hodder pbk £4.99 0450550990

Ogre, Ogre
Orbit pbk £4.99 1857231600

Roc and a Hard Place
NEL pbk £5.99 0340654236

A Spell for a Chameleon
Orbit pbk £5.99 185723250X

Yon Ill Wind
Hodder pbk £5.99 0340654252

Castle Roogna
Orbit pbk £5.99 1857232879

Chaos Mode Harper
Collins pbk £4.99 0586213481

The Colour of Her Panties
Hodder pbk £4.99 0450582337

Crewel Lye
Orbit pbk £5.99 1857232240

Demons Don't Dream
Hodder pbk £5.99 0450598918

Geis of the Gargoyle
Sceptre pbk £5.99 0340622962

Harpy Thyme
Hodder pbk £4.99 0450604381

Out of Phaze
Hodder pbk £4.99 045052471X

Tarot
HarperCollins pbk £8.99
0586206183

JEAN M. AUEL (b.1936)

Jean M. Auel's saga *The Earth's Children* mixes fantasy and romance in the story of life and adventure in prehistoric times. Centred on the life of one woman whose actions shape the destiny of prehistoric mankind, these escapist yarns are not sophisticated but they have their own charm and are the latest examples of a fantasy subgenre that dates back to Edgar Rice Burroughs and before.

Earth's Children Series

The Clan of the Cave Bear
Hodder pbk £6.99 0340268832

The Valley of Horses
Hodder pbk £6.99 0340329645

The Mammoth Hunters
Hodder pbk £6.99 0340393114

The Plains of Passage
Hodder pbk £6.99 0340547421

TERRY BROOKS (b.1944)

Brooks is best known for his Shannara cycle of books. Written as a homage to Tolkien, they chart the struggle of the individual against a pervasive evil which threatens the status quo of the world Brooks brings to life for the reader. The original book, *The Sword of Shannara,* is a traditional quest. A Gandalf-like figure instructs a boy to leave his home and find the legendary missing sword, which vanquished an evil warlord centuries beforehand, and must be found so that it can perform the deed again. The popularity of this tale created a demand for Shannara's pre-history, told in *The First King,* and for stories of Shannara in the centuries after the events described in the first book. These have been explored in Brooks's later novels. The Heritage cycle, for example, tells the stories of three Shannara descendants who must complete their own quests in order to defeat Shadowen, the latest evil which threatens to engulf their homes.

Brooks has also written the popular Landover series of books. In these light-hearted and humorous novels, a jaded lawyer agrees to take on a troubled magic kingdom but neglects to read the small print on the contract. Predictable chaos ensues. Wittily written these books are similar in style to Piers Anthony's *Xanth* stories.

Shannara

The Sword of Shannara
Orbit pbk £6.99 1857231511

The Elfstones of Shannara
Orbit pbk £6.99 1857231104

The Wishsong of Shannara
Orbit pbk £6.99 1857231325

The Scions of Shannara
Orbit pbk £6.99 1857230752

Druid of Shannara
Orbit pbk £5.99 1857233808

The Talismans of Shannara
Legend pbk £5.99 0099255413

Elf Queen of Shannara
Legend pbk £5.99 0099210313

First King of Shannara
Legend pbk £5.99 0099602113

Magic Kingdom of Landover

Magic Kingdom for Sale/sold
Orbit pbk £5.99 1857232569

The Black Unicorn
Orbit pbk £5.99 185723108

Wizard at Large
Orbit pbk £4.99 1857231031

The Tangle Box
Legend pbk £9.99 0099255510

Witches' Brew
Legend pbk £5.99 0099601818

Running with the Demon
Legend hbk £16.99
0099602210

EDGAR RICE BURROUGHS (1875–1950)

Burroughs was responsible for the creation of one of the most famous and widely recognised figures in twentieth century fiction – Tarzan of the Apes. His first published piece, however, was a science fiction short story, *Under the Moons of Mars*, and he went on to produce two series set in alien worlds – Barsoom (Mars) and Pellucidar (the hollow interior of the earth). Burroughs's simple tales of manly heroes battling to win the hearts of beautiful alien princesses are easily mocked but he set in place many of the types and prototypes which other, more sophisticated writers went on to develop.

The science fiction and fantasy of Edgar Rice Burroughs is out of print in the UK. Some large Waterstone's branches may stock imported US editions.

STORM CONSTANTINE (b.1956)

Very much the wild woman of contemporary SF, Constantine blends Goth attitudes with SF and fantasy. Her idiosyncratic visions are crammed with beautiful, sexually ambivalent youths, mysterious cults, exotic dancers and devilish ceremonies, all played out against lavish and often outlandish backgrounds. A dark glamour pervades her work, owing more to the sensuality of Angela Carter and the ambiguities of David Bowie than to the whimsicalities of Tolkien. Her characters, resplendent in eyeliner and attitude, swagger through societies of Wraeththu (mutated homosexuals), Eloim (vampire artists) and Grigori (fallen angels). Her plots, often brutal, always quirky, are extravagant and outrageous. In a genre with more than its fair share of identikit writing, Storm Constantine always invigorates.

Burying the Shadow
Headline pbk £4.99 0747238774

Calenture
Headline pbk £5.99 0747245533

Hermetech
Headline pbk £4.99 0747236097

Sign for the Sacred
Headline pbk £5.99 0747240949

Grigori Series

Scenting Hallowed Blood
Signet pbk £5.99 0451189299

Stalking Tender Prey
Signet pbk £5.99 0451184017

Stealing Sacred Fire
Penguin pbk £5.99 0140268960

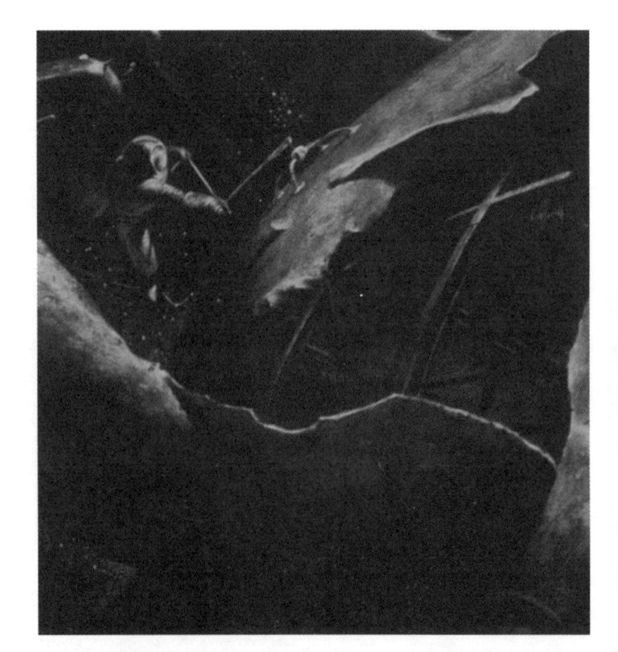

STEPHEN DONALDSON (b.1947)

American writer Stephen Donaldson has done much to provide an alternative to the insipid protagonists and settings that are to be found only too often in modern fantasy. In Thomas Covenant, his most famous character, he has created an anti-hero who, perversely, refuses to believe in, or enjoy, the fantastical world into which he has been thrust. In classic fantasy tradition, Covenant is the prophesied saviour of the land to which he has been magically transported. In his other life, however, he was a leper, forced by his affliction into a state of constant mental vigilance in order to protect his damaged body. Covenant cannot bring himself to abandon his survival habits and attempts to deny the reality of his new world. Just as his central character tries to undermine the fantasy world in which he finds himself, Donaldson uses the cliches of the genre and its language to readjust the reader's perception of what a fantasy novel should be. His Land is peopled by wizards, giants and warriors but Donaldson has brought new life and maturity to them. Covenant is required to deal with a world which *should* be imaginary yet is only too real. Fantasy and reality are subtly intertwined. As well as the two massive *Chronicles of Thomas Covenant the Unbeliever*, Donaldson has written the double volume *Mordant's Need*, set in a claustrophobic world fuelled by mirror magic, and the acclaimed *Gap* sequence of SF novels. In these books, also, Donaldson demonstrates his ability to subvert traditional notions of the hero and create a narrative as compelling as it is intelligent.

Chronicles of Thomas Covenant

Lord Foul's Bane
HarperCollins pbk £5.99
0006152392

The Illearth War:
HarperCollins pbk £5.99
0006152465

The Power That Preserves
HarperCollins pbk £5.99
0006152473

The First Chronicles of Thomas Covenant
HarperCollins pbk £9.99
0006473296

Second Chronicles of Thomas Covenant

The Wounded Land
Voyager pbk £5.99 0006161405

The One Tree
HarperCollins pbk £5.99
0006163831

White Gold Wielder
Voyager pbk £5.99 0006167772

The Second Chronicles of Thomas Covenant
HarperCollins pbk £9.99
000647330X

Mordant's Need

The Mirror of Her Dreams
HarperCollins pbk £5.99
0006173993

A Man Rides Through
HarperCollins pbk £6.99
0006176542

The Gap Series

The Real Story
HarperCollins pbk £4.99
000647019X

Forbidden Knowledge
HarperCollins pbk £5.99
0006470203

A Dark and Hungry God Arises
HarperCollins pbk £5.99
0006470211

Chaos and Order
HarperCollins pbk £5.99
000647022X

This Day All Gods Die: The Gap into Ruin
Voyager pbk £6.99 0006470238

Daughter of Regals
HarperCollins pbk £5.99
0006175546

DAVID EDDINGS (b.1931)

Eddings began writing fantasy relatively late in life but he has made up for this with a prolific output. So far, in addition to some stand-alone novels, he has produced four epic sequences, set in medieval-type worlds in which magic, sorcery and destiny are centrally important and in which powerful gods and multitudes of characters interact. It could be argued that Eddings is not the most original of plotters. All his narratives are built around some version of a quest or fantastic mission, which requires a gathering of different people with different skills to embark on a long journey through strange lands to end up in the right place at the right time, three or five books later, to thwart the powers of evil. Eddings's strength is his ability to create memorable characters. Belgarath the sorcerer, in *The Belgariad,* his daughter Polgara the arch-sorceress and the simple farm boy Garion, who is caught up in the quest to track down the Orb of Aldur, are all wonderful creations and the reader cares, not so much what happens next, but what happens next to *these* characters. In the same way, the driving force of *The Elenium* and *The Tamuli* is not so much the plot but the character Sparhawk, described by one reviewer as 'the best-realised hero in current fantasy.' For those readers who like their fantasy to be ambitious in its scope and like the people who inhabit the fantasy worlds to be convincingly portrayed, Eddings is one of the best contemporary writers.

The Malloreon Series

Guardians of the West
Corgi pbk £5.99 0552130176

King of the Murgos
Corgi pbk £5.99 0552130184

Demon Lord of Karanda
Corgi pbk £4.99 0552130192

Sorceress of Darshiva
Corgi pbk £5.99 0552130206

Seeress of Kell
Corgi pbk £4.99 0552130214

The Belgarath Series

Pawn of Prophecy
Corgi pbk £5.99 055212284X

Queen of Sorcery
Corgi pbk £5.99 055212348X

Magician's Gambit
Corgi pbk £4.99 055212382X

Castle of Wizardry
Corgipbk £5.99 0552124354

Enchanters' End Game
Corgi pbk £5.99 0552124478

Belgarath the Sorcerer
HarperCollins pbk £6.99
0586213155

Polgara the Sorceress
HarperCollins hbk £17.99
0246138440

The Elenium Series

The Diamond Throne
HarperCollins pbk £5.99
0586203729

The Ruby Knight
HarperCollins pbk £5.99
0586203737

The Sapphire Rose
HarperCollins pbk £5.99
0586203745

The Tamuli Series

Domes of Fire
HarperCollins pbk £5.99
0586213139

The Shining Ones
HarperCollinspbk £5.99
0586213163

The Hidden City
Voyager pbk £5.99 0586213171

The Losers
HarperCollins pbk £4.99
0586217592

RAYMOND E. FEIST

Feist's Riftwar Saga is one of the great fantasy series, a major, defining example of the genre. It has all the elements a reader expects – from powerful magic to dwarves and elves. Yet very nearly every fantasy series has these. What sets Feist's work apart is his ability to develop storyline and character and to examine ideas within the context of his richly imagined creation. In the large and magnificently realised worlds of Midkemia and, later, Kelewan the reader is introduced to international politics and inter-racial conflicts, a war between two rival powers, even to the beginnings of time itself. Plot twists and intrigues are stylishly and elegantly interwoven in the books. The characters are three dimensional and develop and grow as the reader progresses through the saga. Often characters that appear peripheral at first turn out to be at the centre of major advances in the narrative. The power to overturn readers' expectations is central to the *Riftwar Saga.* Throughout the Midkemia half of the series a vivid picture is painted of a ruthless and alien enemy that knows no mercy, the Kelewans who seek to conquer Midkemia, apparently at any cost. In the Kelewan half of the saga Feist, writing with Janny Wurts, moves the viewpoint from Midkemia to Kelewan. Now the reader is treated to an enemy's view of the world, cleverly illustrating how easy it is to misjudge a culture when only half the facts are known. Feist, in his presentation of Midkemia and Kelewan, has created worlds on a broad canvas indeed.

The Riftwar Saga

Magician
HarperCollins pbk £6.99
0586217835

Silverthorn
HarperCollins pbk £5.99
0586064176

A Darkness at Sethanon
HarperCollins pbk £5.99
0586066888

Empire Trilogy

Daughter of the Empire
HarperCollins pbk £5.99
0586074813

Servant of the Empire
HarperCollins pbk £6.99
0586203818

Mistress of the Empire
HarperCollins pbk £6.99
0586203796

Midkemia Novels

Prince of the Blood
HarperCollins pbk £5.99
0586071407

The King's Buccaneer
HarperCollins pbk £5.99
0586203222

The Serpentwar Saga

Shadow of a Dark Queen
HarperCollins pbk £5.99
0006480268

Rise of a Merchant Prince
HarperCollins pbk £5.99
0006497012

Rage of a Demon King
HarperCollins pbk£6.99
0006482988

Shards of A Broken Crown
HarperCollins hbk £16.99
0002246546

Faerie Tale
HarperCollins pbk £5.99
0586071393

MAGGIE FUREY

Although a relative newcomer to fantasy writing, Maggie Furey has already gained a legion of admirers for her successful and well-written quartet *The Artefacts of Power.* The series focuses on the Magefolk, a race of immortal and magical beings who are able to command the elements with their thoughts. However such power corrupts and some of the Magefolk, such as the evil Archmage Miathan, have been corrupted. The books follow the battle for supremacy between Miathan and Aurian, child of renegade Mages, and the search for the four artefacts of power, the magical weapons that can bring either destruction or peace. Furey draws on the archetypes of Celtic mythology for some of her material but the quartet is an original and stylish creation and its author is clearly destined to be a force in fantasy writing for many years to come.

The Artefacts of Power

Aurian
Legend pbk £5.99 0099270714

Harp of Winds
Legend pbk £5.99 009927101X

The Sword of Flame
Legend pbk £5.99 0099270919

Dhiamarra
Legend pbk £5.99 0099698110

Heart of Myrial
Legend hbk £16.99 0099698218

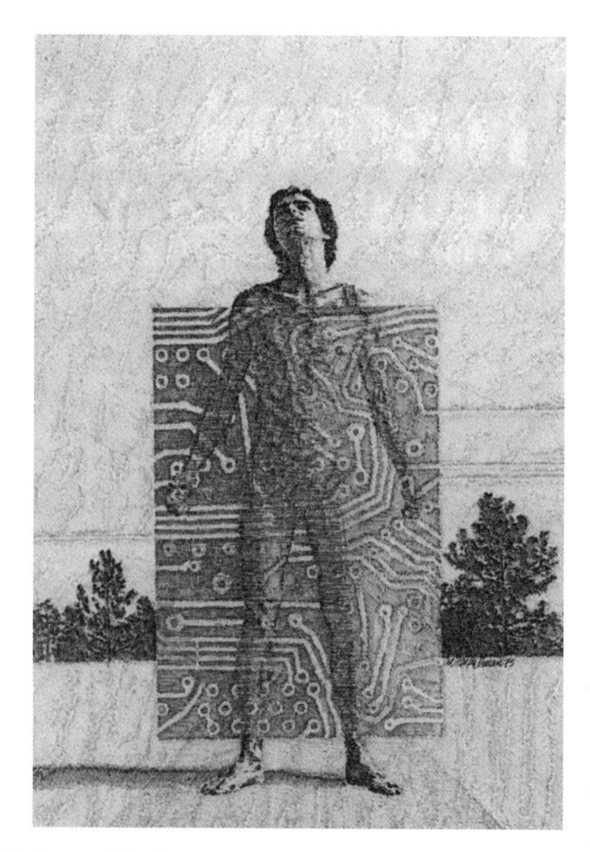

DAVID GEMMELL

David Gemmell is probably the best heroic (as opposed to epic) fantasy writer working in Britain today. His twenty-two novels to date show diversity of characterisation and background detail and are set in a range of fantasy worlds – from far-future post-holocaust Earths to ancient Greece to Arthurian Britain. Gemmell's constant obsession is with the duality of good and evil and, for his characters, heroism and courage emerge in action rather than being inherent, unchanging elements of personality. In Gemmell's books actions have reasons. It is not simply that the good guys wear white hats and the bad guys wear black ones. His grasp of motive and circumstance is sophisticated. His best-known series are the *Sipstrassi* tales, in which the world's history is subtly influenced down the ages by Atlantean gods and magic, and the *Drenai* sagas, the tales of Druss the Legend, his brothers-in-arms and their descendants. Of all of them, his first novel, *Legend*, is perhaps the most powerful, written at a time when the author was fighting against a life-threatening medical condition, the life and death struggle of a lonely fortress is a direct and poignant reflection of the author's own state of mind at the time. *Knights of Dark Renown* is possibly the best example of Gemmell's treatment of themes of good and evil, and a recent offering, *Winter Warriors*, is a good example of the way his refreshingly direct world-view renders common themes startlingly original. His work is highly recommended for those who like their fantasy slightly grittier and with a harder edge than most.

Drenai Novels

Legend
Legend pbk £5.99 0099470209

The King Beyond the Gate
Legend pbk £5.99 0099470101

Quest for Lost Heroes
Legend pbk £5.99 0099643405

Waylander
Legend pbk £5.99 009947090X

Waylander II
Legend pbk £5.99 0099892502

The First Chronicles of Druss the Legend
Legend pbk £5.99 0099261413

The Legend of Deathwalker
Corgi pbk £5.99 0552142522

Winter Warriors
Corgi pbk £5.99 0552142549

Sipstrassi Novels

Wolf in Shadow
Legend pbk £5.99 0099534703

The Last Sword of Power
Legend pbk £5.99 0099619601

Ghost King
Legend pbk £5.99 0099565501

The Last Guardian
Legend pbk £4.99 0099643308

The Lion of Macedon
Legend pbk £5.99 0099703505

Dark Prince
Legend pbk £5.99 0099703602

The Hawk Queen

Ironhand's Daughter
Legend pbk £5.99 0099892901

The Hawk Eternal
Legend pbk £5.99 0099893002

Bloodstone
Legend pbk £5.99 0099355310

Dark Moon
Corgi pbk £5.99 0552142530

Knights of the Dark Renown
Legend pbk £5.99 0099639505

Morningstar
Legend pbk £4.99 0099228912

TERRY GOODKIND

Of the fantasy writers who have emerged in the last few years, Terry Goodkind is one of the most interesting and original. He may work within the well-tried conventions of heroic fantasy inherited from Tolkien, but he does so with intelligence and individuality, easily transcending the formulaic. Piers Anthony hailed his first book as 'a phenomenal fantasy, endlessly inventive' and Goodkind has so far produced four books, all part of the same ongoing sequence. Each book in *The Sword of Truth* is a separate story in the saga of Richard Cypher, the reluctant wizard hero, and his lover Kahlan, the Mother Confessor. The massive narrative presents a classic confrontation of good and evil, although Goodkind's characters are subtly presented and few are wholly black or wholly white. Ambivalence also exists in the treatment of magic within the novels. Is magic inherently evil and corrupting, as Richard Cypher sometimes fears, or does it reflect the intentions of its users? Goodkind works within an established fantasy tradition to produce a narrative that is hugely enjoyable and carries the reader into a richly coloured and imagined world.

The Sword of Truth

Wizard's First Rule
Millennium pbk £6.99 1857982355

Stone of Tears
Millennium pbk £6.99 185798305X

Blood of the Fold
Millennium pbk £6.99 0752806661

Temple of the Winds
Millennium hbk £16.99 1857985060

BARBARA HAMBLY

In addition to a number of Star Trek and Star Wars novelisations, Barbara Hambly has written a variety of rewarding and tightly plotted fantasy novels, all informed by historical learning and peopled by convincing and morally complex characters. Her wide cast of characters in varying worlds are linked by a central idea and she gives herself the freedom to manouevre them skilfully. A minor character in one novel can become the heroine of another. She has also written vampire novels, like *Travelling with the Dead* and other more occult fantasy such as *Bride of the Rat-God*, in which a silent screen star becomes entangled with ancient devil-gods of Manchuria.

The Mother of Winter
Voyager pbk £5.99 0006482295

Sorcerer's Ward
Voyager pbk £4.99 0586217819

Travelling With the Dead
Voyager pbk £5.99 0006480292

ROBIN HOBB (b.1952)

Robin Hobb, who has also written under the name of Megan Lindholm, provides a refreshing breath of air in a genre often criticised for producing nothing but the same old story time and again. A fantasist of the highest order, she creates characters, dramatic plots and visionary imagery that have an originality that really does have to be read to be believed. One of the school of writers that believes no character should be just black or white (unless they truly be a Fool) the figures who inhabit Robin Hobb's landscapes are alive with a thousand shades of vibrant and scintillating colour. In a genre in which every angle seems to have been covered so many times already, it is a pleasure to discover a writer with a talent for surprise and all fans of Raymond E. Feist, J.V. Jones and George R.R. Martin will find much to admire in Robin Hobb's books.

The Farseer Trilogy

Assassin's Apprentice
Voyagerpbk £5.99 0006480098

Royal Assassin
Voyager pbk £6.99 0006480101

Assassin's Quest
Voyager pbk £7.99 00648011X

The Liveship Traders

The Ship of Magic
hbk £16.990002254786

ROBERT HOLDSTOCK

(b.1948)

Beginning his writing career as an SF author with novels like *Eye Among the Blind* and *Where Time Winds Blow*, Robert Holdstock is best known today for the extraordinary, haunting fantasy *Mythago Wood* and its sequels. Skilfully interweaving Jungian archetypes and Celtic mythology in the story of a stretch of English woodland, Ryhope Wood, which turns ancients secrets and legends into physical reality, Holdstock produced a major work of fantasy. *Mythago Wood* won the World Fantasy Award and subsequent excursions into Ryhope Wood have been equally acclaimed. As one critic wrote in The Times, 'These are the visions of a real artist.'

Ancient Echoes
Voyager pbk £5.99 0006480004

The Fetch
Warner pbk £4.99 0751500844

The Hollowing
Voyager pbk £5.99 0586212930

Mythago Wood
Harper collins pbk £4.99
0586065857

J. V. JONES (b.1963)

This Liverpool-born fantasy writer shot to the top of the US book charts with her first trilogy of novels *The Book of Words* and she has repeated that success in the UK, rapidly making her impression on the genre. Her storytelling style is similar to that of greats of the genre like David Eddings. She creates worlds with complicated politics and histories but she doesn't allow these to get in the way of constructing an exciting narrative. *The Book of Words* includes all the essential elements of fantasy – the damsel in distress, the usurped royals, the evil wizard and the young innocent destined to bring about his downfall – but Jones adds her own particular brand of bawdy humour and rich characterisation. All her characters, from the mad King Kylock and the wizard Baralis to the baker's boy Jack, from the widowed Melliandra to the disgusting palace guards Bodger and Grift, endlessly discussing the best ways to bed women, are thoroughly memorable. Jones's popularity is well-founded and she holds great promise of further achievement in the future.

The Book of Words

The Baker's Boy
Orbit pbk £6.99 1857233751

A Man Betrayed
Orbit pbk £6.99 1857234022

Master and Fool
Orbit pbk £6.99 1857234715

The Barbed Coil
Orbit hbk £16.99 185723510X

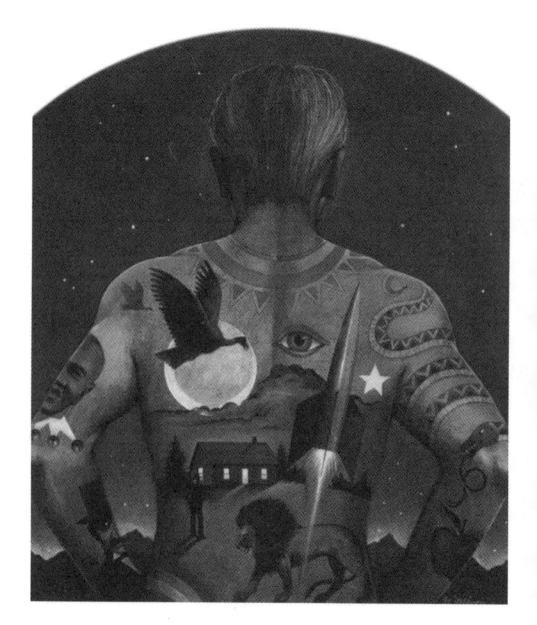

ROBERT JORDAN (b.1948)

Decorated Vietnam veteran Robert Jordan has published both historical works and a number of books about Conan, the musclebound hero originally created by Robert E. Howard. However he is best known for the saga he is currently engaged in writing, *The Wheel of Time.* The basic story of *The Wheel of Time* is a simple one. Every millennium a Dragon is born, a man who can wield the 'One Power' and must use it against the evil let loose on the world. Yet this power is unstable in the hands of men and can lead to their madness and destruction and the descent of the world into chaos. At the beginning of the sequence the evil Ba'alzamon is breaking free of his bonds and the prophecies are about to be fulfilled again. An organisation of women, themselves familiar with the 'One Power', set out to find the Dragon Reborn in order to banish the evil forever. On the foundations of this simple story Jordan builds an incredibly elaborate and complex world, a world filled with a richly imagined history and culture, comparable even to Tolkien's Middle Earth. His characters, especially the women, are strong and colourful and Jordan allows them the space to evolve and develop as the narrative unfolds. The main characters begin as naive village children and grow into mature and world-weary protagonists. Seven volumes of the sequence are already complete; three more instalments of this challenging and rewarding saga are promised.

Conan the Barbarian

Conan the Defender
Legend pbk £4.99 0099704013

Conan the Destroyer
Legend pbk £4.99 0099704412

Conan the Invincible
Legend pbk £4.99 0099703912

Conan the Magnificent
Legend pbk £4.99 0099704218

Conan the Triumphant
Legend pbk £4.99 0099704315

Conan the Unconquered
Legend pbk £4.99 0099704110

The Conan Chronicles
Legend hbk £15.99 009978601

The Conan Chronicles 2
Legend hbk £16.99 0099224925

Wheel of Time

The Eye of the World
Orbit pbk £6.99 1857230760

The Great Hunt
Orbit pbk £6.99 1857230272

The Dragon Reborn
Orbit pbk £6.99 1857230655

The Shadow Rising
Orbit pbk £6.99 185723121X

The Fires of Heaven
Orbit pbk £6.99 1857232097

Lord of Chaos
Orbit pbk £6.99 185723300X

A Crown of Swords
Orbit pbk £6.99 1857234030

The World of The Wheel of Time
Orbit hbk £25.00 1857235053

GUY GAVRIEL KAY

Guy Gavriel Kay worked with Christopher Tolkien on the editing of *The Silmarillion* and his own fantasy work, with its magic, elves and complex religious and historical structures, is deeply influenced by the master. However Kay's fiction is defined by his characters and the intense psychological portrayals which shape the stories. The magic appears real, the battles are bloody but inner turmoil and personal anguish are always the more devastating experiences in Kay's work and the true goal is the self-discovery or self-sacrifice of the characters. *The Fionavar Trilogy*, perhaps his best known work, creates a marvellous world of myth and magic as seen and shaped by five young people from present-day Canada. Other novels include *A Song for Arbonne*, which explores the world of courtly love, and *Tigana*, a powerful story in which the boundaries between good and evil, so often clearly fixed in fantasy fiction, are rendered cleverly ambivalent.

Fionavar Tapestry

The Darkest Road
HarperCollins pbk £4.99 0586215247

The Summer Tree
HarperCollins pbk £4.99 0586215220

The Wandering Fire
HarperCollins pbk £4.99 0586215239

Lions of Al-Rassan
Voyager pbk £6.99 0006480306

A Song for Arbonne
HarperCollins pbk £5.99 0586216774

Tigana
RoC pbk £6.99 0140177043

PAUL KEARNEY

Paul Kearney's novels have gained considerable critical acclaim but have been slow to achieve wide recognition. However he is fast developing into a superb writer of gritty, dramatic fantasy that has many of the qualities of David Gemmell. His latest series *The Monarchies of God* is an excellent dark (small 'd') fantasy in which a seemingly implacable foe threatens destruction to a land rife with internal conflict. Kearney provides all the reader can want – great characterisation, action and adventure, pain and sorrow, magic and joy. He is an author of great potential who has already produced rich and rewarding fantasies.

Monarchies of God

Hawkswood's Voyage
Vista pbk £5.99 0575600349

The Heretic Kings
Vista pbk £5.99 0575601868

The Iron Wars
Gollancz hbk 0575063122

PATRICIA KENNEALY-MORRISON

So far Kennealy-Morrison has written seven volumes in her Keltiad but the novelist plans at least as many again. The series is based around the premise that the Celtic races escaped to the stars and founded an interstellar empire. The society that results, described with wit and vigour, is humane and energetic but not without its enemies. In a sequence of trilogies, filled with fascinating characters, Kennealy-Morrison moves back and forth in time to show how the Kelts in varying ages, from the hero Arthur to the fiery queen Aeron, have coped with those enemies. One of the most intriguing aspects of these inventive novels is the use of language, since Kennealy-Morrison has cleverly used a variety of world languages as the bases for her alien tongues.

The Hedge of Mist
Voyager pbk £6.99 0006482309

The other volumes of the Keltiad are currently out of print in the UK.

MERCEDES LACKEY

Immensely popular in the US, the prolific Mercedes Lackey is best known here for her *Heralds of Valdemar* series. Set in a world of feudal societies, repressive religion and magic that is familiar to regular readers of the fantasy genre, her books are, first and foremost, exciting narratives but have a more serious underlying theme of misused power and its consequences. The earlier Valdemar novels, for instance, take place during the mage wars, the repercussions of which are still felt two thousand years later, most devastatingly in the recently published *Mage Storms* trilogy. Lackey's strengths as a writer lie in the realism and credibility of the worlds she creates and the imagination with which she realises alien cultures and species. Other popular series she has written include the *Bardic Voices* and she has also collaborated with several other eminent, female fantasy writers including Andre Norton (*Elvenblood*), Marion Zimmer Bradley (*Rediscovery*) and Anne McCaffrey (*The Ship Who Searched*). She currently lives in Oklahoma with her husband Larry Dixon who illustrates many of her books and co-wrote the *Gryphon* trilogy.

The Black Gryphon
Millennium pbk £4.99
1857982371

The Eagle and the Nightingale
Harper Collins pbk £4.99
0006480365

The Elvenbane (w. Andre Norton)
HarperCollins pbk £5.99
0586216871

Elvenblood (w. Andre Norton)
HarperCollins pbk £5.99
0006480284

Four and Twenty Blackbirds
Voyager pbk £4.99 0006480357

Magic s Pawn
Penguin pbk £5.99 014016751X

Magic s Promise
Penguin pbk £5.99 0140067528

Sacred Ground
Harper Collins pbk £4.99
0006480349

The Ship Who Searched (w, Anne McCaffrey)
Orbit pbk £5.99 1857232054

The Silver Gryphon
Millennium pbk £5.99
1857984978

Storm Breaking
Millennium hbk £16.99
1857982762

Storm Rising
Millennium pbk £5.99
1857984609

Storm Warning
Millennium pbk £4.99
1857982975

The White Gryphon
Millennium pbk £4.99
1857983130

KATHARINE KERR (b.1944)

Katharine Kerr's writing has emerged from her own reading in archaelogy and the history and literature of the Dark Ages and the medieval period mixed with an interest in the role-playing games of the seventies. She has published a series of books based on the world of Deverry and three stand-alone SF novels. Kerr takes the reader through the history of Deverry, focusing on various reincarnations of key characters in a world based loosely around the Celtic way of life, its feudal system and complex clan hierarchy. She blends these Celtic elements with the more fantastical elements of magic, dwarves and elves to produce a highly enjoyable saga that looks set to continue for many years to come.

Deverry

Daggerspell
HarperCollins pbk £5.99
0006482244

Darkspell
HarperCollins pbk £5.99
0006482228

Dawnspell
HarperCollins pbk £5.99
0586207414

Dragonspell: The Southern Sea
HarperCollins pbk £5.99
0586207872

A Time of Exile
HarperCollins pbk £5.99
0586207880

A Time of Omens
HarperCollins pbk £5.99
0586211969

A Time of War
HarperCollins pbk £5.99
0586211977

A Time of Justice
HarperCollins pbk £5.99
000647859X

The Red Wyvern
HarperCollins pbk £9.99
0002243512

Palace
(with Mark Kreighbaum)
HarperCollins pbk £5.99
0006482635

Polar City Blues
HarperCollins pbk £5.99
0586207899

STEPHEN LAWHEAD (b.1950)

Since making his fantasy debut with the well-written *Dragon King* trilogy, Stephen Lawhead has carved out a niche for himself as one of the leading exponents of fantasy fiction based on Celtic culture and history. The *Pendragon* quintet of books were the first to catch readers' imaginations. Basing the work on a combination of Arthurian mythology and other Celtic myths, Lawhead uses the familiar characters of the Arthurian Cycle but entwines them with tales of Atlantis and its fall to create an epic tale that spans centuries, culminating in *Grail*, his most recently published novel. In parallel with the Pendragon books, Lawhead has also written the *Song of Albion* trilogy in which he once again brings his specialist knowledge of the Celtic world to the creation of a universe in which past and present interact. *Empyrion* is a reissue of two science fiction novels in which a group of space travellers are sent to a far distant colony where trouble is brewing.

The Pendragon Cycle

Taliesin
Lion pbk £5.99 0745913091

Merlin
Lion pbk £4.99 0745913105

Arthur
Lion pbk £5.99 0745913113

Pendragon
Lion pbk £4.99 0745927637

Grail
Lion hbk £16.99 0745938825

Song of Albion

The Paradise War
Lion pbk £4.99 0745924662

Song of Albion
Lion pbk £4.99 0745925103

The Endless Knot
Lion pbk £4.99 0745927831

Byzantium
Voyager pbk £6.99 0006482511

Empyrion
Lion pbk £6.99 0745918727

In the Hall of the Dragon King
Lion pbk £4.99 0856488593

The Sword and the Flame
Lion pbk £4.99 0856488755

The Warlords of Nin
Lion pbk £4.99 0856488747

TANITH LEE (b.1947)

Her fairy tale collection *Red as Blood* is subtitled *Tales from the Sisters Grimmer* and this is an apt description of much of Tanith Lee's work, fantasy writing at its darkest. Her work encompasses many standard SF and fantasy plotlines: tales of vampires and werewolves, the alien and the unexplained. Together with her sly rewriting of fairy tales and sword-and-sorcery stories, these combine to produce a fiction which is notable for its compelling storytelling and rich, painterly imagery, surrounding a core of darkness and mystery. Lee is an expert at devious and unexpected endings. Some of her short stories have extraordinary, sometimes shocking denouements. However, although her work explores the darker side of myth and magic, it does so with an entertaining wordplay and a mordant wit that make for compulsive reading.

Black Unicorn
Orbit pbk £4.99 1857232119

Gold Unicorn
Orbit pbk £4.99 1857233018

The Blood of Roses
Legend pbk £5.99 0099678608

Darkness, I
Warner pbk £5.99 0751512192

Elephantasm
Headline pbk £4.99
0747241066

Eva Fairdeath
Headline pbk £4.99
0747243832

A Heroine of the World
Headline pbk £5.99
074724748X

Heart-beast
Headline pbk £4.99
0747239169

Nightshades
Headline pbk £4.99
074724250X

Personal Darkness
Warner pbk £4.99 075150808X

Reigning Cats and Dogs
Headline pbk £5.99
0747250081

Vivia
Warner pbk £5.99 0751515507

When the Lights Go Out
Headline pbk £5.99
0747252165

Women as Demons
Women's Press pbk £4.95
0704341328

FRITZ LEIBER

(1910–1992)

Much of Leiber's output, and he was a wide-ranging and productive author for many decades, is unavailable in the UK. His most accessible and popular work remains the sequence of heroic fantasies, begun very early in his career, featuring his splendid heroes Fafhrd and the Grey Mouser. These enjoyable novels both set the pattern for, and made fun of, the sword and sorcery genre. Leiber was also responsible for many skilfully crafted and award-winning SF short stories and novels.

Return to Lankhmar
White Wolf hbk
£15.991565049284

You're All Alone
Carroll & Graf pbk
£3.990881846791

GEORGE R. R. MARTIN

George R.R. Martin, best known as the editor of the shared-world *Wild Cards* series and a much-respected writer since the early seventies, is now the creator of one of the most powerful and exciting first-in-a-series novels in the fantasy genre. *A Game of Thrones*, the first part of *A Song of Ice and Fire*, has been described as the best fantasy novel since Raymond E. Feist's astonishing *Magician*. Set in a world rich in traditional fantasy imagery and atmosphere, Martin's mastery of storytelling is apparent as seemingly comfortable plot lines suddenly writhe and twist before the reader's eyes into new and wholly unexpected forms. His characters are real and believable and the fantastic imagination is matched by his skill in expressing his ideas. *A Game of Thrones* has set in motion a dynastic saga as strong as Feist and Wurts's *Empire* trilogy and the next installment is eagerly awaited.

A Clash of Kings
Voyager hbk £16.99 000224585X

A Game of Thrones
Voyager pbk £6.99 000647988X

Fevre Dream
Gollancz pbk £5.99 0575600055

L. E. MODESITT JR.

Originally a poet and SF writer, the impressively named Leland Exton Modesitt Jr. crossed over to fantasy with the acclaimed *Recluce* saga. Modesitt formerly worked for a US congressman and was a director at the US Environment Protection Agency, and he has been heavily influenced by this background. Political and environmental issues are a constant theme in his work. As a stylist he is skilful at shifting tense and perspective in his narrative to create different moods and heighten the drama in his novels. His SF work is currently unavailable in the UK but his recent fantasy titles are well worth investigating.

Recluce Series

The Magic of Recluce
Orbit pbk £6.99 1857232011

The Towers of the Sunset
Orbit pbk £6.99 1857232305

The Magic Engineer
Orbit pbk £6.99 1857232720

The Order War
Orbit pbk £6.99 1857233778

The Death of Chaos
Orbit pbk £6.99 1857233867

Fall of Angels
Orbit pbk £6.99 1857234472

MERVYN PEAKE (1911–1968)

Relatively neglected during his lifetime, Peake, who was also a gifted poet and illustrator, found a new audience posthumously for his Gormenghast trilogy. *Titus Groan, Gormenghast* and *Titus Alone* are set in an imaginary kingdom ruled by ancient and stifling ritual. The first two books, published in 1946 and 1950, deal with the rise of the villainous Steerpike and the disillusionment of Titus, the 77th Earl of Groan. Packed with odd and oddly named characters like Fuchsia, Dr. Prunesquallor and Muzzlehatch, the books, illustrated by Peake himself, describe a hermetic world of grotesque and eerie beauty which draws readers in and then surprises them with the poetry and violence of its imagery. Inside the high and crumbling walls of Gormenghast Castle, these characters lead strange and pointless lives entrapped by the constraints of civilization. The third book in the sequence is set outside the walls of the Castle. Titus has escaped and is abroad in a complex and incomprehensible world. In the fifties Peake also published the more overtly allegorical *Mr Pye*, set on the island of Sark, about a man who grows an angel's wings when he does good and a devil's horns when he sins. The isolation of Sark, where Peake lived for a time, and the feudalism of China, where he was born to missionary parents, may have contributed to the creation of Gormenghast, although Peake himself always denied that he intended any direct allegory to be read into his work. Other works, poetry and illustration, are also available.

The Gormenghast Trilogy
Mandarin pbk £12.99 0749314265

Titus Groan
Mandarin pbk £6.99 0749300515

Gormenghast
Mandarin pbk £6.99 0749300523

Titus Alone
Mandarin pbk £5.99 0749300531

'Seven is for something. What's seven for? One for a glorious, golden grave – two for a terrible torch of tin; three for a hundred hollow horses; four for a knight with a spur of spear-grass; five for a fish with fortunate fins, six – I've forgotten six, and seven – what's seven for?'

Mervyn Peake – Titus Groan

MELANIE RAWN

Melanie Rawn is the author of the *Dragon Prince* and *Exiles* series. Essentially stories of birthrights lost and the battles undertaken to regain them, these sequences tell epic narratives and Rawn's writing is pacy and readable. Both series focus on a single family – the royal house of the Desert in the Dragon cycle and the politically influential Ambrais of Exiles. Both families are ousted from their positions of power and must face war and betrayal in the struggle to wrest them back again. The strength of Rawn's writing can be found in the details. In each series she creates a highly credible world with its own religion, mythology and politics. Bold characters clash violently against a dazzling backdrop and plots move so quickly that the reader scarcely has time to keep up. These books spin a good old-fashioned yarn. Magic and dragons, passion and treachery make for good escapism and Melanie Rawn delivers no half measures.

Dragon Prince
Pan pbk £5.99 033031274X

Dragon Token
Pan pbk £7.99 0330328980

The Golden Key
Pan pbk £7.99 0330347764

The Mageborn Traitor
Macmillan hbk £17.99 0333650328

Ruins of Ambrai
Pan pbk £7.99 0330344196

Skybowl
Pan pbk £6.99 0330333186

The Star Scroll
Pan pbk £6.99 0330314041

Stronghold
Pan pbk £6.99 0330326333

Sunrunner's Fire
Pan pbk £6.99 0330317520

KRISTINE KATHRYN RUSCH (b.1960)

In charge of *The Magazine of Fantasy and Science Fiction* since 1991, Kristine Kathryn Rusch took the Hugo Award for Best Editor in 1994. Despite her editorial responsibilities Rusch has found time to be a prolific author of imaginative literature. She has produced Star Trek novelisations, vampire fiction (*Sins of the Blood*) and mainstream SF (*Alien Influences*, the story of a planet on which human and alien children play and interact with unforeseen consequences, was shortlisted for the Arthur C. Clarke Award in 1995). However her most successful work has been *The Fey*, a three volume fantasy set on the Blue Isle, where humans must learn to live with the exotic, shape-changing and warlike Fey.

The Fey

The Fey: Changeling
Orion pbk £6.99 0752809911

The Fey: Rival
Orion pbk £9.99 1857984897

The Fey: Sacrifice
Orion pbk £6.99 1857983106

Alien Influences
Millennium pbk £4.99
1857982495

Facade
Millennium pbk £4.99
1857980751

Heart Readers
Orion pbk £4.99 1857981510

Sins of the Blood
Millennium pbk £5.99
1857982436

Traitors
Millennium pbk £4.99
1857984498

R. A. SALVATORE (b.1959)

R.A. Salvatore has been a prolific author of undemanding, high adventure fantasy in the Dragonlance mould. Although not the most original of fantasy creations, and although Salvatore has few literary pretensions, the *Dark Elf Trilogy* and the *Icewind Dale Trilogy* are entertaining examples of the *Forgotten Realms* series. *The Sword of Bedwyr* is a fantasy set in Eriador, a land enslaved by the Wizard-King Greensparrow. The first volume has just been published in country.

Legacy
Legend pbk £4.99 0099317516

Luthien's Gamble
Warner pbk £4.99 0446603619

The Sword of Bedwyr
Warner pbk £4.99 0446602728

The Woods Out Back
Warner pbk £4.99 0441908721

MICHAEL SCOTT ROHAN (b. 1951)

Michael Scott Rohan is adept at taking the facts of history and geography and weaving them into fantastic narratives, at mingling the real world with worlds of his own imagining. In the trilogy of books, *Chase the Morning, The Gates of Noon* and *Cloud Castles*, an ordinary, though troubled, man is drawn into strange and deadly worlds. A world where tall-masted ships still carry cargoes of spices to the South Seas, but carry them through the clouds, is a world where magic and fantasy intersect with the more mundane realities of our own world. In another book, *A Spell of Empire*, Scott Rohan imagines an alternate Europe in which the Nibelung Empire in the north faces the Tyrhennian Empire based in Sicily and magic and swordplay is plentiful. His is a Wagnerian imagination and his fantasy worlds are well worth visiting.

The Winter of the World

Anvil of Ice
Orbit pbk £5.99 1857230949

The Forge in the Forest
Orbit pbk £5.99 1857231090

The Hammer of the Sun
Orbit pbk £5.99 1857233182

Chase the Morning
Orbit pbk £4.99 185723183X

The Gates of Noon
Gollancz pbk £5.99 0575600322

Cloud Castles
Gollancz pbk £4.99 0575057785

The Ice King (with Allan Scott)
Orbit pbk £5.99 1857230884

The Lord of Middle Air
Vista pbk £5.99 0575602341

Maxie's Demon
Orbit pbk £6.99 1857234626

A Spell of Empire
Orbit pbk £4.99 0708883605

CHRISTOPHER STASHEFF

Stasheff is the author of a number of light fantasy series, including the *Warlock* series and *Starship Troupers* sequence in which a group of unlikely travelling players journey the galaxy, performing Shakespeare. Probably his best books are the engaging *A Wizard in Rhyme*, in which the hero Matt Mantrell finds himself transported to a world where magic is worked by the reciting of verse and becomes Lord High Wizzard. These unpretentious, tongue-in-cheek fantasies, in which Matt deals with beautiful princesses and evil monarchs, drunken dragons and well-spoken cyclops, are ideal, undemanding entertainment.

Her Majesty's Wizard
Legend pbk £5.99 0099556812

The Oathbound Wizard
Legend pbk £5.99 009955691X

The Sage
Atlantic pbk £5.99 0345392396

The Warlock Enlarged
Pan pbk £5.99 0330311166

The Witch Doctor
Legend pbk £5.99 0099557010

SHERRI S. TEPPER (b.1929)

Sherri S. Tepper is often described as a woman's writer. The unspoken assumption, a common one, seems to be that women write books for other women whereas men simply write. True, a lot of Tepper's protagonists are female, but they are real women rather than busty, two-dimensional caricatures. They find their own solutions to challenges in the plots rather than relying on the men in their lives to do it for them. Haunting is a good word to describe Tepper's work. It is also blood-curdling, perceptive, eloquent and humorous. Many of her novels have something of the fairy tale about them. *Beauty* is a wicked re-telling of the sleeping beauty story, complete with fantastic castles, indifferent fairies, stupid fairies and cross-dressing transvestites. *Gibbon's Decline and Fall* is not a chronicle of long-dead Romans but tells of the rise of a Taliban-like, misogynist sect in modern America. The only way for women to overcome it is to enlist the help of lizard women who live in the desert. Her latest novel, *The Family Tree*, is also something of an oddity. It is set again in modern America where the trees are restless and have begun stealing children, closing roads and generally putting mankind in its place. Tepper has a rare ability to discuss environmental issues without becoming either sentimental or patronising. She is a bewitching and intoxicating writer and can even be forgiven for the occasional use of the most irritating and cliched character in fantasy – the mischievous dwarf.

Beauty
HarperCollins pbk £5.99 0586213058

The Family Tree
Voyager Hbk £16.99 0002256231

The Gate to Women's Country
Voyager pbk £5.99 0006482708

Gibbons Decline and Fall
Voyager pbk £6.99 0006482686

Grass
Voyager pbk £5.99 0006482694

A Plague of Angels
HarperCollins pbk £5.99 0006473431

Shadow's End
Voyager pbk £5.99 0006473423

Sideshow
Voyager pbk £4.99 0006480047

J. R. R. TOLKIEN (1892–1973)

Tolkien is one of the great figures, not just of the fantasy genre, but of twentieth century literature. In the recent Waterstone's poll of Books of the Century, *The Lord of the Rings* gained many more votes than any other title and *The Hobbit* is one of the most popular children's books ever written. Virtually single-handedly Tolkien created the fantasy genre we know today and his influence can not be escaped. It is ironic that all this should be the work of a reticent Oxford scholar of literature and linguistics who had no original intention of becoming a novelist and created Middle Earth, in the first instance, as a land to fill with the people to speak his invented languages.

Tolkien first created his fictional world in the trenches of World War I but it was very different from the world of *The Lord of the Rings*. *The Lord of the Rings* may have been the culmination of Tolkien's lifelong fascination with alternative worlds but the early days of the mythology is recounted in *The Silmarillion* and the early version of that is *The Book of Lost Tales*. Tolkien continued to work on *The Silmarillion* up to the time of his death and, like any great mythology, there are many different versions and re-tellings of it. The version Christopher Tolkien published in 1977, four years after his father's death, is only one version. Most of the alternative tellings, including *The Book of Lost Tales*, can be found in the twelve-volume *History of Middle Earth* that Christopher Tolkien has recently finished publishing. *The Lord of the Rings* can be decribed as a great saga in the style of the Norse epics which so influenced it. *The Silmarillion*, the book of the First Age, the Elder Days, is a mythology which Tolkien created for the English, the native mythology that he felt had been swept away by the Norman Conquest. As such it is a vehicle for many of Tolkien's deepest religious and philosophical preoccupations, far more explicitly and deliberately than *The Lord of the Rings*.

The Hobbit was not originally intended to be set in the same land as *The Silmarillion*. It was meant to be simply a children's story but there were hints of and allusions to stories and mythologies already created if not yet published. As Tolkien himself wrote in the introduction to *The Lord of the Rings*, 'there were already some references to the older matter: Gondolin, the High-elves and the orcs, as well as glimpses that had arisen unbidden of things higher or deeper or darker than its surface: Durin, Moria, Gandalf, the Necromancer, the Ring. The discovery of the significance of these glimpses and of their relation to the ancient histories revealed the Third Age and its culmination in the War of the Ring.' As the quote suggests Tolkien realised only gradually, not only the connection between *The Hobbit* and the material in *The Silmarillion*, but the role of the Ring. (In later editions of *The Hobbit* Tolkien made changes to the story to emphasise aspects of the Ring's significance as it developed in his mind.)

The Hobbit remains essentially a children's book. That is not true of *The Lord of the Rings*. Originally intended as a sequel to *The Hobbit*, this developed into the huge, narrative that we know, one which works on all sorts of levels. First and foremost it is a wonderful piece of sustained storytelling. Although Tolkien denied any specific identification of themes, tropes and characters, allegory, of all kinds, can be read into it. Does the whole work refer elliptically to the Second World War and is the Ring symbolic of the A bomb? Some people have thought so. Perhaps the work is driven by hatred of industrialisation and urbanisation. In this reading the Ring symbolises the machine and the Elves and the Three Rings the old ways. On another reading the Hobbits represent the English and their ability to adapt to a new order. However too specific an identification of the allegory limits the sheer scope and grandeur of Tolkien's vision. *The Lord of the Rings* is a huge feat of imaginative construction and to pin it down to precise analogy is to reduce it.

Tolkien, then, is the founding father of modern fantasy, although much of it would probably horrify him. His popularity worldwide indicates something of the timelessness of the mythology he created. Some critics may condescend to his work but he is one of the most enduring and important writers of the century. In fantasy his influence is inescapable and even those, like Michael Moorcock, who are on record as loathing his work, are reacting against it in their own fiction. He is also one of the few fantasy writers to reach a large audience with readers not normally drawn to the genre and, as the victory of *The Lord of the Rings* in the Books of the Century Poll shows, his work has, arguably, had more impact on the public than that of any other novelist.

The Hobbit
HarperCollins pbk £6.99
0261103342

The Hobbit
HarperCollins hbk £12.99
0261103288

The Hobbit (De Luxe)
HarperCollins hbk £60.00
0261103490

The Lord of the Rings
HarperCollins pbk £12.99
0261103253

The Lord of the Rings
HarperCollins hbk £25.00
0261103202

The Illustrated Lord of the Rings
HarperCollins hbk £40.00
0261102303

The Lord of the Rings (Illustrated Boxed Set)
HarperCollins pbk £40.00
0261103415

The Lord of the Rings Boxed Set
HarperCollins pbk £19.95
0261102389

The Fellowship of the Ring
HarperCollins hbk £14.95
0261102311

The Fellowship of the Ring
HarperCollins pbk £6.99
0261103571

The Two Towers
HarperCollins hbk £14.99
026110232X

The Two Towers
HarperCollins pbk £6.99
026110358X

The Return of the King
HarperCollins hbk £14.99
0261102338

The Return of the King
HarperCollins pbk £6.99
0261103598

The Silmarillion
HarperCollins hbk £16.99
0261102427

The Silmarillion
HarperCollins pbk £6.99
0261102737

History of Middle Earth

The Book of Lost Tales Volume One
HarperCollins pbk £9.99
0261102222

The Book of Lost Tales Volume Two
HarperCollins pbk £9.99
0261102141

The Lays of Beleriand
HarperCollins pbk £9.99
0261102265

The Shaping of Middle Earth
HarperCollins pbk £9.99
0261102184

The Lost Road
HarperCollins pbk £9.99
0261102257

The Return of the Shadow
HarperCollins pbk £9.99
0261102249

The Treason of Isengard
HarperCollins pbk £9.99
0261102206

The War of the Ring
HarperCollins pbk £9.99
0261102230

Sauron Defeated
HarperCollins pbk £9.99
0261103059

Morgoth's Ring
HarperCollins pbk £9.99
0261103008

The War of the Jewels
HarperCollins pbk £9.99
0261103245

The Peoples of Middle Earth
HarperCollins pbk £9.99
0261103482

Adventures of Tom Bombadil
HarperCollins pbk £3.99
0044407262

Farmer Giles of Ham
HarperCollins pbk £3.99
0261102087

Smith of Wootton Major
HarperCollins pbk £3.99
004440722X

Poems From The Lord of the Rings
HarperCollins pbk £6.99
0261103121

Unfinished Tales
HarperCollins pbk £9.99
0261103628

Tales from the Perilous Realm
HarperCollins pbk £12.99
0261103423

'Faithless is he that says farewell when the road darkens.'
J. R. R. Tolkien – The Lord of the Rings

MARGARET WEIS & TRACY HICKMAN

This writing team first achieved prominence with their Dungeons & Dragons® based Dragonlance series for TSR. Their first two trilogies, high action fantasy adventures set in the mythical world of Krynn, spawned a vast series of associated novels, novellas and short stories written by a host of other authors, soon making Krynn one of the largest shared-worlds in history. Weis & Hickman then went on to write other fantasy and SF series, all of them a blend of high-octane adventure, magic and excitement. These authors are maybe not as sophisticated as some, but for light reading they're hard to beat.

Death Gate Cycle

Dragon Wing
Bantam pbk £5.99 055340265X

Elven Star
Bantam pbk £5.99 0553402668

Fire Sea
Bantam pbk £4.99 0553403753

Serpent Mage
Bantam pbk £4.99 0553403761

The Hand of Chaos
Bantam pbk £4.99 055340377X

Into the Labyrinth
Bantam pbk £4.99 0553403788

The Seventh Gate
Bantam pbk £4.99 0553403796

JANNY WURTS

Janny Wurts is a U.S. fantasy writer whose reputation continues to grow on both sides of the Atlantic. She is best known for her superb collaboration with Raymond E. Feist on the magnificent *Empire* trilogy, which really set the standard for epic intrigue fantasy, but she has also written several extremely strong stand-alone novels. She is currently working on the second trilogy-instalment of her epic fantasy series, *The Wars of Light and Shadow*, in which the half-brothers Arithon, Master of Shadow, and Lysaer, Lord of Light, cursed into eternal enmity by the demonic Mistwraith, continue their relentless struggle. Highly recommended for fans of Feist, Jordan and Eddings.

Cycle of Fire Series

Stormwarden
Voyager pbk £4.99 0586204830

Keeper of the Keys
Voyager pbk £4.99 0586204849

Shadowfane
Voyager pbk £4.99 0586204857

The Wars of Light and Shadows

The Curse of the Mistwraith
HarperCollins pbk £6.99 0586210695

The Ships of Merior
HarperCollins pbk £5.99 0586210709

The Warhost of Vastmark
HarperCollins pbk £5.99 0006482074

Master of Whitestorm
HarperCollins pbk £4.99 0586210687

Sorcerer's Legacy
HarperCollins pbk £4.99 0586204822

That Way Lies Camelot
HarperCollins pbk £4.99 0006480039

TAD WILLIAMS

Tailchaser's Song and the bestselling trilogy *Memory, Sorrow and Thorn* brought Tad Williams worldwide acclaim as a master of fantasy. The trilogy skilfully blended a pseudo-medieval world, filled with convincing detail and parallels with the reality of twelfth century Europe, with Tolkien-style elves, dragons, monsters and sorcery. The main focus of the story is Simon, a young orphan who dreams of glory and adventure without realising just what his destiny holds for him. He becomes involved with a group of people embroiled in a growing battle with dark forces that threaten the world. The fight is a long one and rages across the whole of the lands that Williams has so imaginatively created. The characters caught up in these physical and magical battles are believable and the whole story is a long, satisfying and intelligent one. Williams's new work, a trilogy begun with the novel *Otherland,* is just as ambitious. Set in South Africa in the near future, in a world dominated by the technology of virtual reality, the novel also reworks stories and myths from the African past and launches the reader into the surreal, fantasy realms of Otherland. It promises to bring Williams as much acclaim as his earlier trilogy.

Caliban's Hour
Legend pbk £4.99 0712650695

Otherland
Legend pbk £7.99 0099661519

Siege: To Green Angel Tower Part
Legend pbk £6.99 009931441X

Stone of Farewell
Legend pbk £6.99 0099848104

Storm: To Green Angel Tower Part 2
Legend pbk £6.99 009938261X

Tailchaser's Song
Legend pbk £4.99 0099959402

The Dragonbone Chair
Legend pbk £6.99 0099704900

GENE WOLFE (b.1931)

Gene Wolfe is a versatile and uncategorisable writer. Does he write science fiction? Or are most of his novels best described as fantasy? Probably Gene Wolfe himself doesn't waste too much time worrying over these questions and neither should the reader. What matters is that he is a subtle and complex writer who has, over the years, skilfully woven elements of both fantasy and SF into his work. His best known work remains the eighties sequence *The Book of the New Sun*, set on a dying world in the far future and telling the story of Severian and his rise from apprentice torturer to ruler of the planet. He has also written much acclaimed shorter fiction and a more recent sequence *The Book of the Long Sun.*

Calde of the Long Sun
Hodder pbk £5.99 045061011X

Castleview
Hodder pbk £5.99 0450562549

Endangered Species
Orbit pbk £4.99 0708883257

Exodus from the Long Sun
Hodder pbk £5.99 0340638362

Lake of the Long Sun
Hodder pbk £4.99 0450606392

Nightside the Long Sun
Hodder pbk £4.99 0450597636

The Urth of the New Sun
Orbit pbk £4.99 0708882684

JONATHAN WYLIE

Jonathan Wylie is the pseudonym of a husband and wife writing team who produce intelligent, literate and inventive fantasy. The *Servants of the Ark* trilogy which many consider their best work is currently unavailable but other, single novels demonstrate their originality. In *Across the Flame* a powerful magician emerges from a painting in which he has been trapped for centuries and twin sisters have to use their own powers to battle him. *Magister* follows a researcher as he realises that the papers of a magician hold secrets connected with his own family.

Across the Flame
Orbit pbk £6.99 1857234685

Magister
Orbit pbk £5.99 1857235150

Horror

Horror and the Supernatural: An Essential Bookshelf *by* Ramsey Campbell

Britain's leading horror writer highlights the classics of the genre

Often readers of bestselling horror ask me what else they should read. Here are just some of the books and authors in the genre I wouldn't be without.

Edgar Allan Poe – the first great writer of modern horror fiction, or was that Hoffmann? Short stories pared to the bone (*The Cask of Amontillado*), studies of murderous psychosis (*The Black Cat, The Tell-Tale Heart*), macabre prose poems (*The Masque of the Red Death*), supernatural horror merging with science (*The Facts in the Case of M. Valdemar*) or with morbid psychology (*The Fall of the House of Usher*), much other key material. *Complete Tales and Poems* (Penguin 0140103848 £10.99) is a bargain.

J. Sheridan Le Fanu (1814–1873) was far more modern than his dates suggest. *Carmilla* influenced Dracula but is much finer. *Schalken the Painter* is subtle erotic horror. *Green Tea* and *The Familiar,* among others, explore that fascinating place where the psychological meets – but doesn't explain – the supernatural. His sombre prose builds up real spectral terror. His best short stories are in *Best Ghost Stories of J. S. Le Fanu* (Dover 0486204154 £9.95). I also recommend the companion volume, *Ghost Stories and Mysteries* (Dover 0486207153 £7.95).

M. R. James (1862–1936) – the most consistently frightening British ghost-story writer, a master of showing just enough to suggest far worse. Genteel settings are invaded by things seldom merely dead, an effect close to surrealism. *Complete Ghost Stories* (Penguin 0140102264 £6.99) collects nearly all his horror fiction.

Arthur Machen (1863–1947) – author of a masterpiece of subtle terror (*The White People*) and of some far more gruesome tales of spiritual horror rendered physical, told in incantatory prose. *Tales of Horror and the Supernatural* (Tartarus 1872621252 £25.00) collects many of them. A novel, *The Hill of Dreams,* makes Wales shine with an old light few people see.

William Hope Hodgson (see entry on page 173) gives the impression of trying to communicate weird visions too large for his narratives to contain. His archaic style can be a hindrance, but do persevere. Best to try *The House on the Borderland, The Boats of the Glen Carrig* or *The Ghost Pirates* before attempting *The Night Land. Carnacki the Ghost Finder* is occult detective stuff, much less interesting.

Algernon Blackwood (1869–1951) wrote magnificent tales of visionary horror (*The Wendigo, The Willows*), superbly modulated stories of black magic (*Ancient Sorceries, Secret Worship*), perfectly constructed ghost stories (*The Empty House, Keeping His Promise, The Listener*). All these and more are in *Best Ghost Stories of Algernon Blackwood* (Dover 0486229777 £8.95). Try this before sampling his lesser work.

H. P. Lovecraft (see entry on page 180) is still the most controversial writer in the field, and one of the greatest. His work unifies the British and American traditions represented above. The Mythos he invented was only one of the stages in his search for the perfect form for the weird tale. The collections *The Haunter of the Dark* and *At the Mountains of Madness* are essential. His revisions and so-called collaborations are mostly inferior.

Fritz Leiber (see entry on page 149) is crucial to the development of urban supernatural horror. In his tales the big city is the source, not just the setting, of the weird. Like most writers in my list, he believed that the genre should concern itself with wonder and terror. His collections – *Night's Black Agents, Shadows with Eyes* – and novels – *Conjure Wife, Our Lady of Darkness* – are vital. Sadly they are currently unavailable in the UK.

Like Machen, **Robert Aickman** saw the world as a veil over the supernatural. His tales are often as enigmatic as they are disturbing. No writer in the field is more worth re-reading. As I write, all his books are out of print in Britain.

Thomas Hinde wrote two pioneering novels told by crazed narrators, *The Investigator* (in Hinde's Games of Chance) and *The Day the Call Came.* Other masters of madness to search for: **Paul Ableman** (*I Hear Voices*), **John Franklin Bardin**. All are unfortunately out of print.

Samuel Beckett's novels *The Unnamable* (Calder 071450825X £9.99) and *How It Is* (Calder 0714509523 £6.99) reduce prose to the essence of utter psychological horror. I take them to be nightmares of the afterlife.

Shirley Jackson's work *The Haunting of Hill House* may be the most delicate novel of terror ever written. Included, together with some equally disturbing short stories, in *The Masterpieces of Shirley Jackson* (Robinson 1854874373 £7.99).

T. E. D. Klein sustains what Lovecraft called 'dread suspense' throughout a considerable novel, *The Ceremonies. Dark Gods* collects four shorter but equally admirable tales in the great tradition. Both books are currently out of print.

David Morrell's *Testament* (Headline 0747236690 £4.95) begins with the most terrifying first chapter I've ever read, and lives up to it. If you can read the opening and replace the book on the shelf you're made of sterner stuff than I am.

Dennis Etchison is the finest living American short story writer in the field – a poet of loneliness and alienation who wastes not a word. His collections are *The Dark Country, Red Dreams* and *The Blood Kiss.* These are all unavailable in the UK. His novels, *Shadowman* (Robinson 1854873423 £4.99) and *California Gothic* (Robinson 1854874152 £4.99) repay reading too.

M. John Harrison is as bleak about Britain as Etchison is about America, and as serious a writer, and as rewarding. *The Ice Monkey* remains one of the greatest and most original collections in the entire field. Harrison's novel *The Course of the Heart* touches upon occultism and has much to tell us.

Peter Ackroyd may not thank me for listing him, but here he is. *Hawksmoor* (Penguin 0140171134 £6.99) is a wonderfully resonant novel of the shaping of the present by occult influences from the past. *First Light* (Penguin 0140171150 £6.99) has great fun, but not only that, with archaeology and ancient rites in an English village. Though *Dan Leno and the Limehouse Golem* (Minerva 0749396598 £6.99) barely hints at the supernatural, it certainly delivers horror, and is a thoroughly compelling read. If these books don't fit into the genre, neither do several of mine.

Reading **Thomas Ligotti** (see entry on page 179) can be like experiencing someone else's nightmare based on the masters of the genre, but that formulation is inadequate: he has a unique voice and vision. *The Nightmare Factory* is a bumper omnibus.

The masterpiece of **Kim Newman** (see entry on page 182) so far may be *The Quorum,* a horror novel in which nobody dies, but his alternate histories of vampirism, *Anno Dracula* and *The Bloody Red Baron,* are not to be missed either, nor his short stories (*Famous Monsters* collects many delights). Witty, continuously inventive fiction by a critic with an encyclopaedic knowledge of the field.

Poppy Z. Brite (see entry on page 149) is the most lyrical writer now working in the genre, a quality that makes her horrors all the more powerful. Indeed, *Exquisite Corpse* scared off more than one publisher of her previous novels, *Lost Souls* and *Drawing Blood.* Her considerable range and her respect for the genre are on show in her collection *Swamp Foetus.*

Terry Lamsley has established himself as an inheritor of all the qualities of classic English supernatural horror fiction: wit, detachment, an economy of effect bordering on the poetic, a seemingly effortless originality. His collections so far are *Under the Crust* and *Conference with the Dead.*

Further reading : *Best New Horror,* edited by Steve Jones, (1997 volume Robinson 1854879014 £6.99) is an indispensable annual anthology. With Kim Newman, Jones compiled the admirably eclectic *Horror: 100 Best Books,* although this is currently out of print. The most complete survey of the genre from Hoffmann onward is the *St. James Guide to Horror, Ghost & Gothic Writers,* edited by David Pringle. This is also unavailable at present. *Necrofile* is a quarterly critical journal devoted to horror fiction.

VIRGINIA ANDREWS

Although her books are usually shelved as horror, Virginia Andrews wrote novels that have as much in common with the psychologically tense dramas of writers like Patricia Highsmith as they do with the work of more recent practitioners of the horror genre. Her chilling tales of claustrophobic relationships and dark, evil forces at work in apparently ordinary American families are best exemplified by the quartet of books about the Dollenganger family. This begins with *Flowers in the Attic*, a story of brother and sister imprisoned at the top of a house until an inheritance can be claimed, and continues with *Petal in the Wind*, *If There Be Thorns* and *Seeds of Yesterday*. Other sagas have followed, though none so well constructed and so intense, and Virginia Andrews, perhaps appropriately for a horror writer, has not allowed death to interfere with her productivity. Under the trademark name new works continue to appear.

All That Glitters
Pocket Books pbk £5.99
0671854623

Dark Angel
HarperCollins pbk £4.99
0006174183

Darkest Hour
Pocket Books pbk £4.99
0671852175

Dawn
Pocket Books pbk £5.99
067171550X

Fallen Hearts
HarperCollins pbk £4.99
0006176046

Flowers in the Attic
HarperCollins pbk £5.99
000615929X

Garden of Shadows
HarperCollins pbk £4.99
000617549X

Gates of Paradise
HarperCollins pbk £5.99
0006178219

Heaven
HarperCollins pbk £4.99
0006172059

Hidden Jewel
Pocket Books pbk £5.99
0671854631

If There Be Thorns
HarperCollins pbk £4.99
000616370X

Midnight Whispers
Pocket Books pbk £5.99
0671715771

My Sweet Audrina
HarperCollins pbk £4.99
0006167578

Pearl in the Mist
Pocket Books pbk £5.99
0671853929

Petals on the Wind
HarperCollins pbk £5.99
0006161820

Ruby
Pocket Books pbk £5.99
0671852167

Secrets of the Morning
Pocket Books pbk £5.99
0671715798

Twilight's Child
Pocket Books pbk £5.99
0671715828

Web of Dreams
HarperCollins pbk £4.99
0006178227

Heart Song (The New Virginia Andrews)
Simon & S hbk £16.99
0684821052

Melody (The New Virginia Andrews)
Pocket Books pbk £5.99
0671855735

Tarnished Gold (The New Virginia Andrews)
Pocket Books pbk £5.99
0671855727

JONATHAN AYCLIFFE

(b.1949)

Aycliffe has been an academic – a lecturer in Arabic and Islamic Studies – and has published novels under the name of Daniel Easterman. Horror fiction such as *Naomi's Room* and *Whispers in the Dark* has been well received. Of *The Vanishment,* the story of a wife's disappearance from a Cornish holiday home, the reviewer in *Interzone* wrote, 'this is the best ghost story of recent years and one which, with its Lovecraftian undertones should ultimately be ranked among the greats.'

The Lost
HarperCollins pbk £4.99
0006496156

The Matrix
HarperCollins pbk £6.99
000649319X

CLIVE BARKER

A man of many talents, Clive Barker is an accomplished playwright, director, producer, artist and illustrator as well as as a bestselling author of vivid and psychologically disturbing horror stories. In his twenties he formed his own theatre company for which he wrote, directed and acted. His recent work in the film world, particularly the *Hellraiser* films, has earned him a cult following. Yet he is still probably best known as a writer of exceptional talent. Exploring the fantastical, the erotic, the perverse and the horrific, his dark gothic style pushes back the boundaries of the traditional horror genre and reinvents the universe and the supernatural. Weird and ghoulish figures haunt his imagination and he has the power to bring them to life in his rich and detailed descriptive prose. Yet beneath the intense and nightmarish imagery his works often grapple with serious issues and hold up to scrutiny everyday notions and commonplace ideas. Inventive, thought-provoking and original, Barker digs deep into the psyche and shows an uncanny ability to unearth the fears that lie most deeply hidden within his readers.

Books of Blood Omnibus 1
Warner pbk £7.99 075151022X

Books of Blood Omnibus 2
Warner pbk £7.99 0751512257

Imajica
HarperCollins pbk £6.99
0006178049

The Fifth Dominion: Imajica: Vol 1
HarperCollins pbk £5.99
000649868X

The Reconciliation: Imajica: Vol 2
HarperCollins pbk £5.99
0006498698

Cabal
HarperCollins pbk £4.99
0006176666

The Damnation Game
Warner pbk £5.99 0751505951

Everville
HarperCollins pbk £5.99
0006472257

The Great and Secret Show
HarperCollins pbk £6.99
0006179088

The Hellbound Heart
HarperCollins pbk £4.99
0006470653

Lord of Illusions
Warner pbk £4.99 0751516511

Sacrament
HarperCollins pbk £5.99
0006482643

The Thief of Always
HarperCollins pbk £4.99
0006473113

Weaveworld
HarperCollins pbk £6.99
0006483003

Forms of Heaven: Plays
HarperCollins hbk £16.99
0002255928

Incarnations: Three Plays
HarperCollins hbk £15.99
0002254042

WILLIAM PETER BLATTY

One of the most successful horror films of the seventies, filled with memorably repellent imagery, was William Friedkin's movie *The Exorcist.* The movie and its increasingly forgettable sequels were based on a novel by William Peter Blatty and, more than twenty five years after the original movie was released, the novel stays in print. Perhaps the story, of the demonic possession of an eleven year old girl and the unpleasant symptoms that accompany it, including projectile green vomiting, has graduated from reviled work of exploitation to genre classic.

The Exorcist
Corgi pbk £5.99 0552091561

CHAZ BRENCHLEY

(b.1959)

Brenchley sold his first short story when he was aged eighteen and he has worked as a professional writer ever since. He also writes under the name of Daniel Fox. He has added fresh depth to the genre and his books mix the traditional, bizarre imaginings of horror and violence with an intelligent and sensitive awareness of political, social and psychological issues. In *Dead of Light*, for example, the protagonist's attempt to escape his family is thwarted when they begin, one by one, to die horrible and gruesome deaths and he is drawn back into a personal and political nightmare. Brenchley is recommended to those readers who ask more of the horror genre than a gorefest.

Dead of Light
NEL pbk £5.99 0450610039

Dispossession
NEL pbk £5.99 0340659920

Light Errant
Hodder pbk £5.99 0340685573

Mall Time
Hodder pbk £4.99 0340574488

Paradise
Hodder pbk £5.99 0340589507

POPPY Z. BRITE

Poppy Z. Brite was born in New Orleans and her novels are mostly set amidst the decadence of that city's French Quarter. *Lost Souls* follows the story of an adopted teenage boy called Nothing, half human and half vampire, as he goes in search of his parents and others like him. Clearly influenced more by films like *Near Dark* and *The Lost Boys* than by Bram Stoker, it brought the vampire novel into the nineties. Following this acclaimed debut Brite quickly established herself as a horror writer for Generation X. Her latest work, *Exquisite Corpse*, is a tale of AIDs, murder and necrophilia, studying two very different serial killers as they meet and embark on a fatal love affair. Brite takes you into the minds of vampires and murderers in ways most crime writers would, well, kill to replicate.

Drawing Blood
Penguin pbk £6.99 0140238719

Exquisite Corpse
Phoenix pbk £5.99 185799437X

Lost Souls
Roc pbk £6.99 0140173927

Swamp Foetus
Penguin pbk £6.99 014023506X

RAMSEY CAMPBELL (b.1946)

Ramsey Campbell was born in Liverpool and became a full-time writer in 1973. Since then he has become one of the most prolific and respected of living authors of horror fiction. He has won more awards within the genre than any other writer and his books have been translated into many other languages. Like all the great horror authors, Campbell is adept at creating a chilling atmosphere in which terrors are implied and nightmares lurk behind walls and around corners. However his imagination is unique and distinctive and his handling of pace and skill with language are a match for most mainstream writers. Indeed, as Clive Barker has said, Campbell should be 'read by anyone interested in how horror fiction may be elevated to fine literature.' As well as full-length novels, Campbell has written some superb shorter fiction and most recent anthologies of horror fiction include examples of his work. He is a writer who is accessible to readers interested in trying horror fiction for the first time and his books are also compulsory reading for the horror fan.

Alone with the Horrors
Headline pbk £5.99
0747243492

The Claw
Warner pbk £4.50 0708852580

Cold Print
Headline pbk £5.99
0747240590

The Count of Eleven
Warner pbk £4.99 0751500887

The Doll Who Ate His Mother
Headline pbk £4.50
0747240604

The House on Nazareth Hill
Headline pbk £5.99
0747239967

The Hungry Moon
Headline pbk £5.99
0747246270

Incarnate
Warner pbk £4.50 0708843956

The Influence
Headline pbk £5.99
0747250758

The Long Lost
Headline pbk £5.99
0747239983

The Nameless
Warner pbk £4.50 0708852572

The One Safe Place
Headline pbk £5.99
0747239975

The Parasite
Headline pbk £4.99
0747240612

NANCY A. COLLINS

One of the group of younger writers who has taken the vampire novel from the hills and forests of Central Europe to the urban streets of modern America, Nancy A. Collins has edited anthologies of stories and published several distinctive and stylish novels. *Tempter* is another story which uses the louche atmosphere of New Orleans as a backdrop for occult goings-on but Collins's best books are *In the Blood* and *Paint It Black* in which the central character is Sonja Blue, everyone's favourite schizophrenic, undead punk chick.

In the Blood
Hodder pbk £4.99 0450561968

Paint It Black
Hodder pbk £4.99 0450610101

Tempter
Warner pbk £4.99 0751510270

SIMON CLARK (b.1958)

Simon Clark is a writer who revels in his ability to move rapidly from the everyday, mundane world to dark apocalyptic visions of chaos, blood and death. In *Blood Crazy* a weekend begins normally but descends into horror as adults become murderously insane, infected with an uncontrollable urge to kill the young. In *King Blood* the protagonist looks forward to meeting the brother he hasn't seen in years but finds himself instead in a nightmare world of cities erupting into flames and survivors battling both a devastated landscape and the demons within and without. In all his novels he has shown why one critic declared, 'Not since I discovered Clive Barker have I enjoyed horror so much.'

Blood and Grit
BBR Books pbk £3.99 1872588034

Blood Crazy
NEL pbk £5.99 0340625759

Darker
NEL pbk £5.99 0340660600

King Blood
NEL pbk £5.99
0340660627

Nailed by the Heart
Hodder pbk £5.99
0340625732

DENIS ETCHISON

Although not as widely known as he should be, American writer Etchison is revered by his peers in horror fiction. Peter Straub described him as 'one of horror's most exciting innovative talents' and Stephen King once said of him, simply, that he is 'one hell of a fiction writer.' Best known as an award-winning short story writer, Etchison has also written novelisations of horror movies, including *Hallowe'en II* and *Hallowe'en III,* and novels such as *Shadowman.*

California Gothic
Robinson pbk £4.99
1854873423

Shadowman
Robinson pbk £4.99
1854874152

CHRISTOPHER FOWLER

Fowler divides his time between writing and running a Soho film company and, in his novels, has proven that the horror genre need not be limited to ghosts and gore. Most of his books are set in London and in these the city itself is the most important character. In *Roofworld* tribal gangs live and battle on the rooftops; in *Disturbia* a young journalist must use his knowledge of London's history and mythology to survive a lethal journey around its most famous landmarks ; in *Rune* a mismatched group of Londoners are all that stand in the way of the Devil's return to Earth. Fowler has also written a number of short stories which criss-cross between fantasy, crime and horror and which use the simplest of ideas to great effect. In *Hated,* for example, a man wakes up one morning to find that, suddenly and inexplicably, everybody hates him. In all his work Fowler shows us, as do so many of the best horror writers, that the scariest monsters are not vampires, ghouls and zombies but ourselves.

Darkest Day
Warner pbk £5.99 0751507652

Disturbia
Warner pbk £7.99 0751519103

Flesh Wounds: Short Stories
Warner pbk £5.99 0751514314

Psychoville
Warner pbk £5.99 0751516643

Red Bride
Warner pbk £4.99 075150159X

Rune
Arrow pbk £4.99 0099720000

Sharper Knives
Warner pbk £4.99 0751507660

Spanky
Warner pbk £5.99 0751506990

STEPHEN GALLAGHER

Although many of his novels are shelved in the horror section, Stephen Gallagher is a writer who resists easy categorisation. Certainly he is a master of psychological terror but his novels often draw on the thriller genre as much as horror. *Chimera,* a story of medical research which goes horribly wrong, is nail-bitingly successful at suggesting terrible secrets about to be revealed. *The Follower,* set in Norway, uses a strange, half-man, half-beast character from Scandinavian mythology, to great effect.

The Boathouse
Hodder pbk £4.99 0450562441

Down River
Hodder pbk £4.50 045051112X

Nightmare with Angel
Hodder pbk £4.99 0340596902

Oktober
Hodder pbk £4.99 0450491781

MURIEL GRAY

Although it has a long history as a literary genre, horror writing has, in recent years, been snubbed by most serious readers. So when journalist and TV presenter Muriel Gray chose the horror genre for her debut as a novelist, many people were surprised. However the poorly written gore fodder that gave the genre a bad name has little in common with the work she has produced. Her writing confronts internal struggles and emotional conflicts and it plays upon real fears. Muriel Gray writes horror that touches a nerve and makes the reader think. Like other younger writers such as Christopher Fowler and Tom Holland, she is producing horror writing that can revitalise the genre.

Furnace
Voyager hbk £16.99 0002253135

The Trickster
Voyager pbk £5.99 0006477186

TODD GRIMSON

Todd Grimson has brought horror into the nineties. His characters are pierced, tattooed, drugged-up and cool. Grimson introduces vampires, zombies, magic and fear into the cityscape of a hypermodern Los Angeles. James Ellroy has described him as 'the hippest writer in America today' and his surreal, cinematic writing offers a bleakly satirical view of the contemporary US. For readers who are weary of white-faced, lace-collared vampires and Victorian haunted houses, for readers who need to be convinced that horror is a viable literary genre, Todd Grimson is to be recommended.

Brand New Cherry Flavour
Quartet pbk £7.00 0704380579

Stainless
Quartet pbk £9.00 0704380447

JAMES HERBERT

It is a measure of James Herbert's talent that he has long outlasted the myriad of gore-merchants and imitators who emerged in the wake of his bestselling success with *The Rats* in the early seventies and has confirmed his position as one of Britain's favourite horror writers of the last quarter of a century. The difference between *The Rats* – and its sequel *Lair* – and the blood-spattered works of his followers is that Herbert used images of mutilation and violence, in conjunction with carefully controlled narrative and characterisation, to challenge the reader rather than to disguise weak writing. Herbert's skills have been proven again and again in the two decades since as his work, from the understated *Shrine* and *Fluke* to the apocalyptic *Portent* and *Domain* (the third and best novel of *The Rats* series), has matured and remained always one step ahead of his critics. His triple helping of classic English dark fantasy - *The Magic Cottage, Haunted* and *The Ghosts of Sleath* - have shown new facets of his talent, as has his recent best-selling flame-orgy, *48*, in which he has returned once again to a recurring theme - the gleefully described destruction of his home-city of London. It is safe to assume that Herbert's work will continue to develop in the years to come.

'48
Voyager pbk £5.99 0006476007
The City
Pan pbk £8.99 0330324713
Creed
NEL pbk £5.99 0450547434
The Dark
NEL pbk £6.99 0450049701
Domain
NEL pbk £6.99 0450058220
Fluke
NEL pbk £5.99 0450038289
The Fog
NEL pbk £5.99 0450030458
The Ghosts of Sleath
HarperCollins pbk £4.99 0006475973
Haunted
NEL pbk £5.99 0450493555
The Jonah
NEL pbk £5.99 0450053164
Lair
NEL pbk £5.99 0450045463
The Magic Cottage
NEL pbk £5.99 0450409376
Moon
NEL pbk £5.99 0450389995
Portent
NEL pbk £6.99 0450588858
The Rats
NEL pbk £5.99 0450021270
Sepulchre
NEL pbk £5.99 0450426688
Shrine
NEL pbk £6.99 0450056597
The Spear
NEL pbk £5.99 0450043002
The Survivor
NEL pbk £5.99 0450032418

WILLIAM HOPE HODGSON (1877–1918)

Hodgson is one of the great neglected masters of English fantasy literature, a legendary figure renowned amongst cognoscenti for his mastery of both the short story and the novel. As a writer of the sea, he has been favourably compared to Conrad and Melville. His novels *The Boats of the Glen Carrig* and *The Ghost Pirates* draw on his experiences in the merchant navy and are shot through with the traditional Hodgson trademark of merciless tension and a smell of seawater that is palpable. His two land-based novels are no less remarkable, although land-based is probably a misleading description. The narrator of *The House on the Borderland* finds himself undergoing out-of-body (indeed out-of-solar-system) experiences while his house is being besieged by semi-human pig creatures. The combination of white-knuckle horror and the hallucinogenic rollercoaster of the out-of-body sections make for one of the most remarkable achievements in the literature of the imagination. His last novel, *The Night Land*, has parallels with Milton and Bosch in its depiction of a sunless far future in which the path to redemption through love is littered with soul-destroying monstrosities. The collection *Men of the Deep Waters* contains his most famous short stories, including *The Voice in the Night*, perhaps the most beautiful horror story ever written, and *The Derelict*, an ingenious take on poltergeists. *Carnacki the Ghost-Finder*, the adventures of an occult detective, is both celebration and send-up of the genre. England has never produced a writer quite like William Hope Hodgson.

The House on the Borderland
NEL pbk £5.99 0340675101

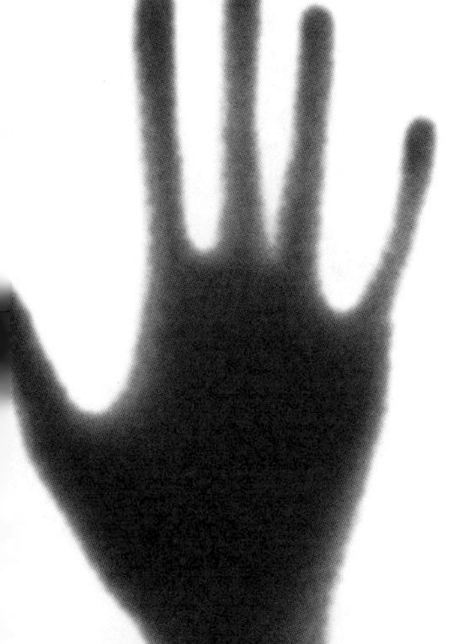

TOM HOLLAND

Tom Holland's novels have brought a welcome breath of fresh air to the romantic vampire myth. Holland's vampires exist against expertly realised historical backgrounds and his novels are ingenious mixtures of fact and fantasy. In *Supping with Panthers* and *Vampyre* we find Lord Byron, Bram Stoker and Henry Irving, all depicted in precise and accurate biographical detail, yet also rubbing shoulders with the undead. In *Deliver Us From Evil* we meet the poets Milton and Rochester in a vampire-infested Europe and discover that the Great Fire was started by combusting zombies. Holland's wit and scholarly intelligence set him in a league of his own amongst recent horror writers and each new novel, bursting with blood, adventure and sexy vampires, is a joy to read.

Deliver Us From Evil
Little, Brown hbk £14.99 0316882488

Supping with Panthers
Warner pbk £5.99 0751514853

The Vampyre
Warner pbk £5.99 075151361X

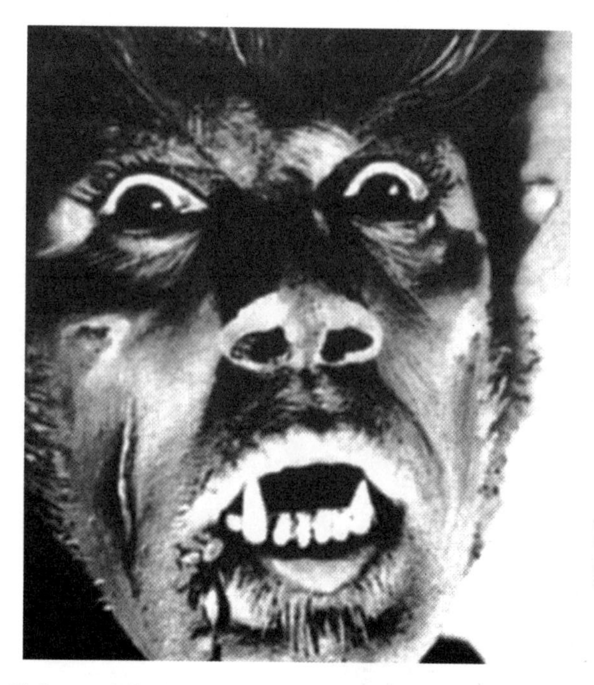

SHAUN HUTSON

The hero of British bloodspatter fiction, Hutson is a writer whose genial personality belies the exhilarating speed, violence and audacity of his work. He's adept at what might be called anti-fiction. His inversion of all the accepted marks of good taste/literary quality argue for a kind of negative aesthetic to be applied to Horror, a genre with different demands and standards from other fiction. What would be crude and offensive written by others is transformed into a kind of heady poetry. His gruesome prose is highly inventive and not without an element of self-parody but his greatest appeal is to the jaded gorehound in search of blood and guts, thrills and chills. Fun for the open-minded, Hutson is definitely not for the squeamish.

Assassin
Warner pbk £4.99 0751501972

Breeding Ground
Warner pbk £3.99 0747407800

Captives
Warner pbk £4.99 0747407991

Deadhead
Warner pbk £4.99 0751501336

Death Day
Warner pbk £5.99 0751504092

Erebus
Warner pbk £4.99 0751513792

Heathen
Warner pbk £5.99 0751501360

Knife Edge
Warner pbk £5.99 0751501263

Lucy's Child
Warner pbk £5.99 0751507695

Nemesis
Warner pbk £4.99 0751506621

Renegades
Warner pbk £5.99 0751514179

Shadows
Warner pbk £5.99 0751514152

Slugs
Warner pbk £4.99 0751514187

Spawn
Warner pbk £5.99 0751513784

Stolen Angels
Warner pbk £5.99 0751501255

Victims
Warner pbk £5.99 0751510750

White Ghost
Warner pbk £5.99 0751507687

PETER JAMES

(b. 1948)

Peter James began his career as a film-maker but has become a much-praised writer of novels of the supernatural whose books sell world-wide. His first novel, *Possession,* was described by one reviewer as 'the sort of book that could knock Stephen King off the top of the bestseller list.' He has since published a number of other novels which skilfully lead the reader from scenes of everyday life to the worst of horrors and nightmares. *Prophecy* is a story of terror emerging from innocent beginnings when a woman answers a personal ad seen by chance in a magazine. In *Dreamer* a woman sees her dreams come terrifyingly true and, in *Twilight,* James fuses modern medicine with the supernatural.

The Alchemist
Signet pbk £5.99 0451179978

Possession
Warner pbk £4.99 0751507571

Prophecy
Signet pbk £4.99 0451174275

Twilight
Signet pbk £5.99 0451174267

STEPHEN KING

There can be few people who have not come across the work of Stephen King, in one of the many film adaptations of his novels if not in the books themselves. King is the source of a huge array of stock on the horror shelves of bookshop and video store alike. In many ways his earlier work remains his best. *Carrie, Salem's Lot, The Shining* and *The Stand* revitalised a dying genre in the seventies and King has matched the ferocious intensity of these books in only a few of his novels since. *It* was one - an epic and thoroughly American portrait of the small town of Derry and the darkness that brings a group of childhood friends back there. *Pet Semetary*, was another. His last outstanding gothic novel, *Misery*, investigated the dangerous relationship between a bestselling author and his readers, a theme that must have had particular resonance for King as his sales headed towards the stratosphere.

As the boom in horror fiction showed signs of slowing down, King moved on to new pastures, exploring other fictional territory with his usual success. The short story collection *Different Seasons* includes non-horror short stories such as *The Shawshank Redemption* and *The Body* (otherwise known as *Stand By Me*) which have been seized on by Hollywood film-makers. Meanwhile fantasy readers have received his sorcery novels in *The Dark Tower* series with great acclaim. The reason for King's continued popularity and his triumph over lesser imitators is not hard to find. First and foremost he is a dissector of character rather than a chronicler of gruesome events and his novels are founded on his insights into the stresses and the fears, the pressures and the nightmares of ordinary people in contemporary society. His books, many of them set in the state of Maine, build upon a realism which is slowly and terrifyingly undermined and destroyed but which provides a bedrock for his imagination. His novels will continue to attract, fascinate and horrify a large readership.

The Dark Tower

The Gunslinger
Hodder pbk £6.99 034070750X

The Drawing of the Three
Hodder pbk £6.99 0340707518

The Waste Lands
Hodder pbk £6.99 0340707526

The Green Mile

Two Dead Girls
Penguin pbk £1.99 0140258566

The Mouse on the Mile
Penguin pbk £1.99 0140258574

Coffey's Hands
Penguin pbk £1.99 0140258582

The Bad Death of Eduard Delacroix
Penguin pbk £1.99 0140258590

Night Journey
Penguin pbk £1.99 0140258604

Coffey on the Mile
Penguin pbk £1.99 0140258612

The Bachman Books
Hodder pbk £8.99 045039249X

Carrie
Hodder pbk £5.99 0450025179

Christine
Hodder pbk £6.99 0450056740

Cujo
Warner pbk £5.99 0751504408

The Dark Half
Hodder pbk £6.99 045052468X

Dark Visions (with Dan Simmons)
Vista pbk £5.99 057560154X

The Dead Zone
Warner pbk £6.99 0751504327

Desperation
Hodder pbk £6.99 0340654287

Different Seasons
Warner pbk £6.99 0751504335

Dolores Claiborne
Hodder pbk £5.99 0450588866

The Eyes of the Dragon
Warner pbk £6.99 0751504572

Firestarter
Warner pbk £5.99 0751504394

Four Past Midnight
Hodder pbk £5.99 0450542882

Gerald's Game
Hodder pbk £6.99
0450586235

Insomnia
Hodder pbk £6.99
0450608484

It
Hodder pbk £7.99
0450411435

Misery
Hodder pbk £5.99
0450417395

Needful Things
Hodder pbk £5.99
045057458X

Night Shift
Hodder pbk £6.99
0450042685

Nightmares and Dreamscapes
Hodder pbk £6.99 0450610098

Pet Sematary
Hodder pbk £6.99 0450057690

Rose Madder
Hodder pbk £6.99 0340640146

Salem's Lot
Hodder pbk £6.99 0450031063

The Shawshank Redemption
Warner pbk £6.99 0751514624

The Shining
Hodder pbk £6.99 0450040186

Skeleton Crew
Warner pbk £6.99 0751504386

The Stand
Hodder pbk £8.99 0450537374

The Talisman (with Peter Straub)
Hodder pbk £7.99 0340674458

The Tommyknockers
Hodder pbk £6.99 0450488357

DEAN KOONTZ (b.1945)

After beginning his career as a writer of SF stories, Koontz turned to horror in the seventies and he rapidly became one of the genre's most important figures. Since turning his hand to horror he has had twenty nine of his books feature in the international best-seller lists. Koontz spent his childhood in Pennsylvania and a difficult relationship with his father has been the emotional wellspring of much of his later writing. Readers of Koontz's work have often noted that it is often at its most frightening when one senses that the writer is portraying his own fears. If we take the portrait of Koontz in Katherine Ramsland's biography into account, it would seem that his own demons *are* being exorcised in his novels and it is the authenticity of terror that makes his work so powerful. His more recent books have shown a new maturity as he has blended, with great confidence, elements of SF, fantasy and horror within the format of an action thriller.Like James Herbert he has moved away from the formulaic and, in recent books like *Sole Survivor* and *Fear Nothing,* has demonstrated to his readers that, in the purging of his own fears, he can play even more skilfully on theirs.

The Bad Place
Headline pbk £6.95 0747234442

Chase
Headline pbk £5.99 0747235252

Cold Fire
Headline pbk £6.95 0747236054

Dark Rivers of the Heart
Headline pbk £6.95 0747244499

Darkness Comes
Headline pbk £5.99 0747235201

The Dean Koontz Companion
Headline pbk £5.99 0747245290

Dean Koontz Omnibus
Headline pbk £7.99 0747208050

Dean Koontz Omnibus 2
Headline pbk £6.99 0747210314

Demon Seed
Headline pbk £5.99 0747234892

The Door to December
Headline pbk £6.99 0747237050

Dragon Tears
Headline pbk £5.99 0747241678

The Eyes of Darkness
Headline pbk £6.99 0747237697

The Face of Fear
Headline pbk £5.99 0747232962

The Funhouse
Headline pbk £5.99 0747238987

Hideaway
Headline pbk £6.99 0747238154

The House of Thunder
Headline pbk £6.99 0747236615

Icebound
Headline pbk £5.99 0747247404

Intensity
Headline pbk £5.99 0747248400

The Key to Midnight
Headline pbk £6.99 0747236461

Lightning
Headline pbk £6.99 0747231648

The Mask
Headline pbk £6.99 0747232628

Midnight
Headline pbk £6.99 0747232725

Mr Murder
Headline pbk £6.99 0747242232

Night Chills
Headline pbk £6.99 0747235228

Oddkins
Headline pbk £6.95 0747279926

Phantoms
Headline pbk £6.95 0747235244

The Servants of Twilight
Headline pbk £6.95 0747236380

Shadowfires
Headline pbk £6.99 074723681X

Shattered
Headline pbk £5.99 0747235236

Sole Survivor
Headline pbk £5.99 0747254346

Strange Highways
Headline pbk £5.99 0747248397

Strangers
Headline pbk £6.99 0747235163

Ticktock
Headline pbk £5.99 0747249725

Twilight Eyes
Headline pbk £6.99
0747235171

The Vision
Headline pbk £6.99
074723518X

The Voice of the Night
Headline pbk £6.99
0747235198

Watchers
Headline pbk £6.99
0747230617

Whispers
Headline pbk £6.99
074723521X

Winter Moon
Headline pbk £6.99
0747242895

THOMAS LIGOTTI

Not a name known widely to the reading public, Ligotti is one of horror's darkest writers and one of those most admired by aficionados and by his peers. Like many of the finest horror writers he is a skilful exponent of the short story and he has produced exceptional collections such as *Noctuary* and *The Nightmare Factory*. In many ways his most original work remains *Grimscribe*, a book of linked short stories in which the eponymous addict of the paranormal relates his encounters with a shadow-world, and its inhabitants, that is, simultaneously, horribly other and horribly familiar.

Grimscribe: His Lives and Works
Robinson hbk £13.95 1854870904

The Nightmare Factory
Robinson pbk £8.99 1854874365

Noctuary
Robinson hbk £14.99 1854872338

Songs of a Dead Dreamer
Robinson pbk £5.99 185487022X

H. P. LOVECRAFT (1890–1937)

In his relatively short life H.P. Lovecraft wrote more than sixty five stories, dozens of articles and maybe as many as 100,000 letters. He enjoyed little success in his lifetime and his stories only saw the light of day in legendary pulp magazines of the twenties and thirties such as *Weird Tales*. However he did win a devoted following amongst a small group of fantasy and horror aficionados and, through the pulps, he made contact and corresponded with numerous other authors of the macabre. These included established writers like Clark Ashton Smith and Robert E. Howard as wll as younger writers such as Frank Belknap Long, August Derleth and a teenage Robert Bloch.

Lovecraft is best remembered for his tales of the *Cthulhu Mythos*, a cycle of loosely connected stories, linked by common references to characters, places and mythology. Lovecraft's work lacks a central structure to indicate a carefully thought out and preconceived history and mythology. Rather the patterns of the Mythos emerge through the process of the writing and in his encouragement of others to explore his world in their fiction.

Lovecraft's writing is usually described as 'horror' but much of his best work is borderline SF, occupying the same kind of territory now explored by The X Files. Indeed one of his masterpieces, *The Whisperer in Darkness*, a tale of aliens quietly, alnost invisibly, going about their business in the Vermont hills, can be seen as a sort of prototype X File. An insidious paranoia seeps through everything. Mail is always intercepted, everyone is being continually watched, attempts to uncover the truth always fail. Only glimpses are possible into what could be going on behind the mundane, everyday world presented by the media and establishment 'experts'.

What all his stories, his dream narratives and his poetry convey is a sense of menace surrounding all human endeavour, of man on 'a placid island of ignorance in the midst of black seas of infinity.' Through his unique prose style that moves between the two poles of clinical detachment and highly charged outpouring, Lovecraft portrays his own uncomfortable vision of a universe much bigger and stranger than we had ever thought possible.

Crawling Chaos: Selected Works:1920-1935
Creation Press pbk £9.95
1871592720

At the Mountains of Madness
HarperCollins pbk £6.99
0586063226

Dagon and Other Macabre Tales
HarperCollins pbk £5.99
0586063242

The Haunter of the Dark and Other Tales of Horror
HarperCollins pbk £6.99
0586063234

BRIAN LUMLEY

An ex-army man who taught himself to write during solitary night duties at checkpoints in the middle of German forests, Lumley is now established as one of Britain's most popular horror writers. His work has two focuses. He has produced a series of tales expanding on Lovecraft's Cthulhu Mythos, many of which are sword and sorcery rather than the usual pastiches involving archaic tomes and shunned houses where something unspeakable dwells. Secondly Lumley has written original and hard-edged vampire novels, including the *Necroscope* sequence, which meld the usual bloodlust with a cold war spy narrative. Huge and pacy, these novels combine the macho with the intelligent and have gained an increasingly large and appreciative audience over the past few years. One day Lumley, with his abundant and fertile imagination, will surely be rewarded with the massive bestseller he deserves.

'There flapped rhythmically a horde of tame, trained, hybrid winged things . . . not altogether crows, nor moles, nor buzzards, nor ants, nor decomposed human beings, but something I cannot and must not recall.'

Brian Lumley's Mythos Omnibus: Vol I
HarperCollins pbk £6.99
0006499376

Brian Lumley's Mythos Omnibus: Vol II
HarperCollins pbk £6.99
0006499384

The Compleat Crow
NEL pbk £5.99 0340695447

Dagon's Bell / Other Discords
Hodder pbk £5.99 0340618361

The House of Cthulhu and Other tales
pbk £4.99 0747235732

The House of Doors: Second Visit
Hodder pbk £16.99
0340708239

Return of the Deep Ones & Other tales
RoC pbk £4.99 014017303X

The Second Wish / Other Exhalations
Hodder pbk £4.99 0340623004

Tarra Khash: Hrossak
Headline pbk £3.99
0747236100

Necroscope Series

Necroscope
HarperCollins pbk £5.99
0586066659

Necroscope II: Wamphyri
HarperCollins pbk £5.99
0586200002

Necroscope III: the Source
HarperCollins pbk £5.99
0586201947

Necroscope IV: Deadspeak
HarperCollins pbk £5.99
0586209042

Necroscope V: Deadspawn
HarperCollins pbk £5.99
0586209050

Necroscope: the Lost Years: Vol 1
NEL pbk £6.99 0340649623

Vampire World

Vampire World: 1. Blood Brothers
Roc pbk £5.99 0140169938

Vampire World: 2. The Last Aerie
RoC pbk £5.99 0140169946

Vampire World: 3. Blood Wars
RoC pbk £6.99 0140169954

GRAHAM MASTERTON

A prolific author of historical fiction and SF disaster novels as well as the horror fiction for which he is best known, Masterton is an interesting writer, more reliant on ideas than the exploitation of blood and gore. In his books ordinary people are forced to adapt to manifestations of the supernatural and infernal. Masterton, described by James Herbert as 'one of the few true masters of horror', creates imaginative and scary plots, whether they be of serial killings and dark secrets beneath the streets of Warsaw, in *The Chosen Child,* or malevolent figures from the greenwood and strange genetic experiments, in *Flesh and Blood.*

Black Angel
Mandarin pbk £5.99 0749309636

Burial
Mandarin pbk £6.99 0749313722

The Chosen Child
Mandarin pbk £5.99 0749323418

Flesh & Blood
Mandarin pbk £5.99 0749316713

The House That Jack Built
Mandarin pbk £5.99 0749320214

The Hymn
Warner pbk £5.99 0751500577

Night Plague
Warner pbk £4.99 0751502413

The Pariah
Warner pbk £4.99 0747404941

Prey
Mandarin pbk £4.99 0749309504

Ritual
Warner pbk £4.99 0751504823

The Sleepless
Mandarin pbk £5.99 0749315768

KIM NEWMAN (b.1959)

Not only one of the most exciting of young British horror writers, Kim Newman is also a film reviewer for *Empire* and *Sight and Sound* and a skilled writer of science fiction. Whatever genre Newman works in, he demonstrates a rich imagination, a stylish prose and an attention to detail which mark him out from most of his contemporaries. Like that of Tom Holland, Newman's work often mixes historical fact into even the most extravagant of fictions and the results are novels which are both witty and genuinely scary.

Anno Dracula
Pocket Books pbk £4.99 0671715917

The Bloody Red Baron
Pocket Books pbk £5.99 0671854518

Famous Monsters
Pocket Books pbk £4.99 0671853007

Jago
Pocket Books pbk £6.99 0671855808

The Original Dr Shade and Other Stories
Pocket Books pbk £4.99 0671715623

The Quorum
Pocket Books pbk £4.99 0671852426

(Ed.)The BFI Companion to Horror
Cassell pbk £19.99 030433216X

EDGAR ALLAN POE (1809–1849)

The beginnings of many genres and sub-genres can be traced back to the work of Edgar Allan Poe. Historians of detective fiction, for example, cite stories like *The Murders in the Rue Morgue* as early examples of the art. A collection of his 'science fiction' has also been compiled which includes stories, like *Mellonta Tauta*, set in the far future. Poe's clearest influence, however, has been on the development of horror fiction. His trapped and tortured protagonists battle unsuccessfully against fate, death and the supernatural. In *The Fall of the House of Usher*, Roderick Usher is caught in a terrifying dance of death with his sister, whose premature burial echoes one of Poe's own innermost fears. In *The Pit and the Pendulum* the prisoner of the Inquisition describes, in Poe's most purple prose, the horrible tortures he has to endure. The murderer in *The Tell-Tale Heart* confuses reality and fantasy and, trapped by a delusion of his own making, confesses to his crime. Poe's own terrible end, found ill and delirious on the streets of Baltimore, seems prefigured in the fates of his characters. In the century and a half since his death, his influence has been immeasurable and it has become clear that, with a dozen or so short stories of genius, Poe expanded the boundaries of psychological horror fiction in a way no one else has matched.

The Complete Tales and Poems
Penguin pbk £10.99 0140103848

The Fall of the House of Usher & Other Writings
Penguin pbk £2.50 0140432914

The Narrative of Arthur Gordon Pym & Related Writings
Oxford UP pbk £5.99 0192828444

The Science Fiction Of Edgar Allan Poe
Penguin pbk £6.99 0140431063

Selected Tales
Oxford UP pbk £2.50 0192832247

ANNE RICE

The lush city of New Orleans, Anne Rice's home town, is also the setting for many of her supernatural novels. Her best known series, the Vampire Chronicles, begins with the classic *Interview with the Vampire*, and recounts the activities of a group of vampires in present-day America. *Interview with the Vampire* is narrated by Louis, a two-hundred year old vampire; in later books his maker and mentor Lestat takes up the tale. Rice's unique touch is that she tells vampire legend from the point of view of the vampires themselves and these are not caped and fanged Draculas but real personalities whose troubled musings on death and decay are at odds with their predatory vampire nature. So her wide-ranging forays into Ancient Egypt, the catacombs of nineteenth century Paris and blood cults of India are set agains the efforts of Louis, Lestat and their kind to find meaning and purpose in their undead, and often cruel, existence.

Rice is a very scary writer. *Interview with a Vampire* has a sustained atmosphere of foreboding and menace which all the special effects of the film version failed to reproduce. At the same time her epic adventures are a gripping, entertaining read, particularly those told in the dry voice of the incorrigible Lestat. The undead also feature in Rice's other novels such as the Egyptian-set *The Mummy or Ramses the Damned* or the frightening tales of the Mayfair Witches, a New Orleans family with a generations-old relationship with a demon. An overwhelming aura of decadence and gothic decay pervades Rice's work and her opulent prose is the perfect vehicle for her tales of the dead and the undead.

THE VAMPIRE CHRONICLES

Interview with the Vampire
Warner pbk £4.99 0708831702

The Vampire Lestat
Warner pbk £5.99 0708831532

The Queen of the Damned
Warner pbk £6.99 0708860729

The Tale of the Body Thief
Penguin pbk £6.99 014013204X

Memnoch the Devil
Arrow pbk £5.99 0099603713

Cry to Heaven
Penguin pbk £6.99 0140132023

Lasher
Penguin pbk £6.99 0140170995

Servant of the Bones
Arrow pbk £5.99 0099184427

The Mummy: Or Ramses the Damned
Penguin pbk £5.99 0140132015

Taltos
Arrow pbk £5.99 0099436817

Violin
Chatto & W hbk £16.99 0701165200

The Witching Hour
Penguin pbk £6.99 0140132031

JAY RUSSELL

Jay Russell writes horror novels with a strong bias towards detective fiction. Or are they detective stories with strong elements of the horror novel? All three of Russell's books read like fairly standard private eye stories until the blood starts to flow and then the weird stuff really hits the fan. Russell's brutal 'in-your-face' style makes it impossible for readers to hide behind the defences of their own, less graphic imaginations. Russell undertakes to do most of the imagining for them and his is a mind that spares them few of the unpleasant details. Elegant style may not be a strong point and characterisation can be stereotypical but narrative pace carries the reader through these bloody and brutal horror stories.

Celestial Dogs
Robinson pbk £5.99 1858474292

Blood
Robinson pbk £5.99 1854874667

Burning Bright
Robinson pbk £5.99 1854874675

DAN SIMMONS

A native of the Rocky Mountains, Colorado, Dan Simmons is another imaginative writer who refuses to be corralled by a particular genre. He has won awards for high calibre work in SF, fantasy and horror and has won praise from very different fellow-writers. Stephen King has said, 'I am in awe of Dan Simmons' and Harlan Ellison has described him as 'a breathtaking writer.' As well as in his novels, his versatility and imagination are apparent in his collections of short stories where tales of ancient magic can be found alongside gripping fictions set in the cold infinities of space.

Carrion Comfort
Headline pbk £4.99
0747234051

Children of the Night
Headline pbk £4.99
0747238995

Fires of Eden
Headline pbk £5.99
0747250057

Lovedeath
Headline pbk £5.99
074724345X

Phases of Gravity
Headline pbk £4.50
074723602X

Prayers to Broken Stones
Headline pbk £5.99
0747238162

Song of Kali
Headline pbk £4.99
0747230447

Summer of Night
Headline pbk £4.99
0747236534

The Hollow Man
Headline pbk £4.99
0747238146

Endymion
Headline pbk £6.99
074723826X

Hyperion
Headline pbk £6.99
0747234825

The Fall of Hyperion
Headline pbk £6.99
0747236046

BRAM STOKER (1847–1912)

Born in Dublin, Stoker was for twenty seven years the business manager for the legendary Victorian actor Sir Henry Irving. However he is remembered today as the author of the most famous of all tales of vampirism, *Dracula,* first published in 1897. The story, told in diary form, of the solicitor Jonathan Harker's journey to Count Dracula's castle in darkest Transylvania and its consequences, is a strange but still effective melange of Victorian period detail, Victorian period moralising and genuinely macabre atmosphere. Stoker wrote other novels and short stories of horror and the supernatural but none has the impact of *Dracula.* The character of the vampiric count himself has, of course, become, like Frankenstein's monster, one of the iconic fictional figures of the twentieth century, appearing in dozens of films, stage adaptations and TV series.

Dracula (Everyman)
J M Dent pbk £3.99
0460871897

Dracula (Penguin Classics)
Penguin pbk £2.50 0140433813

Dracula (World's Classics)
Oxford UP pbk £2.50
0192824627

Dracula's Guest
Brandon pbk £4.99
0863221203

Jewel of the Seven Stars
Oxford UP pbk £4.99
0192832190

The Lady of the Shrouds
Sutton pbk £5.99 0750906898

The Lair of the White Worm
Brandon pbk £4.99
0863221246

The Mystery of the Sea
Sutton pbk £6.99 0750914688

The Snake's Pass
Brandon pbk £4.99
086322119X

GUY N. SMITH

Guy N. Smith is not a subtle writer. In his directness and relish for unflinching descriptions of blood and gore he makes James Herbert look like James Joyce. Yet there is something refreshing about a horror writer who goes so unashamedly for the jugular and there is also an occasional hint of tongue-in-cheek self-mockery in his blood-spattered prose. Since the appearance of *Night of the Crabs* in the seventies, Smith has had a cult following and, although, he is not readily available at present, his books are sure to return to print some day soon.

The novels of Guy N. Smith are currently out of print in the UK.

PETER STRAUB

As a contemporary writer of literary horror fiction, Straub has few peers in his native US. Straub is best known for his collaboration with Stephen King, *The Talisman*, but his novel *Ghost Story* is a seminal work that pays homage to past masters of the genre while expanding its parameters for a late twentieth century readership. It should be widely read because few authors have done as much justice to a tale of haunting since the likes of M.R. James, Henry James and Ambrose Bierce. Straub, whose other work, contains elements of detective fiction and Vietnam veteran angst, is more deserving than most of his competitors of the wide popularity that goes with bestseller status.

Ghost Story
Warner pbk £5.99 0751507024

The Hellfire Club
HarperCollins pbk £5.99 0006498485

Houses Without Doors
HarperCollins pbk £4.99 0586212027

Mystery
HarperCollins pbk £5.99 0586209581

Shadowland
HarperCollins pbk £5.99 000616546X

The Throat
HarperCollins pbk £5.99 0586218491

FREDA WARRINGTON

Freda Warrington is a versatile writer who has written books in a number of different styles. However she is best known for her erotic and imaginative vampire novels. *A Taste of Blood Wine* is the story of an ongoing conflict between two vampires, Karl and Kristian, which culminates in a confrontation amidst the carnage and devastation of World War I. In *The Dark Blood of Poppies* a ballerina is turned into a vampire yet strives to protect her fellow dancers from the depredations of Sebastian, vampire-in-chief. Freda Warrington's skill in the sub-genre was acknowledged when she was invited to write a sequel to the granddaddy of all vampire novels, Bram Stoker's *Dracula.* In *Dracula the Undead* the vampire re-animates himself and pursues the Harker family to London.

The Dark Blood of Poppies
Pan pbk £5.99 0330338501

Dark Cathedral
Signet pbk £5.99 0451184025

Dracula the Undead
Penguin pbk £5.99 0140268804

Sorrow's Light
Pan pbk £4.99 0330333488

Science Fiction in the media

SF IN THE MEDIA

Waterstone's Nick Rennison looks at some of the movies and TV series which have drawn on SF novels and themes.

From the time of film pioneer George Melies and his 1902 *A Trip to the Moon* to the blockbusting, SFX-filled epics of today (*Starship Troopers, Independence Day, The Fifth Element*), the cinema has found inspiration in SF stories, themes and tropes. Many movies have been hackneyed, over-reliant on their effects, childish in plot and character. Nonetheless there have also been some remarkable achievements in the translation of SF and fantasy novels and ideas to the screen. In the thirties *Things to Come,* taken from a work by H.G. Wells, was an early indication of the visual grandeur that film could lend to visions of the future. The decade also saw what still remain the most resonant versions of *Frankenstein* and Wells's *The Invisible Man.*

The following decade produced little notable movie SF, perhaps because reality was apocalyptic enough, but in the fifties American film makers began to relish the potential SF offered to reflect elliptically the society of the Eisenhower years, particularly cold war paranoia. Jack Finney's novel *The Body Snatchers* was memorably filmed by Don Siegel as *Invasion of the Body Snatchers. It Came From Outer Space,* co-written by Ray Bradbury, tackled a similar theme some years earlier. *The Day the Earth Stood Still* saw the arrival of galactic messengers to warn us about the consequences of meddling with nuclear power. *Forbidden Planet* was an interesting attempt to translate Shakespeare to outer space and has the additional delight of Leslie Nielsen in an early and unlikely role as commander of an expedition to Altair 4.

The fifties became the sixties and paranoid drama became bitter, almost nihilistic satire, in *Dr. Strangelove,* camp, soft-porn fantasy in Roger Vadim's *Barbarella* and individualistic takes on genre themes like Godard's uncategorisable and deeply weird *Alphaville.* Another French director, Truffaut, gave us a well-intentioned but unexciting version of Bradbury's *Fahrenheit 451*. A lesser-known novel, Daniel Keyes's *Flowers for Algernon* became an affecting Hollywood movie, *Charly*, starring Cliff Robertson as a retarded man suddenly granted superintelligence. The landmark sixties SF movie was, of course Kubrick's extraordinary, imaginative and enigmatic epic *2001 : A Space Odyssey*. The decade, rather less memorably, also gave us Charlton Heston on the *Planet of the Apes* and Raquel Welch in miniaturised form in *Fantastic Voyage*.

Kubrick followed 2001 with a startling and mesmeric version of *A Clockwork Orange*, which used images and music to dazzling effect to tell Burgess's story of gang violence in a near-future UK. In 1970, the year before Kubrick's movie, a low-budget film called *THX 1138* appeared at a handful of American cinemas. Its director was George Lucas who, in 1977, released what is probably the most influential SF movie, for better or for worse, of all time. *Star Wars* and its sequels, *The Empire Strikes Back* and *Return of the Jedi*, their special effects, their archetypal storylines and their spectacular takings at the box office began a boom in SF and fantasy movies which continues today. Star Wars novelisations appeared at the time of the original movie and have continued to appear ever since. Too numerous to list, the books have often been written by well-known writers such as Timothy Zahn and Barbara Hambly. The same year that *Star Wars* appeared another young Turk of the movie industry, Steven Spielberg, directed *Close Encounters of the Third Kind*, which remains an awe-inspiring vision of first contact between alien and human.

Since the huge commercial and, to some extent, critical success of Lucas's and Spielberg's films, SF has become the most bankable of all genres. Hundreds of SF and fantasy movies have been released over the last twenty years. Their quality has varied from the execrable to the excellent. *Dune*, despite or, perhaps, because of being directed by David Lynch, was a disastrously unsuccessful rendering of Herbert's novel. The 1984 version of *1984* was a surprisingly effective telling of Orwell's dystopian tale. Philip K. Dick's *Do Androids Dream of Electric Sheep* became the movie *Bladerunner*. Box office success with one movie has stimulated the money-lust, if not the imaginations, of producers and series have rolled inexorably off the Hollywood production line. *Batman* has been followed by *Batman Returns* and *Batman Forever* and *Batman Forever* has been followed, sadly, by *Batman and Robin*. *Robocop II* followed *Robocop* like night shall follow day. Not all the sequels have meant a reduction in quality. *Back to the Future II* is a better movie than its predecessor and *Alien 3* is, some would say, the best of the series. *Star Trek* and *Star Wars* have both reached a stage of cultural ubiquity that makes criticism almost redundant. It is safe to assume that the flood of SF movies will continue. Most recently it has seemed that comics will provide the storylines of the future. *Judge Dredd* looked to be the role for which Sylvester Stallone was born. The resulting movie proved conclusively that this wasn't, in fact, the case but other, better comic-based movies have appeared since then and Japanese anime movies, based on manga originals, have made considerable impact in the West since the initial success of *Akira* in the late eighties. Film-makers will continue to want to bring to the screen the novels that have meant a lot to them and the second century of SF in the movies beckons.

Other media, too have made fruitful use of SF. Possibly the most famous radio broadcast ever - Orson Welles's *The War of the Worlds* in 1938, which sent hundreds of thousands of panicked Americans in headlong flight from the Martians they supposed were invading - was based on the novel by H.G. Wells. From the fifties onwards TV saw the potential SF held in attracting audiences. Nigel Kneale was the creator of three popular TV series featuring scientific genius Professor Quatermass who saved the nation from alien threat on a number of occasions. These were sophisticated and intelligent series and Quatermass has also appeared in films, a revived series in the late seventies and a novel taken from it.

However the two phenomena of TV SF, both of which began in the sixties and have persisted through the decades, are, of course, *Dr. Who* and *Star Trek. Star Trek* was originally shown in 1966-1969. It has been constantly reshown, feature films have been made, further generations have appeared in new series. The most famous split infinitive of all time, 'to boldly go where no man has gone before', has heralded a global phenomenon. Novelisations, too numerous to list, continue to appear. Some of the original TV episodes were turned into novels by no less a writer than James Blish. Other well-known writers, including Theodore Sturgeon, Barbara Hambly, Joe Haldeman and K.W. Jeter, have contributed books to the series. *Dr. Who* was first broadcast in November 1963 and survived innumerable changes in personnel over the decades. Originally intended for children, the series always attracted an adult audience and the Doctor and his Tardis have become familiar worldwide. Dozens of novelisations, many of them written by the prolific Terrance Dicks, have appeared over the years and very many are still in print. TV has spawned many other SF series, from *Space 1999* to *Blake's Seven, Battlestar Galactica* to *The X-Files.* None has yet approached the popularity of Dr. Who and Star Trek or been the source for so many books, although *The X-Files* has become an industry in itself. It seems safe to assume that Waterstone's will be selling *Star Trek, Star Wars* and *Dr. Who* books well into the 21st century.

Star Trek, Star Wars and Dr Who books are widely available in most branches of Waterstone's.

Graphic Novels

WRITING AND WEREWOLFING

Neil Gaiman on dreams, the imagination, Sandman and wanting to be a werewolf.

When I grew up, I wanted to be a werewolf. Or a writer. But writer was definitely number two alternative. Werewolfing was an easy number one.

I expected it would begin with the onset of puberty. Instead I got a number of other things, all of them a lot of fun. I got everything, pretty much, except turning into a wolf when the moon was full.

So far I still haven't turned into a wolf, not as far as I know.

But I once dreamed I did, so I know what it's like.

I forget most of my dreams on waking, and do not write them down. Fragments of them sometimes creep into stories, but writers cannibalise all of themselves for stories, and there is no reason that dreams should escape. However, most of the ones I can remember are plotless, set in huge houses I have never lived in, with rooms both topographically impossible and dark. Dreams and houses have always been linked for me, and I do not know why.

But let's leave dreams for a moment and talk about mythology and comics.

Mythologies have always fascinated me. Why we have them. Why we need them. Whether they need us.

And comics have always dealt in myths: four-colour fantasies, which include men in brightly coloured costumes fighting endless soap opera battles with each other (predigested power fantasies for adolescent males); not to mention friendly ghosts, animal people, monsters, teenagers, aliens. Until a certain age the mythology can possess us completely, then we grow up and leave those particular dreams behind, for a little while or forever.

But new mythologies wait for us, here at the crazy end of the twentieth century. They abound and proliferate: urban legends of men with hooks in lovers' lanes, hitchhikers with hairy hands and meat cleavers, beehive hairdos crawling with vermin; serial killers and bar-room conversations; in the background our TV screens pour disjointed images into our living rooms, feeding us old movies, news-flashes, talk-shows, adverts; we mythologise the way we dress and the things we say; iconic figures — rock stars and politicians, celebrities of every shape and size; the new mythologies of magic and science and numbers and fame.

They have their function, all the ways we try make sense of the world we inhabit, a world in which there are few, if any, easy answers. Every day we attempt to understand it. And every night we close our eyes, and go to sleep, and, for a few hours, quietly and safely, we go stark staring mad.

The ten volumes of Sandman were my way of talking about that. They were my way of looking at the mythologies of the last decade of the twentieth century; a way of talking about sex and death, fear and belief and joy – all the things that make us dream.

We spend a third of our lives asleep, after all.

It's a paradox that one of the greatest strengths of comics is also one of its greatest weaknesses. I'm talking about the often serial nature of the medium. Getting a chunk of a story every month allows for reading and re-reading, and means that one can actually genuinely build up the kind of reader involvement that as a rule hasn't been seen in literature since 1841, when a crowd of six thousand people packed the New York wharf at which the ship carrying the final magazine installment of *The Old Curiosity Shop* was due to dock, calling anxiously to the sailors, 'Does Little Nell die?'

These days novelists get to write their novels in peace, polish them, and then publish them in one volume, without people phoning up to plead for the lives of favourite characters.

Since few of us are Charles Dickens, this makes life easier for novelists. For example, if a sudden plot twist occurs to you half way through your novel, it is the work of a moment to go back to chapter one and add the couple of lines that show you knew what the story was about from the word go.

This is not an option for a monthly comic. By the time you've thought of your plot twist, Chapter One has not only been drawn, it's also been printed, and read by a hundred thousand people.

There are two solutions to this. Either you plan out what you're doing meticulously in advance, issue by issue. Or you just head off blindly into the dark, hoping it'll all come out right in the end, and trusting to blind luck.

Sandman was always a bit of both for me. Mostly it worked. The stories collected in the ten volumes of *Sandman* became a huge, intricate, two thousand page story, and most of the accidents were happy ones. The joy of writing *Sandman* was that the territory was wide-open. I wrote it in the world of anything goes: history and geography, superheroes and dead kings, folk-tales, houses and dreams.

Horror and fantasy (whether in comics form or otherwise) are often seen simply as escapist literature. Sometimes they can be, offering quick catharsis, a plastic dream, an easy out. But they don't have to be. When we are lucky they offer a road-map — a guide to the territory of The Imagination, for it is the function of imaginative literature to show us the world we know, but from a different direction.

It's a strange place, The Imagination. A lot of fun by day, when there are all sorts of reassuring and familiar sights and people around. But it's scary, and cold at night, and places you knew perfectly well by daylight aren't the same after the sun's gone down. You can get lost easily there, and some people never find their way back. You can hear a few of them, when the ghost moon shines, and the wind's in the right direction. They scream for a while, and then they stop. And in the silence you hear something else: the sound of something large and quiet, tentatively beginning to feed.

The imagination is a dangerous place, after all, and you could use a guide to the territory — a guide like the volume you are holding.

Even if you never got to be a werewolf when you grew up.

GRAPHIC NOVELS

The term graphic novel is generally attributed to the great comic artist Will Eisner, who coined it in the late seventies, but it did not become a widely-used term until the mid-eighties. The term refers to a form of storytelling in which illustrations are not mere adornments to the text but actually form and drive the narrative. During the eighties a new style of comic writer appeared. Many readers had grown up with comics such as *2000 AD, Batman, The Fantastic Four* and others. Now they were too old for these titles to hold their interest but still wanted a form of comic that could appeal to a maturer audience. To fill this void, writers emerged in the eighties who were as different from each other as they were from the comics that had preceded them.

Art Spiegelman's black and white re-telling of the holocaust in *Maus* was an innovative use of a visual storytelling technique which allowed for a narrative rich in striking imagery and haunting expressions. This form of storytelling was extremely cinematic in style and delivery, a method which was taken even further by the next group of writers and artists.

Watchmen by Alan Moore and Dave Gibbons told a tale of a world in which superheroes were a reality, examining how ordinary people would react to such beings and how the heroes themselves would cope with the psychological stresses imposed upon them. The apocalyptic storyline is told in an original manner through Dave Gibbons's art work, which uses slow pull-back and panning techniques, borrowed from the movies, to draw the reader's eye through the unfolding scenes.

Frank Miller's re-invention of a fifty-year old hero in *Batman – The Dark Knight Returns* stands alongside *Watchmen* as one of the key texts which jump-started the graphic novel genre and also gave a shot in the arm to the comic book industry, prompting more mature output such as DC's *Swamp Thing, Hellblazer* and *Vamps.* Many of these would later be collected and issued as graphic novels.

Much of the graphic novel ouput is composed of material first printed in monthly comic book format, rebound into single volumes. This is not necessarily a bad thing since readers who would not wish to buy comics every month have access to these stories. Many comics writers create storylines with one eye on adaptation to trade paperback form. Especially fine comic-to-graphic novels include Todd McFarlane's alternative super-

A very small selection of the best graphic novels:

MIKE CARLIN (ED)

The Return of Superman
Titan pbk £9.99 1852865148

NEIL GAIMAN & DAVE MCKEAN

Black Orchid
Titan pbk £12.99 1852863366

Mr. Punch
Gollancz pbk £8.99
0575053186

Signal to Noise
Gollancz pbk £9.99
0575052848

Violent Cases
Titan pbk £6.99 1852869593

NEIL GAIMAN

The Sandman Series

The Book of Dreams
Voyager pbk £5.99 0006482783

The Doll's House
Titan pbk £10.99 1852862920

The Dream Country
Titan pbk £8.99 1852864419

Fables and Reflections
Titan pbk £12.50 1852864974

A Game of You
Titan pbk £9.99 1852864788

The Kindly Ones
Titan pbk £12.99 1852866837

Preludes and Nocturnes
Titan pbk £10.99 1852863269

Seasons Of Mists
Titan pbk £9.99 1852864478

hero for the nineties, *Spawn*, long-running Batman epics such as *Contagion* and *Knightfall*, *The Return of Superman*, *Elektra Assassin* by Frank Miller, Martin and Hewlett's *Tank Girl* and Alan Moore's *V for Vendetta*.

Perhaps the finest British writer in the field is Neil Gaiman. Working with long-time collaborator Dave McKean, he produced the graphic novel *Violent Cases* in 1987. He followed this with an eight-year run on DC's 'mature' comic *The Sandman*. This award-winning series, available in a range of graphic novels, tells the tale of Morpheus, the Lord of Dreams and his family. In addition to this Gaiman created the TV series *Neverwhere* and the (rather better) book which accompanied it, co-authored *Good Omens* with Terry Pratchett and worked on *Signal to Noise*, *Black Orchid* and *Mr. Punch* amongst others. His writing is wonderfully lyrical and romantic and demonstrates a fine eye for detail. His ability to mix history and mythology decisively but unobtrusively into the narrative is also remarkable.

Other highly original works by other writers include *Preacher*, the in-your-face series by Garth Ennis and the wonderfully painted *Kingdom Come*, a story which owes much to *Watchmen*. Older characters, such as *Dan Dare*, *The ABC Warriors*, *Judge Dredd* and the Celtic berserker, *Slaine*, have been given a new lease of life. And, of course, there's always Japanese manga. Fine examples include *The Dirty Pair*, *Tank Police*, *Crying Freeman* and the epic *Akira*. The graphic novel, then, is a broad genre which can encompass everything from superheroes to God, the Devil and kangaroos.

The Wake
Titan pbk £12.99 1852868074

The World's End
Titan pbk £12.50 1852866098

Death – The High Cost of Living
Titan pbk £7.99 1852864982

Death – The Time of Your Life
Titan pbk £7.99 1852868171

Neverwhere
Penguin pbk £5.99 0140266518

JAMIE HEWLETT & ALAN MARTIN

Tank Girl
Penguin pbk £8.99 0140243143

MANGA

Crying Freeman Volume 1
Titan pbk £7.99 1900097036

Crying Freeman Volume 2
Titan pbk £7.99 1900097052

The Dirty Pair
Titan pbk £7.99 1900097044

FRANK MILLER

Batman – The Dark Knight Returns
Titan pbk £10.99 1852867981

Elektra Saga
Marvel pbk £11.95 0871355760

Sin City
Titan pbk £9.99 1852864680

Sin City: A Dame to Kill For
Titan pbk £8.99 1852865741

Sin City: The Big Fat Kill
Titan pbk £11.99 1852866985

Sin City: That Yellow Bastard
Titan pbk £10.99 1852868422

ALAN MOORE

Watchmen (with Dave Gibbons)
Titan pbk £11.50 1852860243

V for Vendetta (with David Lloyd)
Titan pbk £13.99 1852862912

ART SPIEGELMANN

Maus 1
Penguin pbk £9.99 0140173153

Maus 2: A Survivor's Tale
Penguin pbk £11.00 0140132066

MARK WAID & ALEX ROSS

Kingdom Come
Titan pbk £9.99 1852868163

Services *at* Waterstone's

THE PRICE PROMISE

If you find any book cheaper locally we shall happily refund the difference (ask a bookseller for details).

BOOKSEARCH

If the book you want is no longer in print, Waterstone's Booksearch Service will try to locate a second-hand copy for you. Booksearch, 32-40 Calverley Road, Tunbridge Wells, TN1 2TD

fax 01892 521 400

MAIL ORDER

We can send any book in print to anywhere in the world. Orders over £45 within the United Kingdom are sent post-free. Waterstone's Mailing Service, 4-5 Milsom Street, Bath BA1 1DA
tel 01225 448 595

fax 01225 444 732 or 01225 420 575

SIGNED FIRST EDITIONS

Waterstone's Signed First Editions Collection offers a choice of up to 150 of the year's finest fiction and non-fiction titles – all signed by the author and posted to you for a subscription of only £6. Waterstone's Signed First Editions Collection, 4–5 Milsom Street, Bath BA1 1DA
tel 01225 448 595
fax 01225 444 732 or 01225 420 575.

BOOK VOUCHERS

Accepted in over 500 bookshops in the United Kingdom and Ireland, including all branches of Waterstone's and WH Smith. As well as posting them anywhere in the world, we provide a card free of charge.

WRAPPING, ORDERING AND POSTING

Most branches will happily gift-wrap your book in a choice of papers. If the book you are looking for is unavailable in the branch, we can order it for you and even post it to any destination in the world.

WATERSTONE'S RECOMMENDS

All the books in a Waterstone's bookshop are bought and selected by the booksellers working in the branch. No matter the subject, please ask for their advice or look out for the Book of the Month or our monthly selection of the best new books – Waterstone's Recommends.

WATERSTONE'S BOOKSHOP ON THE INTERNET

Order any book securely by credit card to be delivered direct to your door or anywhere around the world and join our on-line club at www.waterstones.co.uk

W MAGAZINE

Waterstone's own literary quarterly, available from all branches, price £1.

USEFUL ADDRESSES

THE SCIENCE FICTION FOUNDATION

A charitable organisation which aims to bring together people with a research interest in science fiction, to disseminate information about sf and to promote an understanding of science fiction among the public and the media. For further information, contact:

Andy Sawyer,
Librarian/Administrator,
Science Fiction Foundation Collection,
University of Liverpool Library,
PO Box 123,
Liverpool L69 3DA

THE BRITISH FANTASY SOCIETY

Organisers of the UK FantasyCon and the British Fantasy Awards, producers of magazines on books, authors, fans, conventions and more. For information write to:

The BFS Secretary (F),
c/o 2 Harwood Street
Stockport SK4 1JJ

THE BRITISH SCIENCE FICTION ASSOCIATION

An important source of information on all things sf, organisers of regular events, publishers of Vector *magazine.*

The BSFA Membership Secretary,
1 Long Row Close,
Everdon, Daventry,
Northants NN11 3BE

THE TOLKIEN SOCIETY

A charitable organisation dedicated to furthering the work of J. R. R. Tolkien.

Tolkien Society
Membership Secretary
16 Gibsons Green
Heelands, Milton Keynes
Buckinghamshire MK13 7HN

BBR

Run by Chris Reed, the one-stop source for small and independent press publications in the UK. For a full catalogue, write to:

BBR
P. O. Box 625,
Sheffield S1 3GY

ZENE

The regular review magazine dedicated to the small and independent press. For further information send an s.s.a.e. to:

TTA Press,
5 Martins Lane,
Witcham, Ely,
Cambs CB6 2LB

INDEX BY AUTHOR

Where to find your nearest Waterstone's

ABERDEEN
236 Union St
Tel: 01224 571655

AMSTERDAM
Kalverstraat 152
Amsterdam
The Netherlands
Tel: 00 312 0 638 3821

BATH
4–5 Milsom St
Tel: 01225 448515

University of Bath
Claverton Down
Tel: 01225 465565

BELFAST
Queen's Building
8 Royal Avenue
Tel: 01232 247355

BIRKENHEAD
188/192 Grange Rd
Tel: 0151 650 2400
(May 1998)

BIRMINGHAM
24/26 High St
0121 633 4353

BOLTON
32–36 Deansgate
Tel: 01204 522588

BOURNEMOUTH
14/16 The Arcade
Tel: 01202 299449

BRADFORD
University of Bradford,
Great Horton Rd
Tel: 01274 727885

Management
Centre Bookshop, Emm Lane
Tel: 01274 481404

The Wool Exchange
Tel: 01274 723127

BRIGHTON
55–56 North St
Tel: 01273 327867

BRISTOL
27–29 College Green
Tel: 0117 925 0511

University of Bristol
Tyndall Avenue
Tel: 0117 925 4297

Cribbs Causeway
33 Lower Mall
Tel: 0117 950 9813
(March 1998)

The Galleries Broadmead
Tel: 0117 925 2274

BROMLEY
20–22 Market Sq
Tel: 0181 464 6562

BRUSSELS
Boulevard Adolphe Max 71-75
B1000 Brussels
Belgium
Tel: 00 322 219 2708

BURY
4 Union Arcade
Tel: 0161 764 2642

CAMBRIDGE
6 Bridge St
Tel: 01223 300123

CANTERBURY
20 St Margaret's St
Tel: 01227 456343

CARDIFF
2a The Hayes
Tel: 01222 665606

CARMARTHEN
Trinity College
Tel: 01267 238100

CHELTENHAM
88–90 The Promenade
Tel: 01242 512722

CHESTER
43–45 Bridge St Row
Tel: 01244 328040

COLCHESTER
16 Culver Precinct
Tel: 01206 767623

University of Essex
Wivenhoe Park
Tel: 01206 864773

CORK
69 Patrick St
Tel: 00 353 21 276522

Boole Library
University College
Tel: 00 353 21 276575

CROYDON
1063 Whitgift Centre
Tel: 0181 686 7032

DERBY
78–80 St Peter's St
Tel: 01332 296997

DORKING
54–60 South St
Tel: 01306 886884

DUBLIN
7 Dawson St
Tel: 00 353 1 679 1260

The Jervis Centre
Tel: 00 353 1 878 1311

DUNDEE
35 Commercial St
Tel: 01382 200322

DURHAM
69 Saddler St
Tel: 0191 383 1488

EASTBOURNE
120 Terminus Rd
Tel: 01323 735676

EDINBURGH
128 Princes St
Tel: 0131 226 2666

13–14 Princes St
Tel: 0131 556 3034/5

83 George St
Tel: 0131 225 3436

EPSOM
113 High St
Tel: 01372 741713

EXETER
48–49 High St
Tel: 01392 218392

FOLKESTONE
1–2 Guildhall St
Tel: 01303 221 979

GATESHEAD
17 The Parade
Metro Centre
Tel: 0191 493 2715

GLASGOW
153–157
Sauchiehall St
Tel: 0141 332 9105

GUILDFORD
35–39 North St
Tel: 01483 302919

HANLEY
The Tontines Centre
Parliament Row
Tel: 01782 204582

HEREFORD
18–20 Commercial St
Tel: 01432 275100

HULL
University of Hull
Tel: 01482 444190

The Grand Buildings,
Jameson St
Tel: 01482 580234

INVERNESS
50–52 High St
Tel: 01463 717474

IPSWICH
15–19 Buttermarket
Tel: 01473 289044

KETTERING
72–76 High St
Tel: 01536 481575

KING'S LYNN
76–77 High St
Tel: 01553 769934
(April 1998)

KINGSTON-UPON-THAMES
23–25 Thames St
Tel: 0181 5471221

LANCASTER
2–8 King St
Tel: 01524 61477

LEAMINGTON SPA
1 Priorsgate
Warwick St
Tel: 01926 883804

LEEDS
36–38 Albion St
Tel: 0113 242 0839

93–97 Albion St
Tel: 0113 244 4588

LEICESTER
21/23 High St
Tel: 0116 251 6838

LIVERPOOL
52 Bold St
Tel: 0151 709 0866

LONDON

CAMDEN, NW1
128 Camden High St
Tel: 0171 284 4948

CHARING CROSS RD, WC2
121 Charing
Cross Rd
Tel: 0171 434 4291

CHEAPSIDE, EC2
145–147 Cheapside
Tel: 0171 726 6077

THE CITY, EC3
1 Whittington Ave
Leadenhall Market
Tel: 0171 220 7882

COVENT GARDEN, WC2
9 Garrick St
Tel: 0171 836 6757

EARL'S COURT, SW5
266 Earl's Court Rd Tel: 0171
370 1616

GOLDSMITHS', SE14
Goldsmiths' College, New
Cross
Tel: 0181 469 0262

HAMPSTEAD, NW3
68 Hampstead High St
Tel: 0171 794 1098

HARRODS, SW1
87 Brompton Rd
Tel: 0171 730 1234

IMPERIAL COLLEGE, SW7
Imperial College Rd
Tel: 0171 589 3563

IMPERIAL COLLEGE SCHOOL OF MEDICINE
Charing Cross
Campus
Reynolds Building
St Dunstan's Rd
Tel: 0181 748 9768

Hammersmith Campus
Commonwealth Building
Du Cane Road
Tel: 0181 742 9600

ISLINGTON, N1
11 Islington Green
Tel: 0171 704 2280

KENSINGTON, W8
193 Kensington High St
Tel: 0171 937 8432

NOTTING HILL, W11
39 Notting Hill Gate
Tel: 0171 229 9444

OLD BROMPTON RD, SW7
99 Old Brompton Rd
Tel: 0171 581 8522

WIMBLEDON, SW19
12 Wimbledon Bridge
Tel: 0181 543 9899

MAIDSTONE
19 Earl St
Tel: 01622 681112

MACCLESFIELD
47 Mill St
Tel: 01625 424212
(May 1998)

MAILING SERVICE
Tel: 01225 448595
Fax: 01225 444732

MANCHESTER
91 Deansgate
Tel: 0161 832 1992

MANCHESTER AIRPORT
Terminal 1 Airside
(April 1998)

MIDDLESBROUGH
9 Newton Mall
Cleveland Centre
Tel: 01642 242682

University of Teesside
Middlesbrough
Tel: 01642 242017

NEWBURY
64 Northbrook St
Tel: 01635 569998

NEWCASTLE
104 Grey St
Tel: 0191 261 6140

NORTHAMPTON
19 Abington St
Tel: 01604 634854

NORWICH
21–24 Royal Arcade
Tel: 01603 632426

University of East Anglia
Tel: 01603 453625

NOTTINGHAM
1–5 Bridlesmith Gate
Tel: 0115 9484499

PERTH
St John's Centre
Tel: 01738 630013

PETERBOROUGH
6 Queensgate
Tel: 01733 313476

PLYMOUTH
65/69 New
George St
Tel: 01752 256699

PRESTON
3–5 Fishergate
Tel: 01772 555766

READING
89a Broad St
Tel: 01189 581270

RICHMOND-UPON-THAMES
2–6 Hill St
Tel: 0181 332 1600

SALISBURY
7/9 High St
Tel: 01722 415596

SHEFFIELD
24 Orchard Sq
Tel: 0114 272 8971

SHREWSBURY
18–19 High St
Tel: 01743 248112

SOUTHAMPTON
69 Above Bar
Tel: 01703 633130

Southampton Medical School,
Southampton General Hospital
Tel: 01703 780602

University of Southampton
Highfield
Tel: 01703 558267

SOUTHEND-ON-SEA
49–55 High St
Tel: 01702 437480

SOUTHPORT
367 Lord St
Tel: 01704 501088

STIRLING
Thistle Marches
Tel: 01786 478756

STOCKPORT
103 Princes St
Tel: 0161 477 3755

STRATFORD-UPON-AVON
18 The High St
Tel: 01789 414418

SWANSEA
17 Oxford St
Tel: 01792 463567

SWINDON
27 Regent St
Tel: 01793 488838

TAUNTON
County Hotel
East St
Tel: 01823 333113

TUNBRIDGE WELLS
32/40 Calverley Rd
Tel: 01892 535446

ULSTER
Central Buildings
University of Ulster
Cromore Rd
Coleraine
Tel: 01265 324 735

WATFORD
174–176 The Harlequin Centre, High St
Tel: 01923 218197

WINCHESTER
1/2 Kings Walk
Tel: 01962 866206

WORCESTER
95 High St
Tel: 01905 723397

YORK
28–29 High Ousegate
Tel: 01904 628740